Abraham Cowley (1618-1667)

A Seventeenth-Century English Poet Recovered

18TH CENTURY
MOMENTS

Eighteenth-Century Moments is dedicated to outstanding, memorable works of scholarship, from early modern to enlightenment and Romantic literature, history, and culture. Emphasizing depth of research, quality of thought, and accessibility of style—rather than genre, ideology, or methodology—Eighteenth-Century Moments includes books of various kinds—not only critical, historical, and theoretical considerations from within the British, American, and global Anglophone contexts, but also collections of essays, biographies, book-histories, historiographies, single-author studies, and scholarly editions.

Series Editor
Greg Clingham

Abraham Cowley (1618–1667)

A Seventeenth-Century English Poet Recovered

Edited by
Michael Edson and
Cedric D. Reverand II

CLEMSON
UNIVERSITY
PRESS

First Edition, 2023

ISBN: 978-1-63804-072-9 (print)
eISBN: 978-1-63804-073-6 (e-book)

Published by Clemson University Press
in association with Liverpool University Press

For information about Clemson University Press,
please visit our website at www.clemson.edu/press.

Library of Congress Cataloging-in-Publication Data
CIP Data available on request

Typeset in Minion Pro by Carnegie Book Production.
Printed and bound by CPI Group (UK) Ltd, Croydon CR0 4YY.

Acknowledgments

This project was the brainchild of Mark Pedreira. As we mention in our introduction, his long-standing interest in Abraham Cowley led him to propose a panel on the poet for the 2021 American Society of Eighteenth-Century Studies (ASECS) conference, which garnered so many would-be contributors that it had to be split into two panels. Greg Clingham, well-known in the field for a long history of developing scholarly projects into impressive books, liked what he heard, and suggested Mark turn this into a book; the two of us became involved when Mark asked us to contribute chapters. Although he had lined up the contributors and had most of the abstracts in hand, before he could complete the book proposal, he suddenly, and unexpectedly, died of a heart attack. As a matter of fact, we were both in the middle of writing our chapters when we learned the terrible news. We stepped in to complete the project, but of course, this is really Mark Pedreira's book. It was his idea, and it was his enthusiasm, typical of Mark, that inspired all of us; we hope the result lives up to his expectations. We thank him, and we also thank Greg Clingham, Alison Mero, and John Morgenstern for their continued support of all our efforts.

Tribute to Mark Pedreira

Kevin L. Cope

C offee: a delicacy that often animates conference panels concerned with eighteenth-century mercantilism, cookery, or sociability but that seldom suffuses memorial minutes. Peculiar as it may be, my most cherished memories of my dear late friend, Mark Pedreira, swirl like latte cream atop the cheerful brew. Decades ago, for reasons that will now forever remain unknown, Mark began sending me an annual Christmas parcel containing a selection of the finest Caribbean and Central American plantation coffees, usually accompanied by a Christmas card expressing gratitude for "help" and for good deeds that I could never identify. Those annual (and probably undeserved) gifts capture the energetic uniqueness of Mark: the singular ease with which he performed magnanimous as well as surprising acts that, like a clever line from his favorite poet, Abraham Cowley, would happily startle, complexly delight, and joyfully ravish their beneficiary.

Mark had a congenially apparitional quality to him. One would often go months without hearing a word from him, then, presto, a letter would appear in an email box with a dazzling proposal, or he himself would step onto the stage of an academic convention, there to refresh an enduring friendship. Mark did not always have an easy life—his university and even his living conditions in Puerto Rico routinely bogged down under the pressure of hurricanes, epidemics, power outages, earthquakes, student unrest, and worse, yet one always suddenly and reliably "saw" Mark, dapperly dressed, across the table at some fine upscale restaurant in one of the deluxe ASECS conference cities. Seemingly unscathed by a world that, in sad fact, hammered him, he could always be counted on to pop up whenever cheerful conversation or lively debate animated a venue. From the fine intellectual filaments running through topics such as rhetoric, metaphor, and late neo-Baroque post-metaphysical poetry, he wove both an extensive web of publications and a vast network of friends, correspondents, and colleagues, not one of whom ever spoke an ill word of him, and every one of whom lauded him without hesitation.

Like Abraham Cowley, the poet whose legacy he was reviving when his life culminated, Mark embraced the contradictory and loved the peculiar. He could talk with endless enthusiasm about his extensive rare book collection while also wondering when and where he would regain the electrical power that dehumidified these tokens of merry old English eighteenth-century culture; he could inspire scholars normally concerned with "hot" topics to direct their attention to the peculiar panegyrics and bizarre conceptions of a poet like Cowley; he could, in sum, draw an entire world in the aforementioned cream atop his coffee. We thank you, Mark, for a life well lived, and, per your name, for leaving an indelible mark on the friendly world of long eighteenth-century studies. His death came as a real shock to me, and I shall I miss him, dearly.[1]

Contents

Figures

THE

WORKS

OF

Mr Abraham Cowley.

Confifting of

Thofe which were formerly Printed:

AND

Thofe which he Defign'd for the Prefs,

Now Publifhed out of the Authors

ORIGINAL COPIES.

LONDON,

Printed by *J. M.* for *Henry Herringman,* at the Sign of the
Blew Anchor in the Lower Walk of the *New*
Exchange. 1668.

Abraham Cowley, *The Works of Mr Abraham Cowley*
(London: Printed by J. M. for Henry Herringman, 1668)

Abbreviations

Cowley, *Six Books*
> Abraham Cowley, *The Third Part of the Works of Mr Abraham Cowley, Being His Six Books of Plants, Never before Printed in English: . . . Now made English by several Hands. With a Necessary Index* (London: Charles Harper, 1689)

Cowley, *Verses*
> Abraham Cowley, *Verses Written Upon Several Occasions* (London: Henry Herringman, 1663)

Cowley, *Works*
> Cowley, *Miscellanies*
> Cowley, *The Mistress*
> Cowley, *Pindariques*
> Cowley, *Davideis*
> Cowley, *Verses Written*
>> Abraham Cowley, *The Works of Mr. Abraham Cowley. Consisting of Those which were formerly Printed: And Those which he Designd for the Press* (London: J. M. for Henry Herringman, 1668). (Since each section is separately paginated, and the poems have no line numbers, we will refer to the title of the poem, the section, and the pagination within that section.)

Dryden, "Discourse"
> John Dryden, "Discourse concerning the Original and Progress of Satire," *The Satires of Decimus Junius Juvenalis. Translated into English Verse By Mr. Dryden, And Other Eminent Hands. Together with the Satires of Aulus Persius Flaccus* (London: Jacob Tonson, 1693 [1692]), i–[liv]

Johnson, *Lives*
> *Samuel Johnson: The Lives of the Most Eminent English Poets: With Critical Observations on Their Work* (1779–81), ed. Roger Lonsdale, 4 vols. (Oxford: Oxford University Press, 2006), online at Oxford Scholarly Editions database, www.oxford-scholarlyeditions.com/view/10.1093/actrade/9780199284795.book.1/actrade-9780199284795-work-1. The "Life of Cowley" is online at www.oxfordscholarlyeditions.com/view/10.1093/actrade/9780199284795.book.1/actrade-9780199284795-div1-8

Pope, *Poems*

> Alexander Pope, *The Poems of Alexander Pope: A Reduced Version of the Twickenham Text*, ed. John Butt (New Haven: Yale University Press, 1963), used for all quotations from Pope

Sprat, "Account"

> Thomas Sprat, "An Account of the Life and Writings of Mr. Abraham Cowley. Written to Mr. Clifford," from Cowley, *Works*, sig. A1r–e1v

SECONDARY SOURCES

Allsopp, *Poetry*

> Niall Allsopp, *Poetry and Sovereignty in the English Revolution* (Oxford: Oxford University Press, 2020)

Moul, *History*

> Victoria Moul, *Literary History of Latin and English Poetry: Bilingual Verse Culture in Early Modern England* (Cambridge: Cambridge University Press, 2022)

Nethercot, *Cowley*

> Arthur H. Nethercot, *Abraham Cowley: The Muse's Hannibal* (London: Oxford University Press, 1931)

Royalists, ed. Major

> *Royalists and Royalism in 17th-Century Literature: Exploring Abraham Cowley*, ed. Philip Major (New York: Routledge, 2020)

Trotter, *Poetry*

> David Trotter, *The Poetry of Abraham Cowley* (London: Macmillan, 1979)

Introduction

Michael Edson & Cedric D. Reverand II

> Of the English poets he [Milton] set most value upon
> Spenser, Shakespeare, and Cowley.
>
> —Samuel Johnson (*Lives*, 1:174)

When a centenary of a noted author's birth, or death, rolls around, we can generally expect commemorations, special volumes of scholarly essays devoted to the author, and conferences—Dryden's tercentenary produced three such conferences (at the University of Bristol, UCLA, and Yale)—yet when the latest centenary of Abraham Cowley (1618–67) occurred, nothing happened. Nobody noticed. Although period specialists know who Cowley is, most "common readers," to use Johnson's term, don't, and that includes both English majors and graduate students. Little wonder. It would be difficult to find any Cowley in the English literature anthologies commonly used in university courses. And although the term "metaphysical poetry" was coined, by Samuel Johnson, specifically to describe Cowley's verse, you would be hard pressed to find any of his poetry in modern anthologies of English metaphysical poetry.

And yet, as Milton's comment attests, Cowley was one of the major authors of his age. Writing in 1700, Daniel Defoe put Cowley and Milton at the front of his list of Restoration literary worthies:

1

Cowley, Milton, Ratcliff, Rochester,
Waller, Roscommon, Howard, and to *Bhen* [sic]
The Doubtful Fight the better to maintain;
Giants these were of Wit and Sense together.[1]

Shakespeare, Spenser, Milton, Dryden. Notice how Cowley keeps coming up, always in good company, especially in the first few decades after his death. Speaking of death: John Evelyn reported "neere an hundred Coaches of noble men & persons of qualitie following" in Cowley's funeral train to Westminster Abbey, where he was buried, in good company, near Chaucer, in what subsequently became known as Poet's Corner.[2] As Thomas Sprat reported, in his tribute to his late friend, "Whoever would do him right, should not only equal him to the Principle Ancient Writers of our own Nation, but should also rank his name amongst the Authors of true Antiquity, the best of the *Greeks* and *Romans*" ("Account," sig. e3v). We should, but we haven't. What exactly happened? And why? This collection will attempt to answer those questions.

Cowley seemed destined from his youth to match Dryden's and Milton's literary acclaim. Cowley was a child prodigy, publishing his first book at age fifteen, who went on, in adulthood, to write across many modes and genres, publishing love lyrics, Pindaric odes, Latin poems, two (unfinished) epics—one of which influenced Milton's *Paradise Lost*—four stage comedies, and *Plantarum Libri Sex* (1668), a heavily footnoted, 7,000-line Latin poem on the properties and uses of plants and herbs. As this last work indicates, he was also a "natural philosopher" who celebrated the New Science in both poetry and prose, the latter including his *Proposition for the Advancement of Experimental Philosophy* (1661), one of the proposals that led to the founding of the Royal Society. Fighting for Charles I during the English Civil War, Cowley wrote many of his works over the twelve years he lived in exile in France serving Charles's widow, Queen Henrietta Maria. After advancing the Royalist cause on the Continent as a messenger and spy, Cowley returned to England in 1656 and reluctantly "submitted to the conditions of the *Conqueror*," Oliver Cromwell ("Preface," *Davideis*, sig. A4r). After Cromwell's death in 1658, however, Cowley fled to Paris, resumed working with the Royalists, and returned with Charles II at the Restoration in 1660. Because of his acquiescence to Cromwell, however, he had difficulty convincing the restored regime of his loyalty to the Crown and repeatedly failed to gain preferment, especially the mastership of the Savoy Hospital, for which he had long angled. He retired first to Barn Elms, on the outskirts of London, and then to Chertsey, in Surrey, where he became an amateur horticulturist, and died at age forty-nine. A year after his death, Bishop Thomas Sprat's "Account," the first biography of Cowley, appeared, and it is important to note that it was written not by a fellow poet or *littérateur*, but by one of the founding members of the Royal Society, fitting for a polymath such as Cowley, whose writings mixed genres and bridged science with poetry. The hybrid, experimental quality of Cowley's poetry is one of the central issues, and a connecting theme, in the present collection.

Despite Sprat's efforts as biographer to buttress his friend's legacy and shield him from criticism for his perceived political flipfloppery, despite Cowley being considered as Milton and Dryden's peer, and despite his poetry being much more widely published, in the seventeenth and eighteenth centuries, than that of Donne, Herbert, Marvell, or Crashaw, Cowley's reputation faded toward the end of the eighteenth century. This is generally attributed to Johnson, who dismissed the poet's bloodless verse and overwrought "metaphysical conceits," qualities that T. S. Eliot, no fan of Cowley's, would later attribute to a "dissociation of sensibility." However, in providing examples of supposedly terrible Cowley metaphors in his "Life of Cowley," Johnson also cited many passages from Donne, whom he found equally guilty. And in his "Life of Milton," after extended, lavish praise of *Paradise Lost*, a work Johnson regarded as "great," Johnson went on to extended, lavish examples of the work's shortcomings: "The plan of *Paradise Lost* has this inconvenience, that it comprises neither human actions nor human manners"; "*Paradise Lost* is one of the books which the reader admires and lays down, and forgets to take up again"; and, most memorably, "None ever wished it longer than it is" (*Lives*, 1:244, 252). Yet the modern reputations of Donne and Milton don't seem to have suffered much.

By the 1950s, Cowley's poems had all but vanished from anthologies and syllabi, while the works of his erstwhile equals, Milton and Dryden, joined by his contemporaries, Donne and Herbert, became reliable hubs for the explicatory and editorial labors of the midcentury New Critical scholarly industrial complex. As Philip Major reminds us in the introduction to his fine 2020 collection, *Royalists and Royalism in 17th-Century Literature: Exploring Abraham Cowley,* no monograph devoted to Cowley has appeared since 1979 (David Trotter's *The Poetry of Abraham Cowley*), with Major's volume being the first edited collection on Cowley ever. Obviously, we, as the editors of the second collection on Cowley, heartily agree with Major's sense that Cowley deserves more attention. But inferring Cowley's current diminished status from the dearth of full-length books on him is a bit misleading. Single-author studies started to drop off in the 1990s for reasons related to the economics of academic publishing, making the lack of monographs on Cowley in the last thirty years not terribly surprising. By the measure of the single-author study, both Dryden and Pope could also be declared to have fallen nearly as far as Cowley, at least in the last decade, with Milton not far behind them. But anyone attending to articles and chapters knows this is not the case, not with Pope and Dryden, nor with Cowley. Since 2000, Christopher D'Addario, Niall Allsopp, Scott Black, Jane Darcy, Paul Davis, Alan De Gooyer, Richard Hillyer, David Hopkins, Theodore Kaouk, Kathryn R. King, Margaret Koehler, Simon Malpas, Tom Mason, Andrew Mattison, Henry Power, Adam Rounce, Joshua Scodel, Elizabeth Scott-Baumann, Nathaniel Stogdill, Joseph Wallace, and Thomas Ward, among others, have published articles or book chapters on Cowley.[3] He also features in recent work by Victoria Moul and others on neo-Latin poetry (*History,* chapter 5). Then there are the student editions of Cowley selections as well: Julia Griffin's for Penguin (1998), and Hopkins and Mason's for Carcanet (1994). Earlier, in 1989, the University of Delaware Press launched a projected six-volume authoritative edition of Cowley's works, edited by Thomas O. Calhoun, which should have marked the beginning of a Cowley revival. It even had the backing of a major National Endowment of the Humanities grant, which was renewed after the first volume was published in 1989, and the second in 1993 (the NEH referees who recommended renewing the grant were James Anderson Winn and Cedric Reverand). But posthumous bad luck struck again. Calhoun died, and despite Delaware's continuing efforts to find a new general editor, the whole editorial project fizzled out.

Cowley remains in limbo, seeming to be ever on the edge of reentering the canon, even as the field seems to be leaving the traditional canon behind. One could see this as just more of the same hard luck that sunk the poet's reputation. But his reputation may not be as low as we tend to assume. When Mark Pedreira proposed a session on Cowley for the 2021 American Society for Eighteenth-Century Conference (held online via Zoom), he was inundated by so many proposed papers, that he had to split the panel into two separate, well-attended sessions (well attended "virtually," of course). Indeed, the steady drip of new articles and chapters on Cowley in the last two decades, leading up to the 2021 conference, suggests that there was, and continues to be, much interest in Cowley, even if bad luck and uncertainty in academic publishing have combined to keep him out of sight and out of mind. Hence the title of this collection: our contributors seek to recover what was always there.

Even before his bad luck, Cowley suffered from bad timing. According to Major, Cowley's royalism rendered him unappealing to generations of literary critics who admired revolutionaries over conservatives (introduction, *Royalists*, 1–19, especially 7). Major is probably right, but this isn't the whole story. As the nine contributors to this volume show in their different ways, Cowley's initial popularity and later disappearance had more to do with poetics than politics. In bridging disciplines (botany and poetry), modes (prose, verse), and genres (lyric, ode, epic) in unexpected ways, Cowley's poetry was challengingly experimental, either far ahead of its time or, depending on your perspective, ages behind it. We see Cowley as being far ahead of everyone. Demonstrating how he blended neoclassical and baroque, metaphysical and baroque, poetry and prose, epic and history, science and verse, the essays to follow reveal Cowley as a daring poet whose innovative works fell between recognized categories and periods and therefore fell through the cracks of literary history.

Cedric Reverand sets the stage by examining the very question that animates this collection: how did Cowley, a poet regarded as major throughout the seventeenth and most of the eighteenth centuries, disappear from the canon? After charting how he fell from grace, Reverand proceeds to ask why, proposing that "the problem is not with Cowley; it's with our conception of literary categories." As it turns out, critics in assembling the canon could never quite fit Cowley into their conceptions of literary genres: the poet for whom Johnson coined the term "metaphysical poetry" wasn't metaphysical enough, but rather Cavalier, or Spenserian, or Miltonic, or Augustan, or neoclassical, or (when the commentators are hedging), transitional. Reverand goes on to examine a typical Cowley poem, demonstrating that it seems to be both baroque (like Dryden's ode to Anne Killigrew) and metaphysical (like Donne's lyrics) at the same time. What we discover, which other contributors to this volume explore, is that Cowley is too rich, too variegated; his verse shifts shape across genres, thereby eluding critics when they try to piece together a coherent (and linear) literary history.

Further suggesting that Cowley's merging of genres, styles, and traditions has frustrated generations of academics looking for tidy categories and clear distinctions, Kevin Cope focuses specifically on the strange mix of difficulty and "pop" accessibility in Cowley's poetry. Ranging across his lyrics, from the "Hymn. To Light" and "Ode upon Doctor Harvey," to one of his most famous and anthologized pieces, "The Grasshopper," Cope traces how Cowley invents dizzyingly complex conceits only often to spend the rest of a poem breaking these ideas down, workmanlike, into their component parts. Zooming in and then out, and also abruptly changing perspectives, to tease out every nuance in his metaphors, Cowley in his seemingly difficult poetry in fact offers an "easy-reading experience that seldom challenges the intellect," a quality that won Cowley popularity in his day but left many later readers scratching their heads. This habit of breaking down complex images and ideas, or Cowley's "segmented baroque," Cope argues, combines idioms and voices, including metaphysical, neoclassical, and Anacreontic, to create some startlingly poetic effects, much to the alarm of overly category-conscious scholars.

Cowley's experimental poetics often give priority to textual elements usually seen as secondary or marginal. Ian Calvert considers Cowley's re-prioritizing of digressions in his scriptural epic, *Davideis* (1656). While an expected feature of epic, the digressions in *Davideis*, as Calvert shows, often overshadow Cowley's "main" narrative in both size and importance. Through these digressions, Cowley gives his poetry a Royalist sublimity, a divine tranquility distinct from the enthusiasm associated with Puritan zeal. These digressions become vehicles for Cowley's hope that what seemed like the main plot of the 1650s—republican rule—"would ultimately turn out to be a digression from a Royalist norm." Questions of historical and political priority manifest in the poem's own structure, forcing readers to ask what is central and what is marginal, what is plot and what is digression, questions that the narrative's unfinished state only further intensifies.

Just as Calvert sees in *Davideis* a plot challenged for primacy by its own digressions, so Joshua Swidzinski finds in Cowley's *Pindariques* verse "eclipsed" by its own accompaniment of notes. As Swidzinski demonstrates, Cowley challenged contemporary expectations in presenting vast prose notes as essential complements to poetry, not as secondary or disposable appendages. Accumulating parallel passages or analyzing the poetry's images, these notes allow Cowley to play both the poet and scholar without violating decorum. While later readers such as Johnson criticized Cowley's too-complex poetry, a complexity his notes on the technicalities of his own metaphors magnified, Cowley's "prosimetric ode" influenced many eighteenth-century poets for whom "the mixture of verse and prose ... [became a] distinctive feature" of their own writings.

Adam Rounce continues the discussion of the notes in *Davideis*, following the leveling of hierarchies and mixing of kinds, literally into the margins. As in *Pindariques*, Cowley uses notes in *Davideis* to burnish his scholarly credentials, but his is an ironic, self-conscious pedantry that, once again, makes the verse seem secondary to the annotations. Far from just showing off his learning, however, Cowley often uses his explanations to comment wittily on the absurdity of learning, and on the futility of explanation. In offering a critical history of these notes and tracing Cowley's unique personality and sense of humor in them, Rounce argues for the delightful oddness of Cowley's prose-poetry experiments, an oddness that many later audiences found profoundly disorienting.

"Disorienting" also describes how many critics have regarded the subject of Caroline Spearing's essay, *The Civil War*, the other unfinished Cowley epic. Focusing on the poem's mixing of genres and fragmented tone—careening from epic triumphalism to elegiac grief and back—Spearing challenges the long-standing view of *The Civil War* as an artistic failure. She instead argues for Cowley's mixing of epic and elegiac as his way of gesturing at the alienation involved in civil war, and at the impossibility of true victory in any internecine conflict. By combining in his battlefield depictions the heroic idiom and moral certitude of Virgil with the grotesquerie and moral ambiguity associated with Lucan, Cowley reveals the difficulty of representing war in poetry, the poem's incompleteness thus necessitated by its subject matter.

Many of the chapters in this book, like Spearing's, explore how Cowley combines both genres and classical voices: Pindar, Ovid, Virgil, Lucan. Michael Edson adds Martial to this list, exploring how Cowley mixes verse and prose to lend his *Essays* (1668) a wry, Martialian wit. Noting occasional tensions between Cowley's idealistic poetry and his ironic or skeptical prose, Edson presents *Essays* as combining modes to foster contrasting perspectives, with Cowley indulging in the same self-mocking humor that Rounce finds in the notes to *Davideis*. Pointing out sly jokes throughout the *Essays*, Edson argues that Cowley laughs at his own investment in the retirement poet persona, making Martial, who mocked his own fantasies of escaping Rome, an ideal vehicle for Cowley to express misgivings about retiring to Chertsey. We have missed Cowley's humor for the same reasons we have ignored Martial's role in *Essays*: discomfort with Cowley's supposedly false, mixed wit, a humor for which Martial was the classical exemplar.

Cowley moved in Royal Society circles, and no study would be complete without considering the interplay between natural philosophy and poetry in Cowley's works. As Katarzyna Lecky argues in her chapter on *Plantarum Libri Sex* (1662/1668), Cowley adapts the emerging terms and hierarchies of botany from the Royal Society to a distinctively poetic way of appreciating florae. His fusion of botanical and poetic idioms is subversive, refusing not only the male-dominated utilitarianism of the botany practiced by the Royal Society specifically, but also all human attempts to classify and control nature generally. Taking an Ovidian delight in how the disorderly, transforming qualities of plants defeat human agency, Cowley bridges his identities as naturalist and poet at a time when scientific discourse was drifting apart from artistic representation. Ultimately, *Plantarum* offers "an alternate version of expertise" where plants are not defined according to human needs.

To close the volume by returning to the issues of canonization and reception raised in Reverand's opening chapter, Philip Smallwood considers Johnson's response to *Pindariques* as explaining Cowley's appeal to eighteenth-century poets. While Johnson's "Life" is often wrongly thought to have initiated Cowley's slow disappearance from the canon,

Johnson, as Smallwood asserts, was not as critical of Cowley as he could well have been. Johnson objects to Cowley's overdrawn metaphors, but he also tolerates the exuberance of Cowley's metrical irregularities and repeated rhymes, and even applauds his "axiomatic habits" of expression as reminiscent of Shakespeare's own. Prior, Congreve, Watts receive no similar praise from Johnson for their Pindaric labors, and it was Cowley's freedom and energy, even in his defects, Smallwood argues, that Johnson and other poets admired.

As will now be clear, in addition to showing how Cowley challenges artistic hierarchies and expectations in the past, this collection also aims to foreground aspects of his writings that might give new pleasure to readers now and in the future. Critical movements, such as the New Formalism and New Lyric Studies, have recently brought renewed attention to poetics, genre, and generic hybridity. At the same time, the growth of interdisciplinary approaches across academic fields has generated new interest in interdisciplinarity in the past, before the word "interdisciplinary" even existed, especially between science and literature. Scholars today are more interested than ever in writings that defy traditional categories and hierarchies; Cowley, as a poet-botanist working across and between the genres and disciplines defining his era as well as our own, is therefore uniquely positioned to reap the rewards of our changing critical tastes today. In studying his generic shape-shifting and poetic experimentation, this book presents Cowley as a poet who should appeal to seventeenth- and eighteenth-century literature scholars approaching genre, discipline, and canon formation in new ways. Our sense is that the time is right for Cowley's luck finally to take a turn for the better.

CHAPTER ONE

"Who Now Reads Cowley?"

How a Major Poet Disappeared from the Canon

Cedric D. Reverand II

> Who now reads Cowley? if he pleases yet,
> His moral pleases, not his pointed wit;
> Forget his Epic, nay Pindaric Art,
> But still I love the language of his Heart.

—Alexander Pope, "The First Epistle of the Second Book of
Horace Imitated" (1737), ll. 75–78.[1]

The black marble gravestone for the poet, in the floor of Poets' Corner in Westminster Abbey, reads, in extremely large letters,[2]

ABRAHAM COULEIUS

H.S.E.[2]

1667

The top of this stone, above Cowley's coat of arms, bears the following inscription, in much smaller letters:

Near This Stone Lie Buried

Geoffrey Chaucer	1400	John Dryden	1700
Francis Beavmont	1616	Charles de St. Denis	
Sir John Denham	1669	Lord of St. Evremond	1703
Sir Robert Moray		Matthew Prior	1721

My reaction when I first saw this, many years ago, was to laugh, and wonder: what on earth happened? According to Samuel Johnson, "Milton is said to have declared, that the three greatest English poets were Spenser, Shakspeare, and Cowley." Dryden, in his preface to his 1692 translations of Juvenal and Persius, called Cowley "the Darling of my youth." Cowley's funeral hearse was followed to the abbey by nearly a hundred coaches filled with noblemen and persons of quality, according to John Evelyn.[3] Just opposite the floor tablet is Cowley's white marble monument, donated by his patron, the Duke of Buckingham, placed against the western wall of Poet's Corner, to the immediate left of Chaucer's tomb; it features an urn on a pedestal, and a medallion containing a lengthy Latin inscription, written by his friend, Thomas Sprat. In short, Cowley was the great poet of his generation, who overshadowed those now more-familiar names. Yet today, one would be hard pressed to find a single Cowley poem in any of the anthologies commonly used in college English courses.

Well, tastes change. Walter Scott was one of the most popular poets in the first decades of the nineteenth century, but who now reads, or teaches, "The Lay of the Last Minstrel" or "Marmion." Edward Bulwer-Lytton once rivaled his friend Dickens as a popular Victorian novelist, but who now remembers *Pelham* or *The Last Days of Pompeii*? Bulwer-Lytton is now remembered, when remembered at all, for convincing Dickens to write an alternate, happier ending to *Great Expectations*, and for beginning one of his novels (*Paul Clifford*) with the immortal line, "It was a dark and stormy night." Same thing here: tastes change. But tastes always change. That's not a helpful observation. The real question should be, *why* did tastes change? Or, back to my initial reaction, what happened? Answering that question will, I think, not only tell us something about Cowley, but, equally important, will also reveal some of the serious problems, and limitations, modern commentators have encountered in dealing with literary history.

The general consensus is that after his death, Cowley's reputation faded quickly. Part of the blame, or credit, goes to Dryden for comments in his preface to *Fables* (1700):

> One of our late great Poets is sunk in his Reputation, because he cou'd never forgive any Conceit which came his way; but swept like a Drag-net, great and small. . . . For this Reason, although he must always be thought a great Poet, he is no longer esteem'd a good Writer; And for Ten Impressions, which his Works have had in so many successive Years, yet at present a hundred Books are scarcely purchas'd once a Twelvemonth.[4]

But Samuel Johnson is thought to have administered the *coup de grâce*, because of his "Life of Cowley," from *Lives of the Most Eminent English Poets* (1779–81), in which Cowley became the occasion for Johnson to define the genre of metaphysical poetry, and blast the "whole race" because, in their poetry,

> the most heterogeneous ideas are yoked by violence together; nature and art are ransacked for illustrations, comparisons, and allusions; their learning instructs, and their subtilty surprises; but the reader commonly thinks his improvement dearly bought, and though he sometimes admires, is seldom pleased. (1:56)

Then, Johnson proceeds to illustrate their far-fetched metaphors—"Who but Donne would have thought a good man is a telescope?" (1:78)—with a barrage of examples, primarily from Cowley, Donne, and Cleveland.

But, in fact, this generally accepted idea of Cowley's quick fall from grace is incorrect. Johnson didn't put an end to his reputation. Although we remember his disparaging remarks on metaphysical poetry, and his examples of abstruse references, strained metaphors he labels "conceits," overly intellectualized arguments that abound in that poetry, we tend to forget that Johnson also praises Cowley:

> It must be however confessed of all these writers [the metaphysicals], that if they are upon common subjects often unnecessarily

and unpoetically subtle; yet where scholastick speculation can be properly admitted, their copiousness and acuteness may justly be admired. What Cowley has written upon Hope, shews an unequalled fertility of invention. (1:99)

His strength always appears in his agility; his volatility is not the flutter of a light, but the bound of an elastick mind. (1:109)

[The poems in *The Mistress*] are written with exuberance of wit, and with copiousness of learning. (1:119)

In the following odes, where Cowley chooses his own subjects, he sometimes rises to dignity truly Pindarick, and, if some deficiencies of language be forgiven, his strains are such as those of the Theban bard were to his contemporaries. (1:131)

Furthermore, Johnson's "Life of Cowley" is the first entry in *Lives of the English Poets*, which, in itself, suggests something about his reputation at the time. It is also the longest of Johnson's lives, and, according to Boswell, "Johnson himself" considered it "the best of the whole."[5] It is also worth noting that *Lives* does not include biographies of Donne, Herbert, Marvell, or Crashaw. At the time, they weren't even in Cowley's league.

As for Dryden's dismissive comment about "one of our late great Poets" who has "sunk in his Reputation," Dryden never actually says *which* one of our late great poets he had in mind. People have just assumed, probably because he mentions overly ingenious conceits, it must have been Cowley. However, as Dryden was making this comment, the publisher Henry Herringman was about to offer an augmented ninth edition of Cowley's works, which is scarcely what one would call evidence of a sunken reputation; clearly, this contradicts Dryden's statement about so few of this late great poet's books being purchased in a twelvemonth. It seems to me more likely, and more in line with the facts, to think that Dryden may have been alluding to Wycherley or Etherege.[6]

Far from declining, Cowley's reputation remained strong across the eighteenth century, which becomes apparent now that we have access to searchable databases, including Early English Books Online (EEBO) the

Eighteenth Century Collections Online (ECCO), and the Digital Miscellanies Index (DMI). His posthumous works, collected by his friend Thomas Sprat, were reprinted fourteen times before 1721, and then, in various editions, appeared in 1721, 1772, and 1777 [dated 1778].[7] *The Literary Magazine* (January 1758) rated twenty-nine authors: "Pope scored highest with seventy-one, followed by Milton, Dryden, and Addison. At the next level stood the improbable trio of Shakespeare, Cowley, and Swift, each awarded a total of sixty-six."[8] Cowley doesn't come out on top, but he's "reduced" to the same level as Shakespeare. ECCO reveals that, where Cowley was going through at least twelve editions in the eighteenth century, there were but three collections of Donne poems, five of Herbert, three of Marvell, and one of Crashaw. Adam Rounce also observes that Donne and Herbert had "relatively sparse appearances in the DMI" (160), while samples of Cowley abound. Wordsworth, in his "Essay Supplementary to the Preface, 1815," notes: "Turning to my own shelves, I find the folio of Cowley, seventh edition, 1681. . . . I well remember that, twenty-five years ago, the booksellers' stalls in London swarmed with the folios of Cowley."[9] This is only anecdotal information, to be sure, but if Wordsworth is accurate, even though he seems to be reflecting on a decline in Cowley's reputation in 1815, he nonetheless reports that the booksellers' stalls were teeming with Cowley back in the 1790s—and Wordsworth himself owns a seventh edition. When Pope, in 1737, asked, "Who now reads Cowley?," the answer would have been, many, many people. Yet, as Rounce comments, "For all his popularity, it seems to have been the peculiar fate of Cowley to have his reputation continually called into question, whether or not there was any evidence of a decline" (163).[10]

The actual *coup de grâce* for Cowley came in our own times, primarily at the hands of T. S. Eliot in his famous 1921 *TLS* review of H. J. Grierson's *Metaphysical Lyrics and Poems of the Seventeenth Century* (1921), followed by Eliot's further ideas on metaphysical poetry from his 1926 Clark Lectures at Trinity College, Cambridge, and 1933 Trumbull Lectures at Johns Hopkins University.[11] Eliot managed to resuscitate the genre, in large part because of his "belief that this poetry and this age have some peculiar affinity with our poetry and our own age" (43). Indeed, who but a metaphysical poet would have thought an evening was like a patient etherized upon a table? What Eliot admired about Donne was his supposed ability to draw "within the orbit of feeling and sense what had existed only in thought" (51). While Donne succeeding in fusing sense and thought, Cowley, in Eliot's opinion, failed. Cowley imitates Donne, and thus

> comes to resemble him somewhat in spirit as well as form— though no one was less gifted to this end by nature. And yet Cowley, I shall admit in advance, does not satisfy my definition of metaphysical poetry. He fails to make the Word Flesh, though he often makes it Bones. . . . In Cowley we reach the fringes of the metaphysical poetry; and I have elected to give him so much attention, because it was Cowley who represented this age to the next, and who, by a kind of fusion with Denham, Waller, and others, effects a transition, less violent than we are often led to believe by the history books, to the Augustan Age. (61, 63)

"My definition of metaphysical poetry," as Eliot explains, is different from Johnson's definition of metaphysical poetry, and it is something narrower; in particular, it has to merge feeling and reason; when this fails to occur, we get the now well-known "dissociation of sensibility." Somehow, Cowley doesn't successfully combine the two, although, *pace* Eliot, I remain puzzled as to how anybody can actually tell that a poem combined the emotional with the rational, or, for that matter, determine how a poem failed to combine the two. And yet, Eliot's notion of this fusion, and its opposite, the dissociation of sensibility, have caught on and, as we shall see, have influenced many commentators in their approach to the poetry of this period.

The Grierson anthology Eliot reviewed includes, by my count, 35 poems by Donne, 7 by Cowley; other now familiar names represented include Vaughan (11), Herbert (13)—both under "Divine Poems"—Marvell (10), Carew (10), and Crashaw (7).[12] What begins as an assortment of metaphysical and quasi-metaphysical poets, however, narrows in the numerous scholarly studies of seventeenth-century poetry appearing after Eliot's commentary, and Cowley simply disappears. Joan Bennett's *Four Metaphysical Poets* from 1934 featured Donne, Herbert, Vaughan, and Crashaw. Her 1964 *Five Metaphysical Poets* added Marvell. Both J. B. Leishman's *The Metaphysical Poets* (1934) and Helen White's *The Metaphysical Poets* (1936) include Donne, Herbert, Vaughan, and Traherne. Rosemund Tuve's *Elizabethan and Metaphysical Imagery* (1947) covers mostly Elizabethan poets, especially Shakespeare, Spenser, and Sidney. Of the metaphysicals, Donne gets plenty of attention, with passing nods to Traherne and Herbert, but a total of only one mention of Cowley. And so it continues, right up until more recent times: Richard Willmott's anthology, *Four Metaphysical Poets* (1985), includes poetry by Donne, Herbert, Marvell, and Vaughan; Sidney Gottlieb's MLA volume from 1990, *Approaches to Teaching the Metaphysical Poets*, covers Crashaw, Donne, Herbert, Marvell, and Vaughan. Frances Austen's *The Language of the Metaphysical Poets*, from 1992, discusses Donne, Herbert, Crashaw, Vaughan, and Traherne.[13] Compare that to pre-Eliot editions of British poetry: the multivolume *British Poets* series edited by F. J. Child (1822–55) includes Donne, Cowley, and Marvell; Alexander Grosart's *The Fuller Worthies' Library* series from the 1870s includes Donne, Herbert, Cowley, and Marvell.[14] But, once Eliot has spoken, Cowley gets ushered out of the metaphysical mode altogether.

This is how Cowley dropped by the wayside, I think, but the question remains: why? I find hints to a possible answer in Eliot's comment, specifically when he calls Cowley transitional. We should remember that Cowley was a master of many genres, many of which the contributors to this volume will be exploring, including lyrical poems in the Cavalier mode (*The Mistress*), comedies, Anacreontics, essays, an incomplete heroic epic, *Davideis*, which influenced Milton, even poems in Latin, which Johnson admired:

> At the same time were produced from the same university, the two great Poets, Cowley and Milton, of dissimilar genius, of opposite principles; but concurring in the cultivation of Latin poetry. . . . If the Latin performances of Cowley and Milton be compared, . . . the advantage seems to lie on the side of Cowley. Milton is generally content to express the thoughts of the ancients in their language; Cowley, without much loss of purity or elegance, accommodates the diction of Rome to his own conceptions. (1:33, 34)

While we cannot help thinking of Cowley as a metaphysical poet, thanks primarily to Johnson, in Cowley's own day he was known best for his English translations and imitations of Pindar, first published in 1665. The elaborate inscription on his Poets' Corner monument opens with "Anglorum Pindarus, Flaccus, Maro," ("the Pindar, Horace, and Virgil of England").

Basically, Pindaric poems are over-the-top extravaganzas, irregular, impassioned, ambitious, wildly expressive, overreaching—all traits we associate with "the baroque"—as well as loose in logical structure (sometimes veering into the realm of the incoherent), filled with hyperbolic claims and extreme metaphors. And Cowley was the absolute master of Pindar. In fact, Dryden used Cowley's translations of Pindar to define what he meant by a proper translation, which, for Dryden, was not literal, "Confin'd" to an author's "Sense," but a free imitation: only "A Genius so Elevated and unconfin'd as Mr. *Cowley*'s" could handle "So wild and ungovernable a Poet," and "make Pindar speak English."[15] Like the similarly baroque English heroic dramas of the late seventeenth century, this was a mode that was quick to find detractors. Congreve, in his "Discourse on the Pindarique Ode" (1706), took Cowley to task for ignoring Pindar's strophe-antistrophe-epode structure, for turning Pindar's regularity into irregular stanzas, and for producing "a Bundle of rambling incoherent thoughts" and "uncertain and perplex'd Verses and Rhymes" (sig. A1r).

Nonetheless, this was Cowley's forte, of which Johnson took particular notice, in a passage worth quoting at length:

> The Pindarique Odes have so long enjoyed the highest degree of poetic reputation, that I am not willing to dismiss them with unabated censure; and surely though the mode of their composition be erroneous, yet many parts deserve at least that admiration which is due to great comprehension of knowledge, and great fertility of fancy. The thoughts are often new, and often striking; but the greatness of one part is disgraced by the littleness of another; and total negligence of language gives the noblest conceptions the appearance of a fabric August in plan, but mean in the materials. Yet surely those verses are not without a just claim to praise; of which it may be said with truth, that no man but Cowley could have written them. (1:144)

This is begrudging praise, to say the least, but Johnson is admitting, if one accepts the Pindaric ode as valid, that Cowley is the master of that mode, even though he is also the poet who occasioned Johnson's definition of metaphysical poetry. Modern critics find themselves straining to fit Cowley into Johnson's metaphysical mode—remember, Eliot can only get him as far as the fringes of metaphysical poetry—but therein lies the problem. He can't be made to fit, and I think it's because his supposedly metaphysical poems are actually "baroque metaphysical" poems; he straddles two categories, one of which was reborn in the twentieth century because of its resemblance to contemporary poetry, the other of which, epitomized by the Pindaric ode, was short-lived, as Johnson attests—he is willing to praise Cowley's Pindarics because they once enjoyed "the highest degree of poetic reputation." But by the time Johnson was writing, the Pindaric ode was no longer in fashion, and, as anybody who has tried to teach Dryden's ode to Anne Killigrew to undergraduates will attest, it is not likely to return any time soon. As some indication of how alien that mode is to modern sensibilities, one might note that there is a well-known article, by David Vieth, arguing that Dryden is actually satirizing Anne Killigrew (which would have come as an unwelcome surprise to Anne's father, Thomas Killigrew, who was Dryden's friend and sometime business partner). Faced with Dryden's baroque exaltation of a minor poet—the poem ends with the preposterous, but typically baroque, image of Anne leading all mankind to heaven with the raising of the dead at the Last Judgment—Vieth cannot believe Dryden's praise could be genuine.[16] I would add that although the *Norton Anthology of English Literature*, probably the most commonly used anthology in standard college English literature courses, once included the poem to Anne Killigrew in its Dryden selection, it was dropped from editions somewhere in the 1980s. So much for the Pindaric making a surprise comeback to the canon.

In essence, Cowley doesn't qualify for Eliot's canon because he's too baroque to be metaphysical. It is not just Eliot who has a problem trying to see Cowley as a metaphysical poet. F. R. Leavis, who endorses Eliot's account of metaphysical poetry, and who, like Eliot, regards Donne as its supreme practitioner, examines Cowley's "Ode. Of Wit," and struggles:

> In the penultimate short couplet of the first stanza quoted—
>> Such were the Numbers which could call
>> The Stones into the Theban wall
> —and in most of the second stanza, Cowley is clearly lurching into Pindarics. The smoothed and polite Metaphysical of the

poem in general moves towards Mr. Waller. We might reasonably call what is illustrated here "dissociation of sensibility."[17]

Or we might call it category confusion. What starts as a polite metaphysical poem somehow has lurched into the Pindaric, except that just a few pages earlier, Leavis thought the poem wasn't metaphysical at all: "In that poem he discusses and expounds wit in a manner and spirit quite out of resonance with the Metaphysical mode—quite alien and uncongenial to it" (30). It is difficult to understand how it could leave the "polite Metaphysical" mode, when it stood outside that mode in the first place. Like Eliot, Leavis also implies that Cowley is a transitional figure: "He suggests curiously (and significantly) at one and the same time Spenser, a more tenderly and disinterestedly elegiac Milton, and a purified elegiac strain of the eighteenth century (see Gray's sonnet on Richard West)" (26). Similarly, Geoffrey Walton, regards Cowley as "a transitional figure between the Metaphysical and Cavalier Schools and Dryden and the Augustans."[18] Robert B. Hinman observes that "most scholars . . . agree with George Williamson that Cowley is a decadent, transitional writer whose work reflects the growing distrust of imagination in the latter half of the seventeenth century" (20). Williamson is, I think, also worth quoting at greater length:

> Seldom, however, did he [Cowley] synthesize experience into the more complicated expression of the Metaphysical imagination. His wit had a more limited range of feeling, and his learning, though various, more limited systems of invention. . . . In him the Metaphysical complex begins to break up: wit begins to be separated into the Anacreontic or satiric poem, passion transformed into the magniloquence of the Pindaric ode, argument into public discourse. In verse, even in the Pindaric ode, principles of balance exert themselves more and more, and imagination gradually submits to decorum. But Cowley also translates elements of wit and speech into Neo-Classical verse that endured.[19]

First, he's not quite a metaphysical, or he's Miltonic, or Spenserian, but he's shifting into the satiric, or the Pindaric, but then, Eliot, Leavis, Walton, and Williamson maintain, he is finally moving into the neoclassical verse of the next generation. While Williamson sees Cowley straddling several categories, Donald Mackenzie limits the straddling to two genres:

> Cowley, acclaimed in his day as one of the greatest English poets, is now read only by specialists and the occasional random general reader who is likely to find his lyrics in the Metaphysical style imitative and limp—Donne poems rewritten on blotting paper— and his Pindaric Odes a creaky extravagance.[20]

Now, Cowley is insufficiently metaphysical, or too extravagantly Pindaric. The very poet that led Johnson to define metaphysical poetry in the first place has been excluded altogether from the category his poetry defined. The problem is not with Cowley; it's with our conception of literary categories.

I think I can illustrate what I mean by Cowley's baroque metaphysical mode by examining one of his poems, his "Ode: Sitting and Drinking in the Chair, made out of the Reliques of Sir *Francis Drake's* Ship."[21] This was first published in 1663, not part of his "love verses" assembled in *The Mistress* (1647), and not one of his Pindaric odes or imitations—*Pindaric Odes* was first published in 1665. In other words, it is one of his miscellaneous poems, of the sort Johnson presumably had in mind when he described Cowley's metaphysical mode:

> Chear up my Mates, the wind does fairly blow
>   Clap on more sail and never spare;
>   Farewell all Lands, for now we are
>   In the wide Sea of Drink, and merrily we go:
> Bless me, 'tis hot! another bowl of wine,   5
>   And we shall cut the Burning Line:
> Hey Boyes! she scuds way, and by my head I know,
>   We round the World are sailing now
> What dull men are those who tarry at home,
> When abroad they might wantonly rome,   10
>   And gain such experience, and spy too
>   Such Countries, and Wonders as I do?
> But prythee good *Pilot*, take heed what you do,

And sail not to touch at *Peru*;
With Gold, there the Vessel we'll store,   15
And never, and never be poor,
No never be poor any more.

What do I mean? What thoughts do me misguide?
As well upon a staff may Witches ride
       Their fancy'd Journies in the Ayr,   20
As I sail round the Ocean in this Chair:
'Tis true; but yet this Chair which here you see,
For all its quiet now, and gravitie,
Has wandred, and has travailed more,
Than ever Beast, or Fish, or Bird, or even Tree before.   25
In every Ayr, and every Sea't has been,
'T has compas'd all the Earth, and all the Heavens 't has seen.
Let not the Pope's it self with this compare,
This is the only Universal Chair.

The pious Wandrers Fleet, sav'd from the flame,   30
(Which still the Reliques did of *Troy* persue,
       And took them for its due)
A squadron of immortal Nymphs became:
Still with their Arms they row about the Seas,
And still make new, and greater voyages;   35
Nor has the first Poetick Ship of *Greece*,
(Though now a star she so Triumphant show,
And guide her sailing Successors below,
Bright as her ancient freight the shining fleece;)
Yet to this day a quie[t] harbour found,   40
The tide of Heaven still carries her around.
Only *Drakes* Sacred vessel which before
      Had done, and had seen more,
      Than those have done or seen,
Ev'n since they Goddesses, and this a Star has been;   45
As a reward for all her labour past,
      Is made the seat of rest at last.
      Let the case now quite alter'd be,
And as tho[u] went'st abroad the World to see;
      Let the World now come to see thee.   50

The World will do't; for Curiositie
Does no less that devotion, Pilgrims make;
And I my self who now love quiet too,
As much almost as any Chair can do,
            Would yet a journey take,   55
An old wheel of that Chariot to see,
            Which *Phaeton* so rashly brake:
Yet what could that say more than these remains of *Drake*?
Great Relique! thou too, in this Port of ease,
Hast still one way of Making Voyages;   60
The breath of fame, like an auspicious Gale,
            (The great trade-wind which ne'er does fail,)
Shall drive thee round the World, and thou shalt run,
            As long around it as the Sun.
The straights of time too narrow are for thee,   65
Launch forth into an indiscovered Sea,
And steer the endless course of vast Eternitie,
Take for thy Sail this Verse, and for thy *Pilot* Mee.[22]

What would make this poem metaphysical?[23] As Johnson explained, "The fault of Cowley, and perhaps of all the writers of the metaphysical race, is that of pursuing his thoughts to their last ramifications" (1:133), and here we have a whole poem devoted to a chair, with Cowley piling on metaphoric possibilities and allusions. One thinks of Donne's penchant for stuffing an enormous amount of significance into a single object; he has not one, but two poems that are about a "bracelet of bright haire about the bone" ("The Relique," "The Funerall").[24] Admittedly, a chair is larger than an anchor, a coin, or a bracelet, but it is still a single object, which becomes a theme on which Cowley seems to be playing variations.

Johnson commented that "as authors of this race were perhaps more desirous of being admired than understood, they sometimes drew their conceits from recesses of learning not very much frequented by common readers of poetry" (1:65). We start with the speaker "sitting and drinking" in Drake's chair, but as the poem unfolds, Cowley expects the reader to recognize allusions to book 9 of the *Aeneid*, when, as Turnus is watching the Trojan ships burn, they suddenly turn into a "squadron of immortal

Nymphs," not exactly one of the most familiar episodes from the poem. Next, without pause, we encounter an allusion to Jason and the Golden Fleece, which, Cowley tells us, is "now a star," alluding to the constellation Argo Navis. Following this, we encounter a reference to the myth of Phaeton (most fully developed in Ovid), who borrowed the chariot of Helios, his father, for a day, and "rashly" crashed it. That would be three classical allusions, along with a sidelong reference to a constellation, all of which would be not generally known to most "common readers of poetry"—you need footnotes to read Cowley—and notice that Cowley does not even deign to mention either Aeneas or Jason by name; it is assumed that readers will simply recognize the allusions. When it comes to poetry, there are some, like Johnson, who seem to regard too much learning as a dangerous thing.

Unlike Cavalier poets, or Renaissance poets, who can be formal and decorous, Donne has a habit of falling into the vernacular with his opening lines: "Goe, and catche a falling starre"; "For Godsake hold your tongue, and let me love"; "I wonder by my troth, what thou and I / Did, till we lov'd?"; "Marke but this flea"; "Stand still, and I will read to thee / A Lecture." Similarly, Cowley's opening lines are direct and conversational: "Chear up my Mates, the wind does fairly blow, / Clap on more sails and never spare." Donne also likes puns, sometimes puns that rely on the etymological roots of words. He opens "The Relique" with these lines:

> When my grave is broke up againe
> Some second ghest to entertaine,
>   (For graves have learn'd that woman-
>   To be to more than one a Bed)
>   And he that digs it, spies
> A bracelet of bright hair about the bone,
>   Will he not let us alone,
> And thinke that there a loving couple lies.

There are two puns here. One is on "Bed," which is both a bed of earth, and the kind of bed on which women can indulge in their supposedly innate promiscuity. The other pun, which is generally lost on undergraduates, comes in the first two lines. There is an obvious macabre humor in the idea of a grave entertaining a guest—the word "ghest" locks in the idea that "entertaine" means "treat with hospitality," as if the grave is about to lay out some wine and cheese. But "entertaine" comes from Latin *inter + tenere*, "to hold along with," a meaning still employed when we "entertain an idea." It would be the accurate way of describing what is about to happen, that is, the grave is about to hold a second body along with the first.

Cowley uses a similar pun at the end of the second stanza. After explaining how far this chair has traveled, when it was part of a ship, "more, / Than ever Beast, or Fish, or Bird, or Tree before," he ends with the couplet:

> Let not the Pope's it self with this compare,
> This is the only Universal Chair.

This is a snide allusion to the pope's supposed infallibility, and, as such, not unlike Donne's frequent slaps at Catholicism: what emanates from the papal chair is supposed to be universally true, but, instead, Cowley insists that "This is the only universal chair." The Latin root would be *uni + vertere* = to turn once. Drake's chair is literally the only universal chair, because it is the only chair that has gone once around the earth. And, just to double the humor, Drake's chair is in Oxford University's Bodleian Library, which means it is also a university chair, although one is no longer allowed to sit in it, sober or drunk.[25]

Yet this metaphysical poem could just as easily qualify as a Pindaric ode. First, as Congreve complained, it is irregular: the first stanza is seventeen lines long, the second twelve, the third twenty-one, and the fourth eighteen. No two stanzas have the same shape, and even the line length varies: the opening line has ten syllables, the second line eight, the third line eight, the fourth line twelve, and so forth. There is no predictable rhyme scheme: the first stanza runs abba cc aa dd eee ggg; it just rhymes miscellaneously. Next, it has its share of outrageous claims, including the claim that the "breath of fame" shall speed the chair "around the World, and thou shalt run, / As long around it as the Sun," all thanks to "this Verse." The chair, as a ship, is also superior to Jason's "first Poetick Ship of *Greece*," and to Aeneas's ships that became nymphs who "Still with their

Arms they row about the Seas." In part because Pindaric poets strain for transcendence, they also seem to be drawn to the metaphor of flight. Not only does Anne Killigrew ascend, at the end of her poem, to lead mankind to heaven at the Last Judgment, but the poem opens with her as "Thou youngest virgin-daughter of the skies" (l. 1), and proceeds to the poet wondering

> Whether, adopted to some neighboring star,
> Thou roll'st above us in thy wandering race,
> Or in procession fixed and regular,
> Moved with the heavens' majestic pace;
> Or called to a more superior bliss,
> Thou tread'st with seraphims the vast abyss. (ll. 6–11)[26]

In the poem's penultimate stanza, she is "Among the Pleiads, a new-kindled star" (l. 175), serving as guiding light to "her warlike brother on the seas" (l. 165). Cowley's chair takes off in stanza 2, "As well upon a staff may Witches ride / Their Fancy'd Journies in the Ayr," and remains airborne until the end of the penultimate stanza, when, as a "reward for all her labour past," it "Is made the seat of rest at last." And just as Anne is a star guiding her warlike brother, so does Cowley liken the chair to "the first Poetick Ship of *Greece*," which has become "now a star," that serves to "guide her sailing Successors below." I suppose if one is going to indulge in baroque metaphors of flight, stars are convenient, because the higher the better.

When we add this to the other modes of Cowley's vast output, the very notion of categories seems to fall apart. I have to admit, though, that I am guilty of relying on the very categories whose existence I have been questioning, but I use the terms simply because informed readers will know, immediately, what "baroque" means and what "metaphysical" means. Still, if Cowley can be both, does either mode actually exist as a distinct mode? Unlike the French Impressionist painters, who met with each other and shared exhibitions, the metaphysical poets were not a group, and one could argue that there are as many differences between them as similarities. Is Marvell really like Donne? Is anybody really like Crashaw? As convenient as the idea of separate poetic genres is, here it has served to squeeze Cowley out of the canon, since he does not qualify for his own mode. The other modern predisposition that has excluded him from the canon is implicit in the penchant for calling him a transitional figure, because a transition implies a movement, from a, to b, although those who call Cowley a transitional figure have a difficult time determining where he's moving from, and where he's moving to. While comparing modes and building linear histories have been ubiquitous organizing devices, they are also suspect: literature, like life itself, is messy. Maybe a, b, and c, far from being distinct modes, all overlap, and maybe, instead of occurring sequentially, they are all happening at the same time.

One of the prices we pay for these convenient organizing strategies, as I have been arguing, is losing a poet who was considered great in his own times, and remained popular for at least a century and a half afterwards, although one could also argue that the loss is partially offset by the elevation of two important poets, Donne and Herbert, who, believe it or not, were once considered "minor" (Eliot also had kind words to say about Herbert). Both of these strategies are only possible when we have limited data, because only limited amounts of data can be managed and sorted out. In fact, it might even be the case that limited data make organizing that data irresistible, even when we cannot be sure that the data at hand are actually representative. However, with the advent of such databases as EEBO, ECCO, and DMI, on which I have been relying for this essay, our options have changed drastically. We are now confronted with vast amounts of material; furthermore, the data are searchable, as no libraries are. That treasure trove allows us to revise notions of the canon that were constructed on the basis of a limited number of examples. For instance, in the 1950s, we had Alan Dugald McKillop's *The Early Masters of English Fiction* (1956), which traces the development of the English novel using Defoe, Richardson, Fielding, Smollett, and Sterne, as well as Ian Watt's heavily influential *The Rise of the Novel* (1957), which adjusts the list to Defoe, Richardson, Fielding, and a smattering of Sterne (were there no women novelists?). To their credit, McKillop and Watt were doing admirable work with the data available to them. But if we are no longer constrained by limited data, things are different. Working with EEBO and ECCO, Leah Orr, in *Novel Ventures: Fiction and Print Culture in England, 1690–1730* (2017), examined 475 "novels" in the period, coming up with a richer, more nuanced, more detailed account of what was happening to the novel, an account that is not as comfortingly clear as that of McKillop or Watt, but that has the advantage of being much more accurate. As Orr has demonstrated, using those databases reveals that literary history is, indeed, messy, that genres overlap and blur, and that a, b, and c are all happening at the same time, along with d, e, and f.[27] What we are seeing, gradually, is a shake-up of our understanding of both genres and literary periods, which entails a willingness to deal with the messy, the contradictory, the ill-defined. What we may also see is a rediscovery of important writers, like Cowley, who never deserved to be cast into the outer darkness in the first place.

CHAPTER TWO

Ease, Confidence, Difficulty, and Grasshoppers

Abraham Cowley's Segmented Baroque

Kevin L. Cope

A peculiar highlight of the summer prior to the writing of this essay was a long-awaited hatching of seventeen-year locusts, an event that reminded everyone from entomologists to outdoor wedding planners that grasshoppers and their kinetic kin can go everywhere. Limited size, status, and reproductive opportunities pose no obstacles to those of a swarming mentality, whether omnipresent insects or intellectually omnivorous poets. Something short of a leading man, intermittently if profusely productive, and prone to disappear, Abraham Cowley seems an unlikely candidate for the role of voraciously universal intellect. Yet his first editor and biographer, Royal Society historian Thomas Sprat, boasts that "the variety of Arguments that he has manag'd is so large, that there is scarce any particular of all the passions of men, or works of Nature, and Providence, which he has pass's by undescrib'd" ("Account," sig. b2v). Despite marveling at Cowley's repleteness, Sprat honors this unstintingly interdisciplinary poet for his genial incompleteness. Cowley "always leaves off in such a manner, that it appears it was in his power to have said much more." Sprat presciently discerns one of the reasons for the meteoric rise and equally meteoric crashing of Cowley's audience appeal: Cowley's insistence on tackling big topics from improbable, partial, or constrained postures or perspectives. Whether unveiling the Bible through the exploits of young King David, whether imagining that a tiny platoon of traveling tenured professors can gather a world of knowledge, whether reaching for Pindaric heights through a handful of irregular odes on odd topics, or whether versifying in heroic couplets about modest garden herbs, Cowley seems at best multidirectional, at worst confused, and, on most occasions, stretched across and possibly lost in the gulf between the universal and the unique.

One problem with establishing a readership for Cowley has always been finding something by him to read. Until recently, he seems to have escaped the rush by tenure-seeking professors to prepare annotated editions of everyone.[1] Libraries here and there hold a few copies of Alexander Grosart's nineteenth-century quasi-facsimile edition (or its 1967 reproduction from the AMS Press); industrious researchers may find competent partial editions such as Alfred Gough's nineteenth-century version of Cowley's essays; those with university affiliations may sign into electronic databases such as Early English Books Online (EEBO) or Eighteenth Century Collections Online (ECCO), there to thrash through Cowley's individual publications or to navigate the patched-together multivolume edition assembled in the later seventeenth century by Sprat. No complete modern scholarly edition, indeed, no convenient or minimally indexed presentation of this poet's works, will be found.[2]

What might be dubbed "the erasure problem"—the disappearance, from the publishing world, of one of the most prominent poet-playwright-essayists of the modern era—has economic roots. It is hard to imagine that a large market for Cowley's sublime odes will emerge anytime soon. The erasure problem also has institutional origins. English literature anthologies, which both monitor and mandate what university students read and which exert an oversized influence on the humanities side of university general education curricula, routinely omit Cowley. New historicist Stephen Greenblatt's heavyweight *Norton Anthology of English Literature* allots not a single page to Cowley; Canada's softly expansive *Broadview Anthology of English Literature*, which employs a large committee to edit its Restoration and eighteenth-century section, lets Cowley slip out of its inclusive embrace; cutting-edge, open-access, online anthologies such as the *British Literature I* e-resource from the multi-university-funded Open Textbook Library find no room for Cowley despite having access to near-infinite storage space.[3] Even old-fashioned, dedicated anthologies of Enlightenment literature, such as those edited in the pre-woke era by

Geoffrey Tillotson, Paul Fussell, and Marshall Waingrow, or by Peter Gay, or by Louis Bredvold, Alan McKillop, and Lois Whitney, seem to run low on paper when the time comes to print passages from poor old Cowley.

To be sure, there are plenty of institutional reasons for the vanishing, from curricula and anthologies, of a poet, essayist, and playwright who rivaled John Dryden and who surely exceeded Matthew Prior, Lady Margaret Cavendish, and the Earl of Rochester in productivity, celebrity, and popularity. Classroom presence (or absence) is only one part of a writer's legacy. It is rather more puzzling why Cowley, who, Sprat affirms, "handled so many different Matters in such various sorts of Style, who less wants the correction of his Friends, or has less reason to fear the severity of Strangers," should now draw only apathy from lay reading communities that find ways to generate interest in the sprawling novels of Ann Radcliffe or out-of-the-way pamphlets by Daniel Defoe ("Account," sig. A1r). This essay makes no claim to explain the evolution of the literary canon, but it will look at some of the reasons why a poet regarded as accessible and even "pop" in his own time should now seem so obscure, difficult, and unfashionable, even when far more complicated poems and poets—say, the Dryden who dazzles our wits in *Religio Laici* or *Absalom and Achitophel*—seem unlikely to relinquish their places in entry-level humanities courses. This essay will suggest that Cowley himself is something of an anthology: a perfect condensation of genres, idioms, movements, and assorted literary and cultural phenomena that contemporary academe unadvisedly tries to separate from one another. If nothing else, academic professionals want to make clear distinctions so as to formulate equally clear questions for students' final examinations. For better or worse, such distinctions converge, combine, and sometimes coagulate in Cowley's highly miscellaneous verse. Twenty-first-century scholars seek to distinguish neoclassical from baroque practices, but, back in the seventeenth century, Cowley was busily experimenting with these idioms, irreverently exploring their intersections. He merges traditions in a way that represents the cultural history of the "long" eighteenth century better than syllabi and monographs. Cowley is one of the untidiest of high-profile authors. His works defy attempts at any kind of developmental narrative, whether about the growth of the author's mind, or about experimentation with genres, or about any kind of progress at all. This paper will seek to understand, by studying a subset of Cowley's miscellaneous poems, why Cowley's oeuvre never seems like any kind of definable project, even while it tells us much about both the melody and harmony lines of Restoration culture. The paper will progress—if progress is possible in dealing with Cowley's kaleidoscopic works—to an analysis of one of his most peculiar poems, his "Anacreontic" on a grasshopper.

It is always tempting but seldom fruitful to identify the moment when the overlapping baroque and neoclassical periods began and ended. In college and university classrooms, the tendency is always to relegate the baroque idiom to the age of Donne and to raise up Dryden as the torchbearer and Pope as the epitome of neoclassicism. Cowley's career falls between these would-be historical bookends, which reminds us that the baroque and the neoclassical modes interacted over decades, indeed, continue interacting to this day. Scholars have long opined about the alleged differences between these two modes, often juxtaposing neoclassical clarity and simplicity against baroque complexity, difficulty, drama, and ornamentation. Central to these debates is the use of visual elements— what, in earlier ages of literary criticism was called "imagery"—whether as ornament for buildings, or components in paintings, or "conceits" punctuating verse compositions. Received opinion holds that baroque images decorate poems or paintings, adding more action, ocular interest, and perhaps emotional stimulation than disciplined discursive content, while neoclassical images, in contrast, clearly and unambiguously reveal easily understood information. In such accounts, both baroque and the neoclassical images are stable. The reader or the viewer encounters them, understands them, sees their relation to the composition in which they occur, and then moves on to the next line, canvas, statue, musical measure, or structure.

Cowley, who lives amidst both baroque and neoclassical influences, avoids stable images. If a dog appears near the beginning of one of his poems, readers may assume that it will morph into a cat before the stanzas end. Baroque, "metaphysical" poets—the Donnes, Herberts, and Crashaws— create the possibility of multiple meanings through high-impact but stable images. Neoclassical scribblers took more time to provide, in lucid couplets, explanatory or other informative comments about whatever they might present. Cowley finds ways to manage and maximize the confusing interplay of these two idioms. Instead of unveiling stunning conceits and letting the reader quickly interpret them, and instead of writing discursive verses to elucidate the ideas he presents, Cowley continuously modifies images themselves. He steadily adjusts his conceits so that they maintain a degree of baroque immediacy yet gradually disclose more information. One of Cowley's simpler poems, his "Hymn. To Light" opens our eyes to Cowley's continuous changing of what we see: to his "adaptive imagery." Four stanzas near the beginning of this poem show how Cowley transforms the seemingly simple item, light, that is his topic.

> Hail, active Natures watchful Life and Health
> > Her Joy, her Ornament, and Wealth!
> > Hail to thy Husband Heat, and Thee!
> Thou the Worlds beauteous Bride, the lusty Bridegroom He!
>
> Say from what Golden Quivers of the Sky
> > Do all thy winged Arrows fly?
> > Swiftness and Power by Birth are thine:
> From the great Sire they came, thy Sire the word Divine.
>
> 'Tis I believe, this Archery to shew,
> > That so much cost in Colours thou,
> > And skill in Painting do'st bestow,
> Upon thy ancient Arms, thy Gawdy Heav'nly Bow.
>
> Swift as light Thoughts their empty Carreer [*sic*] run,
> > Thy Race is finisht when begun,
> > Let a Post-Angel start with Thee,
> And thou the Goal of Earth shalt reach as soon as He.
> > > > (*Verses Written*, 35)[4]

The titular topic of this panegyric is light, which, even in Cowley's pre-Newtonian time, counted as something rather less corporeal than the average object in the field of vision. Once Cowley introduces this well-known but insubstantial item, metamorphoses begin. Light, it could be argued, is not a proper subject for poetry. Light is less an object for description than a means by which other objects are seen. Cowley gradually converts this source or foundation of perception into a serialized array of perceived things. First, he turns light into a minimally realized personification that is capable of a marriage with heat. Next, radiant light travels to the mundane world via a comparison with arrows in a quiver, a comparison which allows for a subsequent comparison to swift arrows. A daring dislocation then redirects light into the world of fine art curatorship, a world which is also more concerned with showing than being, and a world where pinging arrows of light draw out the colors adorning objects. This dazzling passage wraps up with a return to the idea of swiftness—to a sort of heavenly postal service in which angels deliver the light that makes vision (and understanding) possible.

In this remarkable passage, Cowley is at once complicated, difficult, confident, simple, and easy. With respect to the number and incongruity of the ideas and images presented, Cowley rivals any of the baroque, metaphysical poets. There is nothing more twisted or puzzling in, say, John Donne's "The Flea" than there is in Cowley's tour de force. On the other hand, Cowley makes this disorienting passage, which combines heaven, earth, corporeal, incorporeal, and just about everything else, into an easy-reading experience that seldom challenges the intellect. Readers can follow every step in this metamorphosis without thinking too much about it; indeed, the poem is presented as a hymn, a spontaneous, straightforward expression of praise.[5] The clashing of ideas, images, and even ontologies spreads over several decompressed lines, in an extended, lucid, expository, neoclassical version of the baroque verse composed by Cowley's predecessors. This *segmented* approach to verse—the creating of artful difficulty that is sequentially broken down into easily assimilable bits and pieces, into bridge-building segments that serially carry readers into unexpected thoughts and strange worlds—will prove key to an understanding of Cowley and his "segmented baroque."

Cowley's "Hymn. To Light" prizes both literal and metaphorical lucidity: both light itself and light as a metaphor for the clarity and intelligibility that would become the watchwords of long eighteenth-century neoclassicism. Proposing overwhelmingly complicated thoughts while breaking them into manageable pieces that can be sequentially reviewed and understood allows Cowley to maintain the elaborately decorative practices of baroque writers while satisfying the emerging neoclassical taste for simplicity and for fealty to experience and evidence. The "Hymn. To Light" is thus able to toss off dramatic, extravagant, or attention-grabbing conceits as if they were scientific facts. In the nineteenth stanza of this composition, for example, Cowley requires one image, that of light rays playing on white lilies, to provoke opposing resonances. "The Virgin Lillies in their White / Are clad but with the Lawn of almost naked Light" (*Verses Written*, 37). Light, which sees and clarifies everything, can illuminate the compound, possibly inconsistent idea of virginity mixed with public nudity. Cowley even tosses in a pun relating to lawn, which can be both fabric for clothing or a surrounding for plants. He destabilizes and transforms his images and ideas through what could be called *lensing*: by quickly and frequently using different degrees of magnification or reduction, as if rapidly changing out lenses. Such a rapid oscillation occurs in the opening stanzas of the "Ode. Of Wit," where Cowley describes another immaterial object:

> Yonder we saw it [wit] plain; and here 'tis now,
> Like *Spirits* in a *Place*, we know not *How*.
> [. . .]
>   Some things do through our Judgment pass
>   As through a *Multiplying Glass*.
> And sometimes, if the *Object* be too far,
> We take a *Falling Meteor* for a *Star*. (*Miscellanies*, 2)

First we see wit telescopically but clearly; next, firsthand and up close but with some fuzziness about its unexplained mobility; then we view wit through a multifaceted, fly-eye lens; finally, we view it at astronomical distances with a high degree of potential experimental error—all within ten lines.[6] Between stanzas 8 and 9 of "Hymn. To Light," Cowley abruptly moves from the colossal venue of the solar system to the little luminous microcosm of fireflies in rural brush. Frequent lens adjustments allow Cowley to break up his grandest, most inconceivable topics into series of images or experiences shown at larger or smaller scales. He thus increases the potential for baroque extravagance—for grandeur and immensity or for the novelty of intricate detail—while also multiplying opportunities for clear, didactical, and, in sum, neoclassical exposition.

Cowley's amalgamative, Lego-like construction of complex conceits and ideas is a happily time-consuming process. Spending ten lines to develop a conceit that Herbert or Herrick could squeeze into a handful of syllables opens time not only for teaching and delighting but also for additional thought. Constantly manipulating time, Cowley develops temporal equivalents for the magnifying and distancing that transform the visuals in his verse. In his accolade "To Sir *William D'avenant.* Upon his two first Books of *Gondibert*," Cowley devotes several lines to an intricate dual presentation of history and poetry. Past and present interact, overlap, and exchange places:

> By fatal hands whilst *present Empires* fall,
> Thine from the Grave *past Monarchies* recall.
> So much more thanks from humane kind does merit
> The *Poets Fury*, than the *Zealots Spirit*.
> And from the *Grave* thou mak'est this *Empire* rise,
> Not like some dreadful *Ghost* t' affright our Eyes,
> But with more lustre and triumphant state,
> Than when it *crown'd* at proud *Verona* sate. (*Miscellanies*, 24)

In the first couplet, time flows both forward and backward. Present regimes sink into the past while past regimes turn up in the present. In the last two couplets, entropy is reversed as the regimes of bygone years not only return to our present attention, but also, through the enhancing power of historical poetry, cast off eons of decay to outdo, in glory, Italian city-states, city-states that are discussed in the past tense despite their presentation as objects of present admiration. Such astounding temporal complications lead readers to look and think sequentially about every slice of time and every cross-section of experience, to take time to assemble, disassemble, and reassemble cultural history, discovering ever more details, meanings, and associations.

Zooming, magnifying, and time-distorting are quick and easy forms of information multiplication and effect intensification. Presenting an item or experience from near, far, past, and present perspectives allows for at least four views and commentaries. Showing one thing in so many ways greatly increases its flourish, its ornamentation, and its entertainment value. Why bother looking around for additional topics or images when one item can reveal so much? Multiplying the uses, renderings, and interpretations of any one subject tends to erase the easy distinction between universal and particular that underlies so many efforts of literary criticism. Samuel Johnson applauds "just representations of general nature" in full confidence that readers easily distinguish particular characters, objects, or events from the broader meanings that arise from their interpretation. Cowley, by contrast, confounds distinctions between the particular and the universal. Suddenly adjusting the scale of his scenes, he shows large ideas or even cosmological processes quickly condensing into smaller physical objects and systems. He presents concrete items as far more universal and general than might seem and vice versa. Cowley opens his ode "Upon *Dr.* Harvey," dedicated to the discoverer of the circulation of the blood, with a bizarre conceit in which Harvey, recast as a hunter, chases the hart of nature through the forest:

> Through all the moving Wood
> Of Lives indow'd with sense she took her flight,
> *Harvey* pursues, and keeps her still in sight.
> But as the Deer, long-hunted, takes a flood,
> She leap't at last into the winding-streams of blood;
> Of Mans *Meander* all the Purple reaches made,
> Till at the Heart she stay'd,
> Where turning Head, and at a Bay,
> Thus, by well-purged ears, she was o're-heard to say.
> (*Verses Written*, 12)

Whereupon nature in her totality announces her intention to reside in the comparatively humble circulatory system, there to disclose her secrets to inquirers. With one grand leap, the personification of nature and all its laws dives into the human body. The universal crashes into the particular while the particular turns out to be a generalized everyman. For Cowley, most anything can operate at most any level of particularity or generality. Tiny corpuscles can conceal the secrets of whole planets; one person can be an average citizen or can personify whole sciences. Harvey himself is

presented as such a combined superman and humble auditor. The relent-
less diversity of nature continually reports directly to him:

> From all the Souls that living Buildings rear,
> Whether imploy'd for Earth, or Sea, or Air,
> Whether it in the Womb or Egg be wrought,
> A strict account to him is hourly brought. (*Verses Written*, 13)

Harvey is at once an unusually talented individual person and a universal
auditor to whom unending cascades of information are delivered. A kind
of meta-personification who is always in the process of growing bigger
and more comprehensive, he has to personify more and more of nature
while erasing the boundaries between the individual and the general.
That sounds difficult, even for a scientific virtuoso, but Cowley is quick
to associate this demanding role with a lowbrow milieu. "He [Harvey]
so exactly does the work survey, / As if he hir'd the workers by the day"
(*Verses Written*, 13). For Harvey, building the pyramid of knowledge is
never an astonishing feat of engineering, or of thinking, or of anything
else. Rather, it is a matter of segmentation, of laying out a whole structure,
one brick after another, through the continuous labor of hired hands. In
the preface to his imitation of Pindar's "Second Olympique Ode," Cowley
sets up the ancient Olympic athlete, "Theron, *Prince of* Agrigentum," as
a possessor of formidable athletic skills and virtues, and a suitable topic
for a sublime ode. But he then quickly declares that his poetry "consists
more in *Digressions*, than in the main subject," juxtaposing supernal
subject matter against a collection of trivia (*Pindariques*, 1). Surprisingly,
the effect of this fluctuation in gravitas never leads to the mock-heroic.
Rather, Cowley aspires to be what modern educators and advocates for
the disabled call "accessible." Digressions, detail, and clutter break down
his topic into understandable components that can support daring ideas
and images without depriving the audience of neoclassical ease, clarity,
and simplicity.

Cowley might be the first and only English poet whose poetry merits
comparison to a crash test dummy. Rhetorical and conceptual collisions,
collapses, crashes, and cacophonies are common in his works. These
raucous events, however, never culminate in scenes of destruction or in

the abandonment of poems or in the tarnishing of Cowley's reputation. Rather, they induce rebounds and recoveries, much as crash dummies bounce back from collisions so as to deliver informative data. Cowley's use of extreme, violent, harsh, bizarre, torturous, and outright crazy conceits rivals anything found in Crashaw or Vaughan, yet the effect of his extremity is often mild, amusing, and even instructive. The metaphysical poets produce their jarring effects by packaging a host of conflicting ideas in tight catachrestical images, but Cowley takes a more segmented approach, doffing a startling line or thought here and there and taking the occasion to explore possibility—to look, for a moment, at one possible, perhaps extreme interpretation of a thing, idea, or experience. Probative and exploratory, his verse avoids the obligations imposed by poets like Donne. Rather than saying "Mark but this flea and mark in this" in the imperative voice and with a focusing pronoun, as does Donne in "The Flea," Cowley simply opens up the possibility that an image or idea might suggest something extreme without tightly strapping tenor and vehicle together. This sort of dazzling, quasi-metaphysical realism—this hard and sudden encounter with an offbeat possible meaning of an ordinary thing or experience—is a staple of Cowley's quaintly self-congratulatory "Ode. Mr. Cowley's Book Presenting it self to the University Library of *Oxford*," in which Cowley presents himself as overawed by the company he and his book will keep among the prestigious authors whose works line the shelves of the Bodleian Library. "Hail," Cowley cries,

> Hail Wits illustrious Galaxy!
> Where thousand Lights into one brightness spread;
> Hail living Univers'ty of the Dead! (*Verses Written*, 7)

As Cowley and his tome approach this awesome library, we travel from the thriving brilliance of the Milky Way to the dark recesses of an intellectual necropolis in a mere thirty syllables. We flip from one extreme to another, from galaxy to grave, experimenting with both characterizations of the Bodleian without fully committing to either of them. The sallies and sorties continue into the next stanza, where the Bodley morphs into Egyptian pyramids containing verse-embalmed poets' souls, and where, looking forward and backward in eternal time, one can

all wonders plainly see
That have been, are, or are to be
In the mysterious Library
The Beatifick *Bodley* of the Deity. (*Verses Written*, 7)

Ultimately, the Bodley becomes a placeholder, a scaffold on which one can hang almost any meaning, emotion, or interpretation, at least until the next one comes along. A futuristic sarcophagus in which a vast assortment of possible future ideas will be "embalm'd" so as to provide material for future odes, the Bodley exists in a perpetual semantic rebound, bouncing from one potential meaning to another, building up drama, and keeping interpretations open.

There is something more than a little grotesque about Cowley's treatment of the world's cultural traditions as a vast mausoleum haunted by voyeuristic poets. That sort of grotesquerie is one of the reasons that Cowley has had so much trouble entering classrooms and canons. For most pedagogues, explaining to bewildered students so peculiar a project as Cowley's verse is simply not worth the effort. Cowley, gladly, could respond to his critics. One of his favorite tricks is softening his most extreme conceptions by a dose of literalism: by upending his violent metaphors with a sudden real-world reference. In his celebratory ode "To Dr. *Scarborough*," for example, Cowley wraps up all the various epidemics and wars that plagued seventeenth-century England into the stock, easily understandable metaphor of the destructive sword. "Scarce could the *Sword* dispatch more to the *Grave*, / Than *Thou* [Scarborough] didst *save*" (*Pindariques*, 35). The horrors inflicted by that metaphorical sword are suddenly blunted by the factual report of Dr. Scarborough's medical successes. The "*Sword*" and the "*Grave*" that indirectly connote thousands of casualties are counterbalanced by the more segmented, particularized inventory of the good doctor's helpful treatments. Sometimes such a buffering of harsh ideas and images involves literalizing metaphors. Earlier in the same stanza, Cowley inundates readers with the "*red waves*" of "*Slaughter*" but then laments that "*Albion*," Britain, is nominally "*white*," a sudden recourse to the literal foundation of a metaphor that takes the edge off and bleaches all that gore. This, too, can be seen as a kind of segmentation, with Cowley reminding us that even metaphors are made up of parts, that they have literal and figurative components, then juxtaposing those two parts against one another so as to buffer his most extreme representations. In the Scarborough poem, this practice reaches an early climax in the second stanza, where Cowley relentlessly compares one plague after another to an assortment of historical, cultural, and epic precedents. Fevers compare to Christianity's hell; their treatment refers to metallurgy, specifically refinement through heat; agues elicit a digression into military science; gallstones bring to mind first Sisyphus and his labors, and then Hannibal and his granite-dissolving vinegar; finally, medical practice compares to Moses striking and bringing water from the rock. Through such baroque allusiveness Cowley skirts along the edges of the mock-heroic. He decompresses and distributes, across multiple comparisons, piquant thoughts that might otherwise violate neoclassical decorum.

Cowley, we know from his ode-ornamented essay *Proposition for the Advancement of Experimental Philosophy*, identified with those many wits and ideologues who, in his time, preferred denotative, empirically referential language in which words clearly corresponded to things. In this pursuit of a technical, business-like idiom, Cowley seems more like an avid follower than leader—like an apologist for rather than peer of Sir Francis Bacon, Joseph Glanvill, John Wilkins, John Ray, and Sprat. Nevertheless, Cowley's verse could well be considered avant-garde insofar as it routinely raises fundamental questions about what a highly referential language might be. Just as Cowley blurs the boundaries between universal and particular or between images and their implications, so he shows literal meanings taking surprising turns. In his Pindaric ode "To Mr. Hobs," for example, Cowley shows how digging can equally well refer to everything from commercial mining, to grave robbing, to archaeology:

> We break up *Tombs* with *Sacrilegious hands*;
>   Old *Rubbish* we remove;
> To walk in *Ruines*, like vain *Ghosts*, we love,
>   And with fond *Divining Wands*
>   We search among the *Dead*
>   For Treasures *Buried*,
>   Whilst still the *Liberal Earth* does hold So many *Virgin*
> *Muses* of *undiscover'ed Gold*. (*Pindariques*, 27)

Here there are at least three processes simultaneously under way: prospecting for treasures with divining rods; excavating the classical cultural and philosophical legacy; and probing the interred world of ghosts, ancestors, and maybe a zombie or two. All of these are forms of digging or working "*Buried*" resources; all are very different; but all are presented as literally as English will allow (if, say, we were not digging for the "*Rubbish*" of ancient learning, we would have to *comb* or *hunt* or *rummage* for it, or engage in some other slightly metaphorical process that moves away from the literal). Language, for Cowley, creates a philosophical mirage. Words referring to familiar processes apply somewhat literally to their referents while they figuratively sketch out artful, interactive renderings of a universe full of surprising relationships. This process occurs again and again in both the Hobbes ode and across the entirety of Cowley's canon. In stanza 2 of this poem, for example, he presents a compact review of several senses of "air." Describing the decline of the scholastic philosophical tradition, he laments that

> Then nought but *Words* it grew,
> And those all *Barb'arous* too.
> It *perisht*, and it *vanisht* there,
> The *Life* and *Soul* breath'd out, became but empty *Air*.
> (*Pindariques*, 26)

Air applies nearly—not completely, but nearly—literally to words, to philosophical systems, to life, to breath, and, of course, to the literal atmosphere, which falls away behind this symphony of near-literal uses. In stanza 5, Cowley invokes the familiar notion that language is the dress of thought to begin questioning whether the English language can produce enough verbal fabric to clothe the contributions of a philosophical colossus such as Thomas Hobbes: Could "all the *Wardrobe* of rich *Eloquence*" provide textiles enough "To cloath the mighty *Limbs* of thy [Hobbes's] *Gigantique Sence*?" (*Pindariques*, 27). If we are to think fully literally, a philosophical giant such as Hobbes must have immense "*Limbs*." Thus, and again, Cowley relies on a combination of neoclassical clarity and midcentury enthusiasm for empiricism to produce images and effects worthy of any baroque sculptor.

Through liberality with literal language, Cowley treats experience itself as artful and full of surprises—as a source of what might be styled the "empirical baroque." In his commemorative poem, "On the Death of Sir *Anthony Vandike*, The famous Painter," Cowley asks a colloquial comparison to overturn the simple distinction between originals and representations:

> His [Van Dyck's] pieces so with their *Objects* strive,
> That both or *Pictures* seem, or both *Alive*.
> *Nature* her self amaz'd, does doubting stand,
> Which is *her own*, and which the *Painters Hand*,
> And does attempt the like with less success,
> When her own work in *Twins* she would express.
>   (*Miscellanies*, 9)

Everyone understands "twins"; there is nothing strange or overwrought about that word. Twinning, the production of identical persons or products by prior sources or prolific parents, however, is not, in either neoclassicism or the baroque, the usual understanding of the relation of art to nature or of artifacts to their producers. Rather, *copying* or *imitating* are more common in long eighteenth-century critical treatises. Introducing one clear, distinct, and denotative term—"twin" is certainly less abstract than "imitate" or "represent"—Cowley implies a fraternal rather than causal relation between nature and art, while also implying that nature might be less natural than painters' productions. Indeed, Cowley does not stop with this turn of phrase and fillip of thought. He suggests an even more elaborate relation between nature, art, and the imitative process by wondering whether god is a painter whose easel the late Van Dyck imitates: "Did he not [in heaven] gladly see how all things shine, / Wondrously *painted* in the *Mind Divine*?" (*Miscellanies*, 9). God is not so much making or creating as painting the universe. The new arrival in heaven can hope to copy His brushstrokes. If God works by painting, we must wonder about what, in the period, would qualify as His original. Is God copying or imitating what He has already created? Or is God painting the cosmos into existence? Or is there some other explanation? Cowley is certainly no systematic theologian and must certainly always be suspected of seeking rhetorical effects at almost any cost. He is

Figure 1: The "Drake Chair," a chair assembled from wood salvaged from Sir Francis Drake's ship, *The Golden Hind*, in the Bodleian Library, Oxford

certainly not attempting a revision of the book of Genesis (one can only imagine the scriptural verse: "On the second day, God painted"). Cowley does show just how far one can go with language that is advertised as (more or less) literal and how capable language is of spinning off, one syllable or segment at a time, into extravagant artistic constructions.

Cowley's talent for adding segments to his lines—for generating complexity and multiplicity out of a few simple words—contributes to some of the more eccentric features of his verse. For one, Cowley is Parnassus's foremost exponent of parenthetical remarks. Parenthetical comments are rare in poetry and outright incongruous in the effusive ode form that Cowley favors, yet few of his poems conclude without some sort of parentheses. Parenthetical comments make lines longer while minimally altering them. They add a piece to a line, but are not fully of a piece with it. Set aside within a sentence almost as if they are not there, parenthetical remarks expand on and extrapolate from simple statements without destroying them. They complicate an idea or a poem while bracketed outside of it. In the ode "Upon *Dr.* Harvey," a parenthesis opens after the second word, which happens to be "Nature," then continues for no less than three lines, an expansive interval that allows Cowley to explain that nature is not what it has always appeared to be, that generations of philosophers have left this "Beauteous virgin" to be explored by posterity (*Verses Written*, 12). Nature enjoys a speaking role in what is otherwise a nondramatic poem, but only after a parenthetical "(said she)" that buffers the improbability of a soliloquy by no less than the universe itself. By wedging in that parenthetical "(said she)," Cowley seems to offer a disclaimer regarding the improbability of nature speaking out. He makes a dramatic aside to an unidentified audience to excuse his daring personification and to deflect attention from the awkward mixing of drama with ode. An equally multipurpose parenthetical remark appears within the first sentence of the ode "Upon the Chair made out of Sir *Francis Drakes* ship, Presented to the University Library in *Oxford*, by *John* Davis of *Deptford*, Esquire," a short, highly cerebral, ten-line effusion (one of two poems Cowley wrote on Drake's unusual chair), in which the parenthetical material occupies no less than 30 percent of the available space (Figure 1) (*Verses Written*, 42). Seeming to regard his own rendering of Drake's vessel as a "*Pythagorean* Ship" as lacking in clarity, Cowley devotes a third of his poem to a bracketed explanation as to why a vessel should be comparable to the works of an ancient geometer. So prominent is this parenthetical elucidation that it overshadows the entire poem. Mixing dazzle with pedantry, this parenthetical remark flips the formula for neoclassicism by turning teaching into the primary source of delight.

Unexpected uses of formulaic, stock ideas is both a Cowley specialty and a form of supplementation through segmentation. Cowley follows his favorite recyclable motifs through his verse, watching them accumulate and extend meanings. Comparisons of misguided thought or obsolete philosophy to "painted grapes" occur in works as diverse as the "Ode. Of

Wit" and the great ode "To The *Royal Society*."[7] Comparisons of explorers such as Christopher Columbus cruising beyond the edge of the world to avant-garde philosophers sailing off the horizons of contemporary thought ornament many poems. In "To Sir *William D'avenant*," a Columbus comparison suggests that Davenant has outdone most real-world colonists by seeking and planting not only one, but multiple new worlds. In "To Mr. *Hobs*," Cowley compliments Hobbes by favorably comparing him to Columbus, substituting "the *Golden Lands* of *new Philosophies*" for the real Columbus's West Indies destination (*Pindariques*, 27). In "The Extasie," Columbus travels vertically rather than horizontally (*Pindariques*, 41–43). His voyage of discovery compares to Cowley's own astral-projection journey to a vantage point in outer space, there to evaluate life on earth. A harsh critic could accuse Cowley of indulging in hackneyed repetition. What could be more predictable than comparing something exploratory to the exploits of Columbus? Yet each of these comparisons takes the Columbus theme in entirely new directions, continuously augmenting the recurring Columbian motif.

Cowley's metaphors conjure Columbus insofar as their memorability arises from their motion and mutability. A large portion of what Cowley's chatty verse discusses is either in motion or undergoing transformation. So with another of Cowley's quirks: the specific selection of immobile objects to represent motion. In Cowley's quaint "Ode: Mr. *Cowley's* Book presenting it self to the University Library of *Oxford*," devices for immobilizing precious resources into permanent positions become tickets to any and all destinations:

> Will you allow me th' honourable chain?
>> The chain of Ornament which here
>> Your noble Prisoners proudly wear;
> A Chain which will more pleasant seem to me
> Than all my own Pindarick Liberty:
> Will ye to bind me with those mighty names submit,
>> Like an Apocrypha with holy Writ?
> What ever happy book is chained here,
> No other place of People need to fear;
> His Chain's a Pasport to go ev'ry where. (*Verses Written*, 7)

Already somewhat less than mobile, Cowley's folio volume and candidate chained book reconciles mobility with immobility. Its binding physical connection to the library unexpectedly renders it a jet-setting citizen of an entire world. Cowley achieves a seamless—perhaps link-less—fusion of the tangible with the metaphorical as a shackled book morphs into another paper document, a passport, that, in turn, enables the process of travel, travel that Cowley upgrades into intellectual voyaging. By gradually shifting through and around his cluster of stock ideas, Cowley resolves the contradiction of mobility and immobility, with ease and clarity. In "Sitting and Drinking in the Chair, made out of the Reliques of Sir *Francis Drake's* Ship," the other, much longer Cowley poem on this Drake's chair, he not only surmounts the mobility-immobility conflict, but also reconciles the universal with the particular. Resolving the mobility issue involves a lightly handled reversal of the direction of motion.

> Let the case now quite alter'd be,
> And as thou went'st abroad the World to see,
> Let the World now come to see thee. (*Verses Written*, 9)

Strictly, nothing happens in the poem, but Cowley, the perpetually astonished spectator, observes a reversal in the kinetic flow, noting that the world now comes to the chair rather than the chair (or the ship from which the chair was made) going out to the world. What could be easier than doing nothing other than noticing a change, but what change could be more dramatic? Encouraged by the easy immobility of this globe-trotting bundle of splinters, Cowley extends his reconciling efforts to fundamental contradictions such as the rudimentary opposition of particular and universal:

> In every Ayr, and every Sea 't has been,
> 'T has compas'd all the Earth, and all the Heavens 't has seen.
> Let not the Pope's it self with this compare,
> This is the only Universal Chair. (*Verses Written*, 9)

If we can set aside the arrhythmia induced by Cowley's contorted contractions, we can marvel at his easy, gradual transformation of a widely traveled physical chair into a put-down of the Pope's metaphysical claims to universal dominion. Cowley's habit of segmentation—of breaking big issues, ideas, and images into manageable units and then gradually recombining them into stunningly clear, easily explicated conceits—thus interacts with his near obsession with mobility, with the use of motion and process to smooth over and enlarge his oddly awesome conceptions. Drake's chair, after all, is itself nothing but a wooden pieces from the famed mariner's broken-up ship: "remains of *Drake*" now berthed in "this Port of ease" yet still ready to "Launch forth into an indiscovered Sea" composed not of water but of cascading thought (*Verses Written*, 10). The Drake chair provides Cowley with a template for piecing together immense concepts shred by shred, chip by chip, shaving by shaving—for the grandest sort of constructive segmentation.

Among Cowley's talents is the devising of flashy, grand, or attention-grabbing titles and dedications. Titles condense Cowley's amalgamative, augmentative language. They set a direction for a poem without so much as completing a sentence. By creating the illusion of a theme or purpose, striking titles give Cowley the liberty to wander, segment, and assemble as he pleases, to the extent that the theme allows. Cowley's titles feature prominent organizations, such as the Royal Society, or famous persons, such as Thomas Hobbes, or large-scale public projects, such as the renovation of Somerset House, or compelling topics, such as ecstasies, the plant kingdom, or even reason itself. Such titles and declared topics tell readers that Cowley is going to build from the ground up in a big way, that he will move expeditiously from his designated conceits and paradoxes to some sort of grand climax or pronouncement. More than a few of Cowley's poems begin with an odd or startling title, then, after much miscellaneousness, deliver some sort of monumental, universalizing denouement.

But not every Cowley production follows this pattern exactly. Some works disarm readers through their unappealing presentation. Few works will attract fewer readers than Cowley's unharmoniously titled Latin comedy, *Naufragium Joculare* ("the shipwreck joke"). Many of the assorted compositions conjugated under the attention-deflecting taxon "Miscellanies" are doomed to descend into obscurity along with the persons who inspired them. The inclusively indefinite biotope of Cowley's miscellaneous compositions includes one production that has garnered a tiny bit of lasting attention, his Anacreontic on a grasshopper. This paean to a humble insect epitomizes all that this paper has proposed about Cowley's "segmented baroque."

An assortment of literary encyclopedias credit Cowley as the inventor of the English Anacreontic. Whatever the authority of those tomes, we can, at least, regard him as a benevolent borrower who joined with multi-tudinous eighteenth-century wits in inventing new versions of old literary forms. For the segmenting Cowley, the Anacreontic is just another piece of the growing puzzle that is the ancients: a bit of antiquity that received less attention from Enlightenment literati than did grand genres such as epic or tragedy and a remnant of archaic lore that can be patched into Cowley's mosaic of ideas about the ancients.[8] Creating a modern genre out of assorted ancient leftovers, Cowley assembles a dozen descriptions, appreciations, and depreciations of diversely robust phenomena such as dueling, drinking, swallows, and, of course, grasshoppers. Always setting himself apart from the targets of his sometimes effusive, sometimes critical commentary, Cowley adopts a plethora of poses and perspectives. His assorted postures combine bits and pieces of the distant courtly lover with bits and pieces of the exiled satirist, and with bits and pieces of the dispassionate virtuoso locked away in a laboratory. Difficulties in interpreting Cowley's miscellaneous poems—in figuring out whether he praises, blames, loves, disdains, or simply describes his topic—result from this prismatic dispersal of viewpoint.

"The Grasshopper" epitomizes Cowley's fragmented, partially occluded perspectives. Modern zoological classification blinds us to what attentive persons in the seventeenth century would have seen in an insect. As its Latin root words suggest, the order of insects, in the early Enlightenment, included almost any creature with a segmented, sectioned body: with, say, notches or indentations marking the boundaries between head, thorax, and abdomen.[9] Fragmentary, alien, compact, and remote, the grasshopper embodies Cowley's verse technique, which features continuous motion across incomplete characterizations and partially explored viewpoints—which cross-sects, bisects, dissects, and, in sum, *insects*.

Anacreon's poems generally celebrate realms of human experience, from drinking to eroticism. By contrast, Cowley often showcases some sort of unapproachable figure, whether the superhuman Sir Francis Bacon leading us from the wilderness, or whether Prometheus needing a pardon, or whether a swallow snuggling away in its winter nest, or whether a bit of borage growing in the garden. Cowley shares with baroque poets and artists the habit of offering brief snippets and scenes, of presenting evocative excerpts from a much bigger story. He shares with practitioners of the New Science a robust confidence that every bit of empirical evidence may, as that old song has it, be the start of something big. This omnidirectional incongruity—heroes who are bigger than odes that are already larger than life yet less regular than typical neoclassical figures; celebratory songs that applaud diminutive or dubious phenomena—pervades "The Grasshopper," which presents a world where everything is momentarily startling while permanently out of proportion with everything else (*Miscellanies*, 37). The opening question to the grasshopper, "What can be / In happiness compared to thee?," juxtaposes a universal "what" that covers everything against the most bizarre and particular of creatures while requesting an inventory of all the other particular beings that might be happy. We soon learn that the grasshopper's "nourishment divine," a sort of orthopterous manna, is only "the dewy *Mornings* gentle *Wine*," that the limitless satisfaction afforded to this creature is a time-delimited totality, a supply line doled out in the grasshopper's "verdant Cup," in whatever allotments a blade of grass in a high humidity environment can deliver. Next comes an exclamation of the joys of vegan omnivorousness in which the triple reiteration of "all" counterpoints an assortment of limitations:

> All the *Fields* which thou dost see,
> All the *Plants* belong to *Thee*,
> All that *Summer Hours* produce,
> Fertile made with early juice.

Universal and particular converge in segmented progress as this tiny hopper crunches its way from leaf to leaf and stalk to stalk. This somewhat lucky grasshopper may have all that it pleases so long as summer can produce it, as long as no steaks or pork chops are on the table, as long as the "early" juice of morning dew can hydrate it, and as long as it can keep going. Stationed at the end of a short interval, the growing season, this "*Prophet* of the ripened year" is "Sated" with its "*Summer Feast*" after

Figure 2: Giovanna Garzoni, *Open Pomegranate in a Dish, with Grasshopper, Snail, and Two Chestnuts* (between 1651 and 1662), Galleria Palatina, Florence

a "*Life*" that is "no longer than" its "*Mirth*." In a daring inversion, the life span, which usually contains multiple moods, becomes a mere function of a much shorter mood. Universal and particular, long and short, seasonal and perpetual bounce around in a kaleidoscopic collage in which everything fits because nothing fits, and in which scales of measurement continuously recalibrate. The incongruous images prized by poets of the preceding generation give way to a cacophony of scales, sizes, and proportions in which, per the standards of neoclassicism, everything is perfectly easy, clear, legible, and rational, yet in which little seems to fit together.

Grasshoppers were objects of fascination among late baroque writers and artists. A canvas by Florentine baroque painter and Cowley contemporary Giovanna Garzoni provides a distant lens on not only Cowley's verse technique but also on his interest in enigmatic insects (Figure 2). In her *Open Pomegranate in a Dish, with Grasshopper, Snail, and Two Chestnuts* (1652), Garzoni presents an inquisitive, virtuoso-like grasshopper perched on a pomegranate and looking into the represented scene from a doubly skewed angle of vision, from atop an unpeeling fruit, gazing downward into the picture and at a sharp angle defined by its turned head.[10] The pomegranate reveals its secrets by disassembling itself while the grasshopper displays its own incised, highly articulated structure. Meanwhile, the dried leaves from the old branch suggest an array of other possible perches from which the querying grasshopper could begin assembling a holographic view of the exotic fruit. Chestnuts roll in at the bottom of the painting, reminding viewers of a completely different biological taxon and, with that, a different array of possible viewpoints. We can only conjecture that the snail, like Cowley, is gradually working its way through this complicated scene, a scene that stands before an undefined background like that vast eternity of inquiry into which the chair constructed from the leftovers of Sir Francis Drake's ship is destined to sail.

Contemporary baroque-classical transitional pieces like Garzoni's help us to understand Cowley's love of diverse perspectives that may contribute toward some grander panorama. The changing perspectives in Cowley's compositions include evocations of a large assortment of genres and voices as well as viewpoints outside the usual human frame of vision and reference. In the course of "The Grasshopper," Cowley evokes at least five different literary traditions. Overall, the poem maintains the usual Anacreontic, lyric voice, with an implied spokesperson who addresses both the grasshopper and the audience throughout the poem. Mid-poem, Cowley pops out of the human perspective and explains that pests can flip the servant–master relationship, quipping that "Man for thee does sow and plow; / *Farmer He*, and *Land-Lord Thou*!," thus lightly experimenting with economics and political commentary. Straightaway we shift into the pastoral voice. Cowley, lauding the grasshopper's tuneful ways, announces that "The *Shephard* gladly heareth thee, / More *Harmonious* then *He*." We glimpse the history of philosophy as Cowley congratulates this "Happy *Insect*": "*Voluptuous*, and *Wise* withal, / *Epicurean Animal*!" The poem ends with a hint of the retired posture of the classical satirists, albeit with a severe downside insofar as the grasshopper is congratulated on a permanent withdrawal "to endless *Rest*." It might not seem possible to put together so many voices and traditions in so short and apparently simple a poem, but that is the point. Cowley goes beyond Donne, Herbert, and Crashaw by being metaphysical in a classical way, by cobbling together, in easy, transparent ditties, panoplies of odds and ends from the whole universe of literature, components that simply do not fit together except, perhaps, in this one particular poem.

What makes Cowley a formerly bestselling and now semi-canonical author yet what makes him alien to both the baroque seventeenth and the neoclassical eighteenth centuries is not solely his miscellaneousness—heaven knows, more than a few poets have wandered from their topics—but the relentlessness and universality of that variety in tandem with Cowley's ability to keep his overfilled world neat, organized, properly segregated, and even in correct temporal order. His exile from the canon and the classroom may result from the possibility that reading assignments might never end, that an adequate representation of Cowley would lead from one poem to another in an ever-augmenting progression toward an elusive completeness. It would be out of keeping with Cowley's amalgamative, segmented, sallying approach if what appears like a concluding analysis of "The Grasshopper" did not also induce another short diversion into another poem.

This paper will close by offering, as a Baedeker to Cowley's sprawling canon of verse, an observation or two concerning one of his most daring Pindaric odes, "The Resurrection" (*Pindariques*, 21–22). In the space of the wildly irregular first stanza of this poem, Cowley diverges from his sensational topic to a series of analogies concerning verse. He sequentially compares verse to winds driving a sea voyage, showers refreshing the earth, midwifery and the birth process, ethical philosophy, Egyptian pyramids, and embalming, all while weaving in and out of parenthetical phrases, and all while annotating his flourishes in ample, multilingual footnotes. Cowley analogizes at every possible scale, from the tiniest seed to the mightiest monument, yet he lines up these comparisons in neatly segregated, tempo-differentiated lines, disallowing any kind of metaphysical compression and eschewing anything even remotely catachrestical. The stanza moves in a chronological sequence from meteorological motions to germination processes through assorted antiquities and on through the full run of time and history, culminating in the quickest of mentions of the melting of the universe during the titular resurrection. Such miscellaneous, complicated, intensely analogical and yet easily understandable progressions continue into the second stanza, where Cowley explains how his tune-making duties will gradually be transferred to the player of the last trumpet call, a call through which an ecumenical "Rich *Natures* ancient *Troy*" that was, despite being pre-Christian, "built by *Hands Divine*," will erupt in one final fiery reconciliation of the ancients, the moderns, Rome, Jerusalem, the sacred, and the secular, all while, in the third stanza, atoms from across the universe come flying together to reconstitute resurrected bodies around the world. On that thought, on the expectation that, some day, each of us shall a "*Soul* naked, and shivering stand" while atoms from everywhere "Meet, salute, and joyn their hands" as they remake our flesh in a massive act of disassembly and reassembly, of progressive segmentation, we shall conclude, hoping that an understanding of Cowley's unstinting but organized miscellaneousness will lead to new appreciations of the role of his grasshopper in mediating not only one, but a whole series of long eighteenth-century disputes, contrasts, and conundrums.

CHAPTER THREE

Sacred Calm
The Digressions of Cowley's *Davideis*

Ian Calvert

Introduction

On its first publication, in Abraham Cowley's *Poems* (1656), the *Davideis* was presented as the most substantial achievement of Cowley's career to date.[1] It received the greatest prominence on the title-page's list of contents, and its placement at the end of the book encouraged readers to see it as a culmination of Cowley's poetic skills and ambition (Figure 3). By placing the *Davideis* after lyric collections of increasing complexity and sophistication (*Miscellanies, The Mistress,* and *Pindarique Odes*), Cowley intimated he had progressed through the traditional hierarchy of literary genres to reach the summit of epic. By appending a subtitle, *A Sacred Poem of the Troubles of Davideis*, Cowley also drew attention to the shift in subject matter across the volume from the secular to the devotional, and the move to sacred poetry suggests a maturation not just of Cowley's career, but also of epic as a genre. The poem follows the conventions and expectations of classical epic, but unlike the epics of antiquity the *Davideis* claims a foundation in historical truth and scriptural revelation.

Yet Cowley's discussion of the *Davideis* in the "Preface" to *Poems* undermines these first impressions. Nothing on the title-page indicates that the *Davideis* is incomplete; it is only in the preface that Cowley states it was "designed into *Twelve Books*" but he has "had neither *Leisure* hitherto, nor have *Appetite* at present to finish the work" (*Poems*, sig.

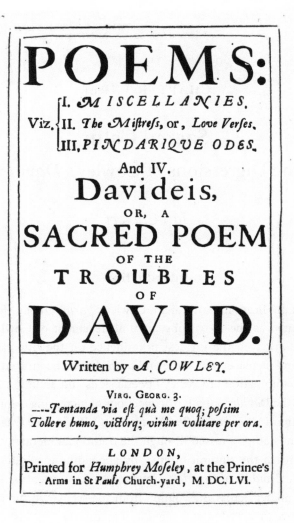

Figure 3: Title-Page, Abraham Cowley, *Poems: Viz. I. Miscellanies. II. The Mistress, or, Love Verses. III. Pindarique Odes. And IV. Davideis, or a Sacred Poem of the Troubles of David* (London: Humphrey Moseley, 1656)

b2v–r). Acknowledging this unfinished quality of the text gives the sense of the four books that appeared in *Poems* as an abandoned, even failed, experiment. The feeling that Cowley saw the *Davideis* as something of a misconceived project is not limited to its status as a poetic fragment.

The poem often seems to have trouble deciding which parts of David's life it should prioritize telling. When Maggie Kilgour describes "the general sense of lack of progress in the poem," she seems to have in mind the material that Cowley did write, not the never-written final eight books.[2] As it stands, the *Davideis* is concerned with the events from a relatively brief part of David's biography as described in 1 Samuel 16–22: his playing before Saul, the threats to his life and his subsequent flights, first to Ramah and subsequently to Nob, Gath, and the kingdom of the Moabites. Cowley frequently suspends this narrative to situate David's troubles in the broader historical and eschatological context: a sleeping David, for example, receives a prophecy from the archangel Gabriel that foresees his coronation and the propagation of a line that culminates in Christ (*Davideis*, book 2). However, Cowley expresses a greater concern with tracing the origins for the story he is telling than for seeing it through to its conclusion. His two most extensive interpolations, the account by David's kinsman Joab of David's victory over Goliath, and David's narration of "how *Saul* came to the *Crown*," look back rather than forward (122).

It was, of course, standard practice in epic to incorporate substantial interpolations. Gabriel's prophecy in book 2 is clearly modeled on the Parade of Heroes in *Aeneid*, book 6, where Aeneas sees the spirits of his own descendants, and the narration of events from the protagonist's own past in the form of retrospective speeches recalls *Aeneid*, books 2–3 and *Odyssey*, books 9–12. Nonetheless, the space granted to the inset narratives expands as the *Davideis* progresses. The inset narratives also occur in reverse chronological order: David's defeat of Goliath happened after Saul's coronation, but it is the first of these two events to be related in the poem. Consequently, the marginalizing of the period of David's life that is the poem's ostensible focus mirrors David's own succession of retreats from Saul. The further the poem progresses, the further it moves back in time and away from its promised end.

The poem's lack of momentum is also a product of its digressions, which, by their very nature, provide material that is extraneous to the main narrative and that delay its resumption. In the table of contents to *Davideis* in *Poems*, passages on the origins of music (13), the priestly college at Ramah (17–22), the praise of love (47–48), and the lives of Abraham and his family (51–53, 89–90) are all formally labeled as digressions. It is these parts of the *Davideis* that I am concerned with in this chapter. Much recent critical discussion of digression follows Ross Chambers's influential study of "loiterature" in associating digression with sideways movement, lingering, peripherality, and teleological delay.[3] I argue that while there are clear parallels between these concerns and the account of the priestly college, and indeed the structure of the poem as a whole, the digressions on music, love, and Abraham's family move along a vertical, not a horizontal, axis; they contribute more to elevation than to loitering or temporal regression. Cowley's emphasis on elevation is the result of his associating digression with sublimity, moving closer toward the divine, and gaining a greater understanding of Providence, the concept that an individual or group of people enjoys the favor and protection of God that is known as Providence. Cowley furthered these connections by drawing on the established Christianized reception of the classical tradition of the *furor poeticus* ("poetic frenzy"), where the poet is possessed by a supernatural force and enters a heightened state of inspiration, either to act as an agent for that force, or to become a passive recipient of that force. While agitation was the accompanying emotional state usually linked to this familiar trope, Cowley, instead, aligns it with calmness and tranquility.

In assuming the role of this new version of the sublimely inspired poet, Cowley illuminates the complex, contested status of the *Davideis* as a site of political commentary. In his digressions on music and love, Cowley adapts a discourse of sublime inspiration that was primarily associated with republicanism during the Interregnum. His digressions on the lives of Abraham also attempt to recode a republican discourse, although there, the focus is primarily on Providence rather than inspiration. His use of terms that carried such a highly republican tone reflects the belief expressed in his "Preface" to the 1656 *Poems* as to why he has written an epic on a biblical instead of a classical narrative:

> Amongst all holy and consecrated things which the *Devil* ever stole and alienated from the service of the *Deity*; as *Altars*, *Temples*, *Sacrifices*, *Prayers*, and the like; there is none that he so universally, and so long usurpt, as *Poetry*. It is time to recover it out of the *Tyrants* hands, and to restore it to the *Kingdom* of *God*, who is the *Father* of it. (*Poems*, sig. b2r–3v)

Through his digressions, Cowley expresses the hope that the 1650s represent a temporary dominance of a tyrannical infernal sublime that Providence will replace with the celestial sublime of true monarchy. Simultaneously, he recognizes that the current situation may well represent the new political status quo. The *Davideis*, consequently, expresses the hope, if not necessarily the expectation, that the republican present of the 1650s would ultimately turn out to be a digression from a Royalist norm. His pragmatic recognition that what he hoped would be temporary might actually become permanent prompted Cowley's digression on the prophets' college. In this, the longest of the five digressions, he enjoys constructing and lingering in an idealized space purged of political debates.

In what follows, before considering the political resonances to the use of the sublime, through its digressions, in *Davideis*, I trace the connections that Cowley made between digression and sublimity, and what precedents he found for sublime writing in classical and biblical literature, especially the works of the Greek lyric poet Pindar and the books of prophecy in the Old Testament. I then consider the influence of these connections in his *Pindarique Odes*, which immediately precede the *Davideis* in the 1656 *Poems*, and which established the preoccupation with the sublime and elevation that Cowley further developed in the digressions of his biblical epic.

Cowley, the Digressive Sublime, and Divine Enthusiasm

English writers have explored the concept of sublimity since at least the sixteenth century, but became especially interested in it during the Interregnum; Philip Hardie has recently championed Cowley's role in establishing it as an aesthetic category during this period.[4] For Cowley and his contemporaries, the key text for thinking about the sublime was the *Peri Hupsous* (*On the Sublime*), a work of criticism from classical antiquity whose authorship and date of composition remain unknown; for convenience, I refer to its author as Longinus, the writer to whom it was attributed in the seventeenth century. The key contention of the *Peri Hupsous* has been neatly summarized by Philip Shaw as "Flawed genius . . . ultimately triumphs over technically perfected mediocrity."[5] As a means of outlining this principle, Longinus asks:

> In lyrics, . . . would you choose to be Bacchylides rather than
> Pindar, or in tragedy Ion of Chios rather than Sophocles? In both
> pairs the first named is impeccable and a master of elegance in
> the smooth style, while Pindar and Sophocles sometimes seem
> to fire the whole landscape as they sweep across it, though often
> their fire is unaccountably quenched and they fall miserably flat.[6]

This is the only direct reference to Pindar in the *Peri Hupsous*, but it was highly influential in fostering associations between Pindar and the sublime. It was thanks to Longinus's praise of Pindar that, as Stella Revard has noted, "sublime . . . is probably the adjective most often applied to Pindar, both in antiquity and in the Renaissance."[7]

The source of Pindar's sublimity, however, did not always remain constant. Anne Cotterill's insight that "the sublime discourse praised by Longinus proceeded from and celebrated the moral elevation of both speaker and listener whose passion could result in disjunction and digression" illuminates what Cowley and his contemporaries saw as the sublime elements of Pindar (*Digressive Voices*, 33). Pindar's poems appeared irregular to seventeenth-century readers because the formal metrical and stanzaic structures that underpin Pindaric lyrics were not fully appreciated in that period. Pindar was subsequently known as a poet whose verses were characterized by digressions and sudden transitions between subjects. This approach to Pindar informs Cowley's references to Pindaric verse as poetry that consists "more in *Digressions*, then in the main *subject*," and that digression is "the fashion of all *Lyriques*, and of *Pindar* above all men living" (*Poems*, 1, sig. b1r). These digressions were interpreted as successive fits of poetic inspiration by a divine power, hence Pindar's ability to ascend to such poetic heights.

Cowley did not only associate sublime digression with Pindar and classical antiquity. He also capitalized on the existing connections earlier writers had found between sublimity, Pindar, and biblical narratives. The origins of these connections can be traced back to Longinus himself, since the *Peri Hupsous* quotes from Genesis (*On the Sublime*, 9.9). For Cowley, though, it was the prophetic passages of the Old Testament that represented the clearest connection between the biblical and the Pindaric sublime: "The manner of the *Prophets* writing, especially of *Isaiah*, seems to me very like that of *Pindar*; they pass from one thing to another with almost *Invisible connexions*" (*Pindariques*, 50). Again, the digressions of the prophetic texts are connected to divine inspiration, since to be "inspired" is to be filled with a supernatural spirit.[8] Cowley's verse collection, *Pindarique Odes*, contains as much, if not more, direct engagement with the Bible than with Pindar. Only the first two of the odes represent English versions of poetry by Pindar himself; the rest are compositions on other topics written in imitation of Pindar's style. The final two poems in *Pindarique Odes*, and so the last poems a reader working sequentially through the volume would read before coming to the *Davideis*, are paraphrases of sections from the Old Testament: "The Plagues of *Egypt*" (from Exodus) and "The 34 Chapter of the Prophet *Isaiah*." Two other poems in *Pindarique Odes*, "Destinies" and "The Resurrection," further indicate that Cowley held the Pindaric form to be the most appropriate mode of including discussions of Christian theology in English poetry.

When describing the structure of "The Resurrection," Cowley notes that "this Ode is truly *Pindarical*, falling from one thing into another, after his *Enthysiastical manner*" (*Pindariques*, 22). In one respect, "*Enthysiastical*" simply affirms the connection between digression and poetic inspiration; like "inspiration," which derives from Latin *in + spirare*, to breathe in, implying being energized by some external force, "enthusiasm" derives from the Greek ἐνθεάζειν, to be inspired or possessed by a god (*OED*). In the *Davideis*, Cowley sought to present himself as an inspired poet in precisely this manner. He states that, thanks to the invocation to God at the beginning of the poem, "the whole work may reasonably hope to be filled with a *Divine Spirit*" (*Davideis*, 24).

While Cowley engages with a long-standing poetic tradition in presenting himself as an inspired poet, his Royalist background makes his use of "inspiration" and "enthusiasm" somewhat surprising. As Anthony Welch has shown, these were hardly neutral terms during the Interregnum:

> Royalists in revolutionary England widely condemned the rhetoric of poetic inspiration. . . . Their attack on inspiration grew out of a widespread conservative horror of religious enthusiasm, the claims of personal illumination by the Holy Spirit that had sprung up among some of the Protestant sects of the Civil War era.[9]

Cowley's presentation of himself in both the *Davideis* and the *Pindarique Odes* as writing in an *"Enthysiastical manner"* ran the risk of being interpreted as an act of a political turncoat, equivalent to his notorious call, in the "Preface" to the 1656 *Poems*, for former Royalists to submit "to the conditions of the *Conqueror*" and *"march* out of our *Cause"* (*Poems*, sig. a4r). The precise nature of his loyalties when he returned to England during the 1650s remains unknown, and the *Pindarique Odes* and *Davideis* have been variously interpreted as expressions of continued Royalist sympathies, anti-monarchist sentiment, and resignation to the republican present.[10] It is entirely possible that Cowley accommodated himself to the new regime; this interpretation of his loyalties was widespread in Cowley's own lifetime, and was a likely cause for his lack of substantial royal patronage and favor in the 1660s.

It was not only Cowley's use of the terms "inspiration" and "enthusiasm" that would have appeared politically suspect in Royalist circles. Sublimity, like these emotional states, was also strongly associated with republicanism. It is not a coincidence that John Hall, who first translated Longinus into English, was a strong supporter of republicanism. John West has described how the 1652 translation of Longinus became "a key component of the Republican literary culture of the midcentury and connected poetical freedom with political liberty."[11]

West's identification of the sublime with political liberty indicates that Cowley's adoption of terms that carried a clear republican charge to describe his own practice as a poet were not limited to inspiration and enthusiasm: Cowley liked to present himself as someone who took poetic liberties. In his gloss to his Pindaric paraphrase of Psalm 114 that he included in the *Davideis*—itself a further incidence of digression within the poem—he states: "For this liberty of inserting an *Ode* into an *Heroick Poem*, I have no authority or example; and therefore like men who venture upon a new coast, I must run the hazard of it. We must sometimes be bold to innovate" (*Davideis*, 37). Even if Cowley was attempting to use "liberty" here in a purely aesthetic context, it could not help but carry political resonances. The same would also apply to his use of "bold." Joshua Scodel has argued that "boldness" was a significant term in Cowley's critical vocabulary, and, in addition, Cowley seems to have associated it with the sublime.[12] He saw Pindar and Isaiah as containing "the highest and boldest flights of *Poetry*," and it was because Cowley presented himself as an inspired poet in the manner of Pindar and Isaiah that he was able to be so bold and innovative (*Pindariques*, 50).

However, when Cowley took liberties, it was within generally established and traditional parameters that were known both to himself and to many of his readers. He tempered his boldness and innovation by claiming that, while he was the first writer in English to include certain formal properties in the *Davideis*, an ancient author still served as a precedent for that specific feature. In the note to his digression on music, he states, "For this second *Invocation* upon a particular matter, I have the authority of *Homer* and *Virgil*" (*Davideis*, 36). He invokes Virgil again in justifying his use of hypometrical lines: "Though none of the *English Poets*, not indeed of the ancient *Latine*, have imitated *Virgil* in leaving sometimes half verses (where the sense seem to invite a man to that liberty) yet his authority alone is sufficient" (*Davideis*, 28). The claim to boldness and temerity Cowley makes in a note when inserting a lyric poem into an epic is the exception to this tendency. Yet in that instance, Victoria Moul has observed, there were, in fact, several precedents in contemporary neo-Latin poetry that Cowley and his readers were likely to have encountered.[13] Cowley habitually extends or builds upon the innovations of earlier poets, even if he is not always open about this practice.

There is a similar tempering to Cowley's self-presentation as a sublimely inspired poet, and of the associations with Interregnum republicanism that came with inspiration and enthusiasm. He felt that the key signifiers of the Pindaric and biblical sublime needed modification in order to be accommodated within English poetry. He states in the "Preface" to *Poems*:

> As for the *Pindarick Odes*, . . . I am in great doubt whether they will be understood by most *Readers*: nay, even by very many who are well enough acquainted with the common Roads, and ordinary Tracks of *Poesie*. . . . The digressions are many, and sudden, and sometimes long. (*Poems*, sig. b1r)

Despite this caveat, in translating Pindar, he felt obliged to include more connecting passages than were present in the original. Without such additions, he argues, "It would be thought that *one Mad-man* had translated *another*" (*Pindariques*, sig. Aaa2r). As with his imitations of Pindar, when paraphrasing Isaiah, Cowley finds the need both to represent and to temper its quality of sublime digression: "The connexion is so difficult, that I am forced to adde a little, and leave out a great deal to make it seem *Sense* to us, who are not used to that elevated way of expression" (*Pindariques*, 50). As Adam Rounce discusses elsewhere in the present volume, Cowley also supplied extensive notes to the *Odes* to aid readers' understanding, a practice that he continued in the *Davideis*.[14] Despite this tempering of the more crabbed aspects of his source texts, Cowley's mode of expression and historical or geographical references still requires explicating, which he invariably does in his notes.

Cowley's moderation of the sublime can also be read as being political, as well as representing a desire to remove barriers to readerly comprehension. Niall Allsopp has suggested that Cowley might have "thought the self-conscious contrivance and difficulty of the Pindaric ode could provide a safe container for the political dangers of inspiration" (*Poetry*, 120). In the *Davideis*, though, Cowley went further than attempting to contain these dangers. By drawing on the rhetoric of divine inspiration, he did not reveal an allegiance to republicanism. Instead, he sought to construct a culturally, if not necessarily politically active, Royalist sublimity. The digressions in the *Davideis* function as a form of poetic restoration. Royalists, as well as republicans, could become divinely inspired, sublime poets. Indeed, for Cowley, it was only Royalists who could truly lay claim to this status. In the *Davideis*, he preserves the frenzied state of sublime inspiration that was associated with radical Protestantism and republicanism, but largely applies it to the forces who are hostile to David, and who, for Cowley, act as agents for infernal forces. As the following section outlines, in his digressions on music and on love, he licenses this frenzy for those who are inspired by the divine, and he usually regards this state of holy sublimity as capable of calming passion and frenzy.

Sublime Elevation: Music and Love

The first digression in the *Davideis* occurs in Cowley's description of David's power to quell Saul's anger through music:

> Tell me, oh *Muse* (for *Thou*, or *none* can'st tell
> The mystick pow'ers that in blest *Numbers* dwell,
> Thou their great *Nature* know[']st, nor is it fit
> This noblest *Gem* of thine own *Crown* t'omit). (*Davideis*, 13)

The movement from plot to digression might seem fairly abrupt and in accordance with the Pindaric model, but Cowley begins the digression within the immediately preceding couplet.

> And true it was, soft *musick* did appease
> Th'obscure fantastick rage of *Sauls* disease. (*Davideis*, 13)

Cowley's references to "soft *musick*" here provide the origin for the account of musical composition. The digression's further shifts of focus, from human to divine composition, are also less abrupt than their counterparts in Pindar's poetry and in the Old Testament. After describing the power of music on earth, Cowley broadens his scope to consider literary as well as musical composition. The creation of the world is then figured as a lyric poem, where God is praised as the original and unsurpassable poet-musician:

> Tell me from whence these heav'nly charms arise;
> Teach the dull world t'admire what they *despise*,
>   As first a various unform'd *Hint* we find
> Rise in some god-like *Poets* fertile *Mind*,
> Till all the parts and words their places take,
> And with just marches *verse* and *musick* make;
> Such was *Gods Poem*, this *Worlds* new *Essay*;
> So wild and rude in its first *draught* it lay. (*Davideis*, 13)

In keeping with the Longinian belief that the sublime lifts people "near the mighty mind of God," digression comes to represent an ascent into sublimity and divinity (*On the Sublime*, 36.1). Unlike in the Pindaric sublime, however, that ascent is more steady than sudden.

Cowley's praise of love preserves the link between the digressive sublime and a state of elevation while tempering the association of the sublime with extreme emotion. While narrating for the first time that

Saul's son, Jonathan, sees David, Cowley is struck by the power of love, which results in a lyric reverie:

> He saw his *Valour* by their *Safety* proved;
> He saw all this, and as he saw, he *Lov'ed*.
>   What art thou, *Love*, thou great mysterious thing?
> From what hid stock does thy strange *Nature* spring?
> 'Tis thou that mov'est the *world* through every part
> And holdst the vast frame close, that nothing start.
>   (*Davideis*, 47)

As in the digression on music, Cowley supplies a transition between the main narrative and the digression. In a further similarity, in his account of love, Cowley moves incrementally, from praise of his ostensible subject, to praise of God. Where the digression on music draws parallels between the poet and God as creators, the digression on love concentrates more on the divine element within creation. Cowley celebrates love as an elemental force: "By *Thee* were all things *Made*, and are *sustain'd*" (*Davideis*, 47). It is the source for fundamental aspects of the world: "How does the absent *Pole* the *Needle* move? / . . . / Or why does *Weight* to th' *Centre* downwards bend?" (*Davideis*, 47). These incidents illustrate God's love for his creation, but they do not lead to greater self-understanding. The love that David and Jonathan have for each other, by contrast, leads to a better awareness of God's love for mankind, and prompts praise of God:

> Such sacred *Love* does he'avens bright *Spirits* fill,
> Where *Love* is but to *Understand* and *Will*,
> With swift and unseen *Motions*; such as We
> Somewhat express in heightned *Charitie*.
> *O ye blest One*! whose *Love* on *earth* became
> So pure that still in *He'aven* 'tis but the same!
> There now ye sit, and with mixt souls embrace,
> Gazing upon great *Loves* mysterious Face. (*Davideis*, 48)

Even against this backdrop of love at work in the world, Cowley sees David and Jonathan's love for each other as especially profound. Such love helps mortals better to comprehend not only themselves, but also the part of God within them.

In presenting love as an elevating force in this manner, Cowley combines the sublime with Platonic and Neoplatonic ideas regarding the role of love in the cosmos. In particular, he draws on the concept of the "Ladder of Love," as originally articulated in Plato's *Symposium* and recontextualized within a Christian framework by Marsilio Ficino.[15] In this formulation, love for another individual represents the lower rungs on the Ladder of Love and acts as the means by which people ascend toward higher forms of love, culminating in God's love. Although Ficino's ideas on love were in wide circulation throughout the Renaissance, they had become newly fashionable in England in the middle decades of the seventeenth century. In a letter dated 1634, the writer and traveler James Howell speaks of how Charles I's French queen, Henrietta Maria, had fostered a cult of Platonic love at court:

> The Court affords little News at present, but that there is a Love call'd *Platonic* Love, which much sways ther of late; it is a love abstracted from all corporeall gross impressions and sensuall appetite, but consists in Contemplations and Ideas of the Mind, not in any carnall fruition.[16]

Cowley would have become familiar with this celebration of Platonic love through his association with the queen's court during the 1640s and the early years of the Interregnum. He had, in fact, lightly satirized Platonic love, specifically the emphasis it placed on love as a union of souls that lacked "carnall fruition." While his collection of amatory verses, *The Mistress,* was published in the 1656 *Poems,* it had first been published as a stand-alone volume in 1647 and is generally considered the product of his time at the queen's court, by then in exile at the Louvre. One of the poems in *The Mistress,* "Platonick Love," begins:

> Indeed I must confess
> When *Souls* mix, 'tis an *Happiness*;
> But not compleat till *Bodies* too do joyne,
> And both our *Wholes* into one *Whole* combine. (*The Mistress*, 12)

A similar claim that true love must involve the body as well as the soul—
"When I'am *all soul*, such shall *my Love* too be"—occurs in "Answer to the
Platonicks," a poem that appears later in *The Mistress* (16).

The element of satire in *The Mistress*'s treatment of Platonic love
comes from a male speaker addressing a female subject. The more sincere
treatment in the *Davideis* is the result of Cowley returning it to its origins,
both in Plato and Ficino, in celebrations of male-male relationships,
which were supposedly superior to male-female relationships because he
repeatedly denies that the former has any connection to bodily desire. Of
Jonathan's love for David he claims:

> Never did *Marriage* such true *Union* find,
> Or mens desires with so glad violence bind;
> For there is still some tincture left of *Sin*,
> And still the *Sex* will needs be stealing in. (*Davideis*, 48)

Cowley, in suitably Neoplatonic fashion, has David and Jonathan represent a union of souls. Their love for each other enables them to ascend
toward God's love. The love of God both reflects and comprises God's
love for his creation and blurs the boundary between the divine and the
human. As in the digression on music, the digression on love advocates
an incremental ascent toward the divine instead of a sudden one. There
is also a much greater emphasis on love as a source of calmness rather
than frenzy. Indeed, it is a "true union" because, Cowley tells us, it lacks
extreme emotion. Stephen Guy-Bray has argued that Cowley's attempts
at denying any aspect of erotic desire from the relationship of David and
Jonathan are not always successful or convincing, and recognizing this
informed Cowley's abandonment of the poem.[17] It is certainly the case
that the love of David for Jonathan is presented in the *Davideis* in more
romantic language than many of the rather bloodless lyrics of *The Mistress*.
But when Cowley uses the discourse of romantic love in his description
of the relationship of David and Jonathan, this is reserved for their initial
encounter; in this example, tranquility very quickly supplants passion.
Cowley even suggests that recognizing tranquility is what drew Jonathan
to David: "He saw what *Mildness* his bold *Spi'rit* did tame, / Gentler then
Light, yet powerful as a *Flame*" (*Davideis*, 47). Sudden as the ascent toward

spiritual love may have been for David and Jonathan themselves, Cowley's account of this ascent and its significance is noticeably more measured.

The Jonathan of book 2 differs, somewhat, from the Jonathan described in the long flashback narrative of book 4. There, Jonathan shares his father Saul's capacity to experience extreme emotional states. What distinguishes Jonathan's passion from Saul's is the source of their inspiration. Saul's wrath is prompted by the actions of the Fury Envy, who has journeyed from the Underworld and (in an imitation of the Fury Alecto in Virgil's *Aeneid*) has cast one of the snakes from her hair into his breast to bring him under her control.[18] When Jonathan is at the head of the army fighting the Philistines, he is struck by a "sacred fury" that reveals to him the path to victory. He tells his companion Abdon:

> What may this be (the *Prince* breaks forth) I finde,
> *God* or some powerful *Spirit* invade my minde.
> From ought but *Heaven* can never sure be brought
> So high, so glorious, and so vast a thought. (*Davideis*, 139)

Not only has Jonathan been struck by thoughts that come from on high, which combine inspiration with sublime elevation, but the course of action that he decides on is also comparable to the state required for musical or poetical composition and for the act of falling in love. Jonathan's ascent is as literal as it is spiritual. To win the battle, he realizes that he must lead his troops up a mountain:

> When th'inspir'd Prince did nimbly *understand*
> *God*, and his *God-like Virtues* high command.
> It call'd him up, and up the steep ascent
> With *pain and labour*, *haste* and *joy* they went. (*Davideis*, 141)

Like his father, Jonathan is in a state of fury, but Jonathan's state is endorsed by the poem as he is inspired to perform God's will where Saul becomes a tool for the Devil's agent, Envy. Cowley has to depart from the biblical narrative in order to make this distinction, since, in the books of Samuel, the evil spirit that visits Saul comes from God, not the Devil. There is an aesthetic and devotional element to this change. It is reminiscent of

Longinus holding that the sublime style of writing leads to greater depths as well as to greater heights of rhetoric: Pindar can, after all, fall "miserably flat" as well as soar higher than any other lyric poet. For Cowley, inspiration can take individuals further away from, and closer to, the divine.

These devotional elements in Cowley's treatment of inspired fury also help to make sense of the poem's politics. While the precise political resonances of the *Davideis* are complex, what can be said is that Cowley generally uses David and his allies as a means of representing Royalist hopes during the Interregnum, and Saul to represent those individuals and forces who sought to frustrate those hopes.[19] In addition, where Saul's default emotional state is frenzied rage, Jonathan's is tranquility. Jonathan channels his fury into a battlefield rampage against the enemies of Israel, but once it has served its purpose, his frenzy dissipates. Since Cowley does not leave it in any doubt to either Jonathan or his readers that what inspires these actions is a divine spirit, rather than an infernal force masquerading as one, the poem is able to sanction Jonathan's actions. Through this framing of events, Cowley associates the infernal sublime with the passionate republican discourse of inspiration and enthusiasm, while attempting to adopt the concept of the sublime to express a standpoint that, if not actively Royalist, was nonetheless associated with Royalist culture and attitudes.

Even though he grants Jonathan the status of an inspired figure, Cowley is careful to have this event recounted retrospectively rather than form part of the main narrative thereby indicating that violence, including divinely sanctioned and mandated violence, lies in Jonathan's past, which is in contrast to his conduct after meeting David. The same impulse likely lies behind Cowley's decision to have David's own act of martial heroism, his victory over Goliath, also appear retrospectively and in a speech by someone other than David himself. It is, in part, thanks to their encounter that both David and Jonathan can replace war with love.

The actions of Saul, Jonathan, and David across the *Davideis*, but especially in its inset narratives, underline Cowley's belief that mortals are forced to surrender themselves completely to a supernatural power, whether infernal or celestial. The question of submission before more powerful forces also informs *Davideis*'s digressions on the life of Abraham and his family, to which I now turn. Rather than tranquility, the dominant emotion in these digressions is resignation and a successful checking of passion in the face of extreme emotional trauma. Despite this shift in emphasis, the digressions on Abraham represent an additional attempt by Cowley to reframe ideas and vocabulary that were primarily associated with republicanism and more extreme versions of Protestantism.

Abraham and Providence

The first of Cowley's digressions on Abraham's family is a work of ekphrasis, since it describes ten tapestries in Saul's palace that depict scenes from Abraham's life. Cowley tells us "But none 'mongst all the forms drew then their eyes, / Like faithful *Abrams* righteous *Sacrifice*" (*Davideis*, 52) of Isaac. As with the digressions on love and music, the shift from narrative to digression is carefully anticipated by and integrated into the narrative. Prior to the digression, we are told that Saul is celebrating the festival of the new moon; Cowley admits the origins of the festival are obscure but may have arisen "From faithful *Abrams* righteous *Sacrifice*" (*Davideis*, 51). The verbatim repetition makes the connection sufficiently clear, but to point the connection even further, the passage between these two lines is mostly dedicated to a lengthy description of the livestock sacrificed as part of the festival.

Cowley grants the scene of Abraham and Isaac extensive attention. As Chloe Wheatley has observed, he dedicates as much time to that one scene as he does to the rest of the images on the tapestries.[20] The source for the expansions is the descriptions of the emotional suffering that Abraham experiences on the journey up Mount Moriah to sacrifice Isaac. At this stage, sublime ascent toward the divine remains defined by extreme passion, rather than by the tranquility that informs the digressions on music and love:

> The sad old man mounts slowly to the place,
> With *Natures* power triumphant in his face
> O're the *Minds* courage; for in spight of all
> From his swoln eyes resistless waters fall. (*Davideis*, 52)

Nonetheless, Nature's power, in the form of his love for Isaac, is only triumphant on Abraham's face and not over his actions. His recognition of the need to obey God forces him to override all other instincts, enabling him to continue the journey. For Allsopp, Cowley's David "exemplifies an ideal submission to God," and Abraham here serves as a precedent for this attitude and a reminder of its benefits (*Poetry*, 137). Nor is it only Abraham's submission that is total. Isaac, too, albeit from a position of ignorance, unquestioningly obeys Abraham: he lies "patiently" on the altar "And did his *Syre*, as he his *God*, obey" (*Davideis*, 52). The syntactic ambiguity of this line suggests both that Isaac obeys Abraham as Abraham obeys God, and also that Isaac obeys both God and Abraham in equal measure. At this moment, of course, Abraham is acting as God's instrument, just as Jonathan acts as God's instrument through his battlefield exploits of book 4.

Isaac's reprieve, when it does come, is presented as highly unexpected. Isaac is saved through an event that even the angelic spectators of the scene had been unsure would actually come to pass:

> A thousand *Spir'its* peep'd from th'affrighted sky,
> Amaz[']ed at this strange *Scene*; and almost fear'd,
> For all those joyful *Prophesies* they'd heard.
> Till *one* leapt nimbly forth by *Gods* command
> Like *Lightning* from a *Cloud*, and stopt his hand. (*Davideis*, 52)

Complete knowledge of the event, and its outcome, is known only to God. It is by submitting completely to God's will, of exchanging passion for patience (both in the sense of "calm, self-possessed waiting" and "the endurance of pain"), that Abraham and Isaac ensure the most positive outcome.[21]

Where Abraham and Isaac show the rewards of completely submitting to God, the other historical digression in the *Davideis*, about the family of Abraham's nephew, Lot, demonstrates the consequences of failing to do so. This digression is again incorporated through ekphrasis, this time through descriptions of the pictures David sees on his arrival at the palace of the Moabites (who, Cowley reminds us, were descended from Lot). As with the tapestries on Abraham, Cowley gives a relatively brief account of Abraham's biography before dedicating the bulk of his attention to one particular event, in this instance, Lot's wife turning into a pillar of salt during the flight from Sodom. Despite being commanded not to look back when leaving Sodom, Lot's wife, "impatient to see what had become of her friends and *Country*," looks back:

> Afar old *Lot* to'ward little *Zoar* hyes,
> And dares not move (good man) his weeping eyes.
> Behinde his *Wife* stood ever fixt alone;
> No more a *Woman*, not yet quite a *Stone*.
> [...]
> Ah foolish woman! who must always be,
> A sight more *strange* then that she turn'd to see! (*Davideis*, 90)

Unlike Isaac, Lot's wife lacks patience (in either of the aforementioned senses) and is ultimately unable to subordinate her allegiance to her family, to her obedience to God.

The events surrounding Abraham, Isaac, Lot, and Lot's wife all act as stark examples of acts of Providence through God's direct intervention in human affairs. As with the sublime, and its associated qualities of inspiration and enthusiasm, Providence was a well-established concept in the Renaissance, but also received a large degree of attention in the middle decades of the seventeenth century: Blair Worden has described this period as the point "when English providentialism took its most intense forms."[22] In a further parallel with the sublime, it was strongly associated with republicanism, because it supplied evidence for God's intervention on behalf of those who fought against the Stuart monarchy, who were then acting as vessels for, and instruments for, God. It also provided an explanation for the extraordinary events of the Civil Wars and an indication of God's favor for the republican cause.

The digressions in the *Davideis* concerned with Providence can, like the engagement with sublimity, enthusiasm, and inspiration elsewhere in the poem, initially suggest changed loyalties, or at least resignation to the republican status quo. But, as Worden and other scholars have established, Providence was not the sole preserve of republicans in the 1650s.[23] Just as the *Davideis* was concerned with a Royalist sublime, so, too, did it establish a Royalist reading of Providence. The digression on Abraham frames a sudden change in fortune and hardship as a trial of loyalty and favor. Such attitudes would naturally have had significant appeal for Stuart loyalists in the 1650s, as they continued to entertain hopes of a restoration of the monarchy. Although there has been some debate about the date of composition of the poem, it is largely accepted that Cowley worked on the *Davideis* during the early 1650s, when politics were highly febrile and unstable, and the prospect of an imminent Stuart restoration remained viable.[24] The situation by the time of the *Davideis*'s publication in 1656 was markedly different, since the Royalist cause was by then at an especially low point and Cromwell's Protectorate government seemed more secure. It is in that context that Cowley's belief in total submission can appear to be an accommodation to Cromwell's regime, but the *Davideis*'s digressions on Abraham and his family emphasize the suddenness with which Providential acts can occur and reverse fortunes accordingly. The digression on Lot's wife prevents these parts of the poem functioning as Royalist fantasies or prophecies: her fate runs counter to that of Isaac, and serves as a reminder that reversals of fortune are not always to be welcomed.

Cowley's attitude toward Providence clarifies his political affinities across the Interregnum and the various fluctuations in Royalist fortunes across that period. As I have argued elsewhere, he used the fragmentary structure of the *Davideis* and the partial telling of David's life before becoming king as a means of expressing his hopes for the future, in the form of a Stuart restoration, while acknowledging that his hopes might never be fulfilled (Calvert, *Virgil's English Translators*, 65–67). The kingly destiny of David of the *Davideis* is made explicit, but when the poem ends, he remains uncrowned, like the future Charles II in the 1650s. Cowley thus holds out for a providential restoration, but while the *Davideis* recognizes this as his desired outcome, it does not suggest that such an event is inevitable. It also acknowledges that the Royalist situation could just as well deteriorate even further as well as improve.

One key difference between the Royalists and Abraham's family members, in the digression, is their sense of what is required of them. Abraham and Lot's wife are both given direct instructions from God, which provide a clear indication of how Providence is to be enacted in the world. The difficulty comes in the severity of those instructions and the challenges people have in executing them, in large part because of the requirement to privilege obeying God over concern for members of their immediate family. It is striking, though, that these instructions are not included in Cowley's account of the episodes. While he could reasonably assume his readers were aware of them, their absence serves as a reminder that he himself and others with Royalist sympathies in the 1650s had no instructions of the type that Abraham and his family were given to follow. Cowley's sense of Providence is founded on the principle that full knowledge of God's plans is rarely available to mortals, and consequently God's instructions can seem (sublimely) cryptic or hostile to human interests, and certainly impossible to predict. It acknowledges that God's will and favor can often seem capricious, hence the need for total submission to Providence. It is acceptance of this powerlessness and the sublime unknowability of God that is rewarded. Crucially, that reward is not guaranteed, even when people have surrendered totally to divine power.

The Prophets' College: Sublime Tranquility

The need for a complete surrender that Cowley advocates in the digressions on Abraham and Lot cannot help but reduce the individual agency of the characters involved. It is in the longest digression of the *Davideis*, the account of the college at Ramah, that Cowley articulates how he and his fellow Royalists might come to terms with this lack of agency, and how they might conduct themselves in a manner that ensures they are largely unaffected by whether or not their desired future comes to pass.

The digression on the prophets' college, like other digressions in the poem, is partly concerned with sublime inspiration. In this case, however, inspiration forms part of the content of the digression instead of serving as its origin. The head prophet of the college is Samuel, and Cowley draws on the long associations in both classical and biblical literature between prophecy and poetry to present him as an inspired bard, like the poet of the *Davideis* himself:

> *Samuel* himself did *Gods* rich *Law* display;
> Taught doubting men with *Judgement* to *obay.*
> And oft his ravisht *Soul* with sudden flight
> Soar'd above *present Times,* and humane sight. (*Davideis*, 19)

Such fits of enthusiasm are, crucially, limited only to Samuel as God's anointed priest. The rest of the college's residents benefit from Samuel's divine inspiration, but their experience of it is secondhand. Even within the priestly elite, the claim to this close connection to God and divine will is limited to a single exceptional individual, as is also the case with Jonathan's experience of "sacred fury" in book 4. In his account of Samuel's fits of inspiration, Cowley attempts to shift the discourse of sublime enthusiasm away from associating with radical Protestantism, toward trusting, instead, an ordained representative to act as an intermediary between God and God's people.

Confining this divine inspiration and enthusiasm to Samuel ensures that the general atmosphere of the college is characterized by tranquility instead of the heightened emotional state that is more usually associated with poet-prophets. The priests, according to Cowley's note on the passage, "separated themselves from the business of the world, to employ their time in the contemplation and praise of God" (*Davideis*, 39). They are sufficiently devoted to their contemplations, which bring them closer to the divine in a measured and steady way, that their lives are free from the trappings of riches, power, or fame. Cowley reinforces the college's status as a haven by drawing on classical descriptions of the Elysian Fields and recording his borrowing in an accompanying note, but it is also hard not to read this account of the priests' lives without thinking of it as an act of wish fulfillment on Cowley's part.[25] The digression on the college gains further significance in light of comments Cowley makes in the "Preface" to the 1656 *Poems*. There, he states:

> My desire has been for some years past . . . to retire my self to some of our *American Plantations*, not to seek for *Gold*, . . . but to forsake this world for ever, with all the *vanities* and *Vexations* of it, and to bury my self in some obscure retreat there (but not without the consolation of *Letters* and *Philosophy*). (*Poems*, sig. a3r–4v)

While this plan never came to fruition, by the time that Cowley published *Poems*, he was dedicating his time to studying botany and medicine, although Sprat, his first biographer, claimed that Cowley used his studies as a cover for further work as a Royalist intelligencer (*Works*, sig. a2v–r). As with several of Sprat's claims, this has been viewed skeptically. Whatever the true nature of his activities in the later years of the Interregnum, Cowley continued to wish for such a scholarly retreat from the world. There are clear parallels between the college of the *Davideis* and the ideal place of learning that Cowley outlined in *A Proposition for the Advancement of Experimental Philosophy*, an essay first published posthumously (*Works*, sig. 2F2r–G2r).

Part of the appeal of the college for Cowley lies in its focus on learning itself over engaging with politics. While he acknowledges that, in his biblical source material, the political intruded even into education, he does so in a manner that ultimately reinforces the status of the college as a haven from politics. Saul sends successive bands of soldiers to extract David from the college, but they find themselves unable to carry out his orders:

> They came, but a new spirit their hearts possest,
> Scatt'ring a sacred calm through every brest:
> The furrows of their brow, so rough erewhile,
> Sink down into the dimples of a *Smile*.
> Their cooler veins swell with a peaceful tide,
> And the chaste streams with even current glide.
> A sudden *day* breaks gently through their eyes,
> And *Morning-b[l]ushes* in their cheeks arise.
> The thoughts of war, of blood, and murther cease;
> In peaceful tunes they adore the *God* of *Peace*.
> New Messengers twice more the *Tyrant* sent,
> And was twice more mockt with the same event. (*Davideis*, 22)

Allsopp has observed how Cowley departs from the biblical narrative in this passage, which has Saul's soldiers struck by an enthusiastic fury, not a sacred calm (*Poetry*, 136). The departure is in keeping with Cowley's practice elsewhere in the *Davideis* of turning sublime frenzy into tranquility. The digression contains elements of both a personal and a Royalist fantasy, since Providence prevents forces that are hostile to the destined monarch-in-waiting from being harmed. However, it is more helpful to see the digression of the college at Ramah as an expression of Cowley's wish to transcend political concerns altogether, in accordance with the desire that in his own society, "the Names of *Party*, and *Titles* of *Division*" could be "extinguished and forbidden" (*Poems*, sig. b1v). Life in such a college would allow Cowley to surrender himself completely to Providence while also remaining insulated from its vicissitudes. As such, its description in the *Davideis* represents a digression that Cowley hoped would become permanent, if not for the nation, then at least for himself.

CHAPTER FOUR

"Verse Loitring into Prose"
Abraham Cowley's Prosimetric Ode

Joshua Swidzinski

When Abraham Cowley's *Pindarique Odes* appeared in 1656, they were surrounded by a scholarly apparatus of self-annotation that eclipsed the poems themselves. To the roughly 12,000 words of verse that make up the fifteen odes, Cowley appended another 16,000 words of commentary spread across 210 notes. Cowley's notes cite, allude to, and pilfer learning from a wide variety of literary, theological, and scientific texts. While a handful of his notes were evidently added later, many are so closely tied to the verse that contemporaneous composition seems more likely.[1] The notes are thus not merely an appendage to but an essential part of Cowley's project and legacy. They offer insight into his idiosyncratic understanding of the nature and function of poetry; additionally, they would serve as a precedent for later poets to mingle verse and prose genres in surprising ways. A study of his notes promises to illuminate not only Cowley's own poetics, but also how poets of the long eighteenth century understood and experimented with verse's relationship to prose genres such as the essay, as well as to forms of knowledge and scholarship more broadly.

My concern in this chapter is with the self-annotation of odes and the generic and discursive experimentation such self-annotation made possible. While it was common for poets of the period to annotate their translations, Cowley's *Pindariques* licensed poets to annotate their original verse with lengthy prose digressions of a scholarly or critical bent.

Cowley, of course, did not associate self-annotation exclusively with the Pindaric ode, for he annotated his Pindarics and *Davideis* (1656) in the same manner.[2] Yet despite some notable instances of self-annotation in epics evidently inspired by Cowley—for example, Samuel Wesley's *The Life of our Blessed Lord & Saviour Jesus Christ* (1693) and Daniel Defoe's *Jure Divino* (1706)—the practice became closely associated with the irregular or Pindaric ode. This chapter, then, describes the origins and later influence of a genre I term the "prosimetric ode"—an irregular ode, modeled after Cowley's, in which the mixture of verse and prose commentary is considered an essential, distinctive feature of the form.[3]

This chapter is divided into two parts. In the first, I explore Cowley's prosimetric practices in the *Pindarique Odes* and argue that he conceives of poetry and scholarship as continuous, complementary activities. I make the case that prosimetric writing enables Cowley to inhabit the roles of poet and scholar simultaneously, allowing him to blur genres and achieve disparate rhetorical purposes without violating perceived rules of decorum. Cowley's Pindarics fashion a prosimetric speaker—a double-voiced poet-scholar capable of operating in distinct registers—that would serve as an influential model of generic innovation for poets of the Restoration and early eighteenth century. In the second part of the chapter, I trace the development and persistence of the prosimetric ode as a form through which eighteenth-century poets experimented with hybrid genres. William Congreve, Lewis Theobald, Aaron Hill, and others employed Cowley's *Pindariques* as a precedent for forms of writing that sought to join the sublime ode with literary criticism, the essay, and physicotheological speculation in surprising and formally inventive ways. Although direct reference to Cowley's Pindarics waned after the middle of the eighteenth century, his prosimetric legacy—a multi-voiced ode capable of assimilating distinct perspectives and forms of discourse within a larger design—continued to influence writers well into the Romantic period.

Cowley was not the first English poet to indulge in self-annotation. He was familiar with Thomas Heywood's copiously annotated *The Hierarchie of the Blessed Angells* (1635) as well as the *Mount-Orgueil* (1641) of William Prynne (whose propensity for notes earned him the sobriquet "Marginal").[4] A more proximate influence may be Henry More's

Philosophical Poems (1647), with its elaborate notes concerning Platonic philosophy, which appears to have engaged Cowley's attention during the months when he began composing the *Pindarique Odes*.[5] Cowley, in other words, did not invent self-annotation any more than he invented the irregular ode—but, like the ode, the license to self-annotate would become closely associated with Cowley throughout the Restoration and eighteenth century.[6]

We know too little about the circumstances under which Cowley composed the *Pindariques* and the *Davideis* to say with certainty where and how he developed his habit of self-annotation.[7] It is evident, however, that the practice required access to a library (the contents of which we can often identify from Cowley's notes) and that it allowed the poet to inhabit the position of a scholar. If—and this is conjecture—the process began with his translations of Pindar's second Olympic and first Nemean odes, Cowley may have started by adding explanatory notes in his capacity as a translator (mimicking the edition of Pindar at his elbow), after which he continued to add notes to his own poetry in the same fashion.[8] Yet, even in these initial notes, which are predominantly focused on issues of translation and indebted to Johannes Benedictus's edition of Pindar (1620), Cowley begins to expatiate, expanding some of Benedictus's hints into lengthy citations of parallel passages from Virgil, Horace, Homer, and Claudian.[9] Regardless of how he may have developed the habit, Cowley eagerly embraced the practice of self-annotation and the scholarly commentary it enabled—in part, perhaps, because it offered him a chance to inhabit the life of scholarship that he felt the Civil Wars had denied him, which he laments losing in both his verse and his essays. This technique of placing verse and prose alongside one another would become a distinctive feature of Cowley's work from the 1650s onward, evident in the *Visions and Prophecies* (1660), *Plantarum Libri duo* (1662), and "Several Discourses by way of Essays, in Verse and Prose" (1668), suggesting that he viewed these modes of writing as complementary and continuous.[10]

Within Cowley's commentary, two activities predominate. The first of these is paraphrase. He regularly offers prose notes that explain the meaning of his verse in a manner that can seem maddeningly redundant. For instance, a passage likening life to a "Vain weak built *Isthmus*, which dost proudly rise / Up betwixt *two Eternities*" elicits from the poet the following superfluous note: "*Isthmus* is a neck of Land that divides a *Peninsula* from the *Continent*, and is betwixt two Seas, . . . in which manner this narrow passage of *Life* divides the *Past Time* from the *Future*, and is at last swallowed up into *Eternity*" ("Life and Fame," *Pindariques*, 39–40). Yet faced by such redundancy, one must recall that the scholarly editions Cowley consulted as he composed the odes exhibit a use of parallel text and commentary that tends to render verse and verse's meaning diffuse. Where, exactly, does the meaning of Pindar reside when, as in Benedictus's edition, he is flanked on all sides by paraphrase, metaphrase, and explication? This diffusion of poem and meaning becomes a creative opportunity for Cowley. For example, in the ode to his physician friend Dr. Scarborough, he laments the limits of the doctor's medical arts using the metaphor of a siege:

> Ah, learned *friend*, it grieves me, when I think
>> That *Thou* with all thy *Art* must dy
>>> As certainly as *I*.
> And all thy noble *Reparations* sink
> Into the sure-wrought *Mine* of treacherous *Mortality*,
> Like *Archimedes*, honorably in vain,
> Thou holdst out *Towns* that must at last be *ta'ne.*
>> (*Pindariques*, 37)[11]

In his note, Cowley makes plain the siege metaphor, but he also adds a new element to the metaphor: "For whilst we are repairing the outward seeming *Breaches*, *Nature* is undermining the very *foundations* of *life*, and draining the *Radical moisture*, which is the *Well* that the Town lives by" (*Pindariques*, 37–38). There is no mention of, or allusion to, a "well" anywhere in the extended metaphor in the verse; this elaboration exists only in the notes. In this way, Cowley uses the notes not only to explain, but also to extend the work of the verse, such that the seemingly scholarly commentary develops the metaphors begun in the poetry.

The second activity on display in Cowley's commentary is digression. He frequently uses his notes to offer up parallel passages from the classics and to share items of historical and literary learning. In his preface to *Plantarum Libri duo*, the poet explains his reasoning for this technique:

Notas autem breves placuit subjungere, non eruditionis oste-
ntandae gratiâ, . . . sed quia . . . non ità multi fortasse Lectores
invenientur qui in historiis Plantarum satìs sint versati ad
ipsa aliquarum nomina intelligenda. Est enim pars quaedam
Philosophiae extra publicas plateas aut itinera usitata, inter avia
atque inculta doctrinae ferè posita. His igitur mihi vicem Lexici
supplere visum est. (*Plantarum*, sig. A4r–v)

[It seemed right, moreover, to subjoin short notes, not for the
sake of showing off learning, . . . but because . . . there are perhaps
not so many readers to be found who are sufficiently versed in
the histories of plants as to understand the very names of some
of them. It is indeed a realm of Philosophy situated beyond the
common roads or familiar paths, almost among the wilds and
uncultivated regions of learning. For these readers, therefore, it
seemed to me proper to supply the recompense of a lexicon.][12]

Cowley expects his verse to be read not only as verse, but also as a lexicon
or reference guide, to regions of learning beyond the realm of poetry. This
is true not only of the explicitly didactic *Plantarum Libri duo*, but also
of the Pindaric odes and of *Davideis*, where he routinely uses the notes
to introduce readers to out-of-the-way learned debates.[13] Prosimetric
writing thus solves a problem of decorum. Cowley is aware that certain
words are unwelcome in verse; indeed, he invokes the figure of the lexicon
on more than one occasion to reveal discursive gulfs between poetry
and the "barbarous" languages of medicine—"What need there here
repeated be by me / The vast and barbarous *Lexicon* / Of Mans *Infirmitie*?"
(*Pindariques*, 36)—and property law:

> Discreet? what means this word *Discreet*
>   A Curse on all *Discretion*!
> This *barbarous term* you will not meet
>   In all *Loves-Lexicon*.

> Joynture, Portion, Gold, Estate,
>   Houses, Houshold-stuff, or Land,

(The *Low Conveniences* of Fate)
                        Are *Greek* no *Lovers understand*. (*The Mistress*, 66–67)

Prosimetric writing allows Cowley to straddle discursive fault lines: he can play the roles of poet and scholar simultaneously, without violating the rules of decorum.

Such digression, however, is not a distraction, but rather an essential feature of the Pindaric and the lyric more broadly, as understood by Cowley. He remarks that "the digressions are many, and sudden, and sometimes long, according to the fashion of all *Lyriques*, and of *Pindar* above all men living" (*Poems*, sig. b1r). In this sense, the notes are digressions continuous with, and related to, the digressive nature of the ode itself: they continue, via scholarly commentary, the main activity of the Pindaric poet. This blurring of distinctions between scholar and poet is visible in Cowley's description of poetry's function. Addressing the muse of lyric poetry, he writes:

> Thou fadom'est the deep *Gulf* of *Ages* past,
>   And canst pluck up with ease
> The *years* which Thou dost please,
> Like shipwrackt *Treasures* by rude *Tempests* cast
>   Long since into the *Sea*,
> Brought up again to *light* and publique *Use* by Thee.
>   (*Pindariques*, 23–24)

In a note, Cowley explains that "*Poetry* . . . makes what choice it pleases out of the *wrack* of *Time* of things that it will save from *Oblivion*" (*Pindariques*, 25). This is a striking definition of poetry. Whereas Sir Philip Sidney memorably characterizes the poet as a godlike creator freely ranging within the zodiac of his own wit, Cowley conceives of the poet as a salvager—as much a scholar as a poet. Indeed, his definition bears a close resemblance to George Herbert's advice to the scholar: "Copie fair, what time hath blurr'd; / Redeem truth from his jawes."[14] If Cowley views poetry as, in part, something that salvages and preserves the past, then his notes play a crucial role in fulfilling this poetic function. The prosimetric quality of Cowley's odes are an effect of his distinctively scholarly theory of poetry.

Later in his preface to *Plantarum Libri duo,* Cowley offers another reason for using notes. In addition to solving a problem of decorum, they also allow the poet to blend distinct functions of prose and verse:

Quia nobis aliquando mentiri concessum est, eâque libertate immodestè abutuntur aliqui, ità in totum fides omnis abrogatur. ... Itaque Testes adhibere volui Idoneos, hoc est, liberâ solutâque oratione usos; ea enim cum Versu comparata sole[m]ne Jusjurandum est. (*Plantarum,* sig. A4v)

[Because it is permitted to us poets to feign sometimes, and some have extravagantly abused that liberty, so all trust in us is entirely dissolved. ... I have therefore preferred to summon suitable witnesses, namely those who have made use of free and loose prose—which, compared to verse, is a solemn oath.]

Cowley possesses a keen sense of the discursive difference between verse and prose: one is the realm of romance and invention; the other, a place of propositional truth and falsity. His sense of this distinction has been overlooked, perhaps, because his literary executor, Thomas Sprat, characterized Cowley's irregular verse as essentially a kind of "Prose" akin to "the style of all business and conversation" ("Account," sig. c1r). Yet Cowley would have been the first to disagree with Sprat's characterization, for one routinely finds him policing the stylistic boundary between prose and verse in both his odes and his essays. In a note to his ode to Hobbes, while tracing classical descriptions of the nearness of fire and snow atop volcanic mountains such as Etna, Cowley remarks that "*Tacitus* has the like expression of *Mount Libanus, Praecipuum montium Libanum, mirum dictu, tantos inter ardores opacum, fidúmq[ue] nivibus.* Shady among such great heats, and *faithful* to the *Snow*; which is too *Poetical* for the Prose even of a *Romance,* much more of an *Historian*" (*Pindariques,* 29). A similar distinction occurs in one of Cowley's essays (framed as a letter to John Evelyn), in which, after an extended biblical analogy, Cowley stops short: "You may wonder, Sir, (for this seems a little too extravagant and Pindarical for *Prose*) what I mean by all this Preface."[15] This sense of distinction recurs across Cowley's writings and illuminates his use of notes. The poet's propensity to invent in verse (indeed, to deceive or to lie, depending on how one translates "mentiri") is mitigated by the authorizing function of the prose: the notes connect the poem to reality and justify its apparent fancies by offering factual evidence to support propositional statements or classical precedents for Cowley's artistic choices.

This division of labor becomes especially clear if we attend to Cowley's handling of the poetic subject. In his odes, he uses the lyric "I" sparingly. He is more likely to refer to himself and his verse obliquely ("my" appears more often than "I") addressing his muse or his verse, or even himself, in the third person—"No matter, *Cowley*, let proud *Fortune* see, / That *thou* canst *her* despise no less than *she* does *Thee*"—than to write from the subject position (*Pindariques*, 31). This is a departure from Cowley's earlier lyric pieces (the first three poems in *The Mistress*, for instance, begin with "I") and, to an extent, from Pindar too. In his headnote to "The Second Olympique *Ode* of *Pindar*," Cowley insists that this form of oblique self-address via the muse is a peculiar feature of Pindaric verse: "The *Reader* must not be chocqued to hear him speak so often of his own *Muse*; for that is a *Liberty* which this kind of *Poetry* can hardly live without" (*Pindariques*, 1). Yet Cowley actually heightens this effect in his translation. At a crucial moment in this ode, when Pindar seems to allude to his own obscurity, he characterizes himself as an archer: "I have many swift arrows under my arm / in their quiver that speak to those who understand, but for the whole subject, they need / interpreters."[16] In Cowley's extended, loose rendering of this passage, however, it is the muse—rather than the poet—who holds the bow:

> To *Theron*, *Muse*, bring back thy wandring Song,
> [...]
> How, noble *Archer*, do thy wanton *Arrows* fly
> At all the *Game* that does but cross thine *Eye*?
>   Shoot, and spare not, for I see
> Thy sounding *Quiver* can ne're emptied be;
> Let *Art* use *Method* and good *Husbandry*,
> *Art* lives on *Natures Alms*, is weak and poor;
> *Nature* herself has unexhausted store,
> Wallows in *Wealth*, and runs a turning *Maze*,
>   That no *vulgar Eye* can trace. (*Pindariques*, 5)

Cowley hands the bow of poetry to the muse and relegates himself to the position of observer: he does not aim or shoot, but merely "see[s]"—and, even then, his "*vulgar Eye*" cannot trace the full reach of the muse's inexhaustible and wandering song.

Yet while the odes may be too sublime to admit Cowley's vulgar "I," the first-person speaker is a crucial presence in the prose notes, where the word "I" appears frequently—indeed, three times more often than it does in the verse. Perhaps taking his cue from Pindar's remark that his listeners need "interpreters," Cowley uses the notes to fashion a first-person speaker whose urbane wit and scholarly interests set him apart from the vatic voice of the odes. Cowley's prose "I," for instance, eagerly discusses matters of literary criticism:

> *Find, Refind*: These kind of Rhymes the *French* delight in, and call *Rich Rhymes*; but I do not allow of them in *English*, nor would use them at all in any other but this free kinde of *Poetry*, and here too very sparingly. . . . They are very frequent in *Chaucer*, and our old *Poets*, but that is not good authority for us now. (*Pindariques*, 37)

He is also given—as both this note and his remark in *Plantarum Libri duo* indicate—to employing the prose notes to authorize facts mentioned and liberties taken in the verse. When the speaker of "The Muse" imagines a place "Where never *Fish* did *fly*, / And with short silver *wings* cut the low liquid *Sky*," his prose counterpart chimes in to defend this likening of sky to sea by citing precedent from scripture, Virgil, Lucretius, and Ovid (*Pindariques*, 23, 25). Although Cowley could tire of such activity—he abruptly ends a note to one of his odes by remarking that "one might cast up a pedantical heap of authorities to the same purpose"—he habitually uses the prose notes to authorize and authenticate the verse's flights of fancy (*Pindariques*, 52).

This division of labor—wherein the poetic "I" soars aloft while the prose "I" plods along behind to explain, expand, and justify—is itself a point of discussion in Cowley's works. In book 1 of *Davideis*, the poet dramatizes the moment when David's "soft *musick* did appease / Th' obscure fantastick rage of *Sauls* disease," spurring Cowley to add both a note (one of his longest) and a digression in verse about music's power to heal the body. In a subsequent note, Cowley addresses the propriety of such digressions as well as the question of who can engage in them:

> *Scaliger* in his *Hypercrit.* [i.e., book 6 of Julius Caesar Scaliger's *Poetices libri septem*] blames *Claudian* for his excursion concerning the burning of *Ætna*, and for enquiring the cause of it in his own person. If he had brought in, says he, any other person making the relation, I should endure it. I think he is too *Hyper-critical* upon so short a *Digression*; however, I choose here upon this new occasion, by the by to make a new short *Invocation* of the *Muse*, and that which follows . . . is to be understood as from the person of the *Muse*. (*Davideis*, 36n33)

Cowley acknowledges that a digression, especially in an epic, is tolerable if spoken by a character, but unwelcome if indulged in the poet's "own person." To obey the neoclassical rules of decorum while at the same time indulging in his beloved practice of digression, Cowley creates a convenient character (here, the muse) through whom he can ventriloquize. Although he leaves it unsaid, one can extend this rationale to the notes: they allow him to say and do things in prose that the mode and register of verse will not allow.

The effect of all this is to create a peculiarly prosimetric type of speaker—possessing two distinct voices operating in different registers and modes—that would become an influential model for poets of the Restoration and early eighteenth century. Not only can these two voices complement each other (as when Cowley the scholar explains and justifies the flights of Cowley the poet), they can also contradict and satirize each other. "The Praise of *Pindar*," Cowley's loose imitation of a poem by Horace, offers a revealing example of this satirical potential. In the ode, the prosimetric speaker throws off constraints and sincerely strives for the sublime, like Pindar, who

> does new *Words* and *Figures* roul
> Down his impetuous *Dithyrambique Tide*,
>   Which in no *Channel* deigns t'abide,
>   Which neither *Banks* nor *Dikes* controul.
> (*Pindariques*, 18–19)

Yet in the prose, the speaker's other voice can gently mock this very sublimity by noting that dithyrambic verse "was a bold, free, *enthusiastical* kind of Poetry, as of men inspired by *Bacchus*, that is, *Half-Drunk*," and adding that, in Horace's attempts to approach the dithyrambic, "He ends like a man ranting in his drink, that falls suddenly asleep" (*Pindariques*, 19–20). To the half-mad poet addressing his muse, Cowley joins a detached, witty scholar whose terse coffeehouse criticism anticipates the sorts of judgments one finds in Dryden's prefaces. (Indeed, Dryden—who described Cowley as "the Darling of my youth"—was not above pilfering material for his prefaces from Cowley's notes.)[17]

Recognizing the prosimetric quality of Cowley's speaker allows us to resolve our often contradictory appraisals of the poet's work. Scholarly discussion of the odes might lead one to suppose the existence of two different Cowleys—one, a sober-minded Baconian and member of the Royal Society who "wishes to create a new kind of ode that is philosophic in design" and capable of "serv[ing] the new philosophy, . . . coming into prominence in the latter part of the seventeenth century"; the other, a dangerous enthusiast whose odes exhibit "disorderly passion, formal unruliness, and licentious degradation," and bear upon their face "the stigma of unreason."[18] These contradictory strands of criticism are, each in its way, correct. Cowley's odes are, simultaneously, frenzied and calm; sincere and wry; brilliantly synthetic and pedantically analytic. They are all these things because Cowley creates and deploys a prosimetric speaker whose double persona—variously, a poet-scholar, poet-wit, and poet-pedant—brings verse and prose into productive relationship with each other in ways that later writers interested in generic innovation would find irresistible.

Early responses to Cowley's odes suggest that readers welcomed, or at least tolerated, such notes as a necessary feature of the genre. When Dryden remarks that "*Pindar* is generally known to be a dark writer, to want Connexion, (I mean as to our understanding) to soar out of sight, and leave his Reader at a Gaze," he leaves open the possibility that readers might need a guide whereby to understand Pindar's flight.[19] Other commentators explicitly welcome Cowley's notes as a complement to his sublime verse: David Lloyd praises Cowley's commentary for "being as Learned as his Poems Ingenious, the one opening what the other coucheth";

and Gerald Langbaine echoes this view, remarking that Cowley "has writ Notes, as replete with Learning, as his Odes with Wit and Fancy, and which most admirably explain the most difficult and abstruse Passages."[20] Crucial here is the idea of "Connexion"—a word Dryden borrows from Cowley, who insists that Pindaric verse "pass[es] from one thing to another with almost *Invisible connexions*," a word that Congreve (whom I will turn to shortly) employs when he remarks of Pindar that "tho' his Digressions are frequent, and his Transitions sudden, yet is there ever some secret Connexion."[21] The fundamental feature of the Pindaric lyric is digression, but it is taken for granted that these digressions are not random or chaotic; rather, they proceed from a latent, logical connection. As Louis de Jaucourt remarks, in the *Encyclopédie*, "All of the sublime transports of the ode must be governed by reason, all of its apparent disorder must be in effect nothing more than a more hidden order."[22] It thus becomes necessary, or at least tolerable, to have these connections illustrated for certain readers, a task the digressive notes fulfill.

William Congreve's handling of the Pindaric ode is instructive here. In 1706, Congreve published an ode to Queen Anne celebrating Marlborough's victory at Ramillies, to which he prefixed "A Discourse on the Pindarique Ode." In many accounts of the modern Pindaric, this preface serves as a turning point in the history of the genre, for Congreve uses his "Discourse" to protest that Pindar's verses were perfectly regular and that "a Bundle of rambling incoherent Thoughts, express'd in a like Parcel of irregular Stanza's" does not constitute a Pindaric ode.[23] Although Congreve is careful to avoid criticizing Cowley directly, he nonetheless recognizes that "those irregular Odes of Mr. *Cowley* . . . have been the principal, though innocent Occasion, of so many deformed Poems since" (sig. A2v). Congreve's ode, in which he strives to model the regularity of Pindar's triadic structure, aims to correct the bad habits that Cowley initiated half a century earlier. Yet Congreve does not repudiate all of Cowley's habits. For when he republished his "Discourse" and ode along with another Pindaric to the Earl of Godolphin in his *Works* (1710), Congreve took the opportunity to add detailed explanatory notes to both poems. Like Cowley, he uses these notes to explain and defend his figures ("They who do not remember *Virgil*, may think this Metaphor too bold") and to cite literary authorities. He even pauses to praise his predecessor's notes directly: "Mr. *Cowley* in his Notes . . . collects a great number of surprising Citations on this Subject."[24] No one was readier than Congreve to censure Cowley's liberties. That he instead emulates Cowley's self-annotation suggests that Congreve viewed it as an acceptable feature of the genre.

The persistence of this feature made the prosimetric ode an ideal vehicle for developing and exploring hybrid genres during the eighteenth century. In 1707, Lewis Theobald, still twenty years away from being immortalized in the *Dunciad*, published his first work, *A Pindarick Ode on the Union of Scotland and England*. In his prefatory remarks, he frankly admits "the Laborious Obscurity of *Pindarick* Writings," a notion echoed in the commendatory poem by J. D., who offers praise, albeit, clumsily phrased, for Theobald's "deep laborious Lines."[25] Theobald's ode, in other words, is willfully obscure. It presumes the existence of notes, without which, at times, it would be nearly incomprehensible. Take, for instance, the poem's opening address to the muse of sacred song (in which I also reproduce Theobald's marginal annotations to give a sense of how frequently he prompts his readers to turn to the notes):

Haste, *Polyhymnia*, haste; thy Shell prepare:
    I have a Message thou must bear,
But to the Carr a Salamander tye;
      Thou can'st not on a Sun-beam play
     And scud it thro' the Realms of Day;
Where Great *Hyperion* sits inthron'd on High.   1
          (Seasons there and Ages stand;
        And measur'd Hours on either Hand;   2
And swift-pac'd Minutes, an Innumerable Band.)
      But thy steep down-ward Journey lyes,
      To th' uncouth *Nadir* of the Skies;   3
          O're whose Dread Yawn,
Th' Intelligent Inhabitants of Air,   4
        Their winged Voyage steer.
Panting aloft, and from the Stench still hast'ning to be gone,
Where Chains and Groans resound the Din of Hell,
            And Spirits yell;
And thousand fictious Monsters dwell. (Theobald, 1)

Some of the accompanying notes are merely ostentatious—the first and third explain the terms "Hyperion" and "nadir," respectively; the second points out how Theobald's verses allude to a passage in Ovid's *Metamorphoses*—but others are load-bearing notes that, like Cowley's, extend and complete the work of the verse. For instance, Theobald's fourth note informs the reader that he here alludes to "the Lake *Avernus*, (that derives its Name from hence,) in *Campania*, o're which, *Virgil* reports, that Birds durst not to fly, by reason of a mortal Stench arising, wherefore it was concluded by the Poets the Passage to Hell" (Theobald, 7). Theobald's use of periphrasis—"Intelligent Inhabitants of Air" for birds, "Dread Yawn" for crater—and his refusal to name Avernus directly force the reader to turn to the notes to make sense of the passage at all. In Theobald's hands, the ode dissolves distinctions between poetry and learning, and between poets and critics. This hybrid genre offers the ideal vehicle for a writer eager to demonstrate creativity and scholarly acumen simultaneously. Indeed, Theobald's first (now largely forgotten) publication fittingly anticipates his later career as a poet-critic who wrote verse and plays in the style of Shakespeare while, at the same time, composing critical works about how best to interpret and amend Shakespeare's darkest passages. This double profession is exemplified in miniature in Theobald's prosimetric ode, where he creates the very cruxes that he then explains in his notes. The generic hybridity of the prosimetric ode thus contributed to the century's fierce debates (waged, most memorably, in Pope's *Dunciad*) about the proper relationship between poetry and criticism, gentlemanly taste and specialized scholarship.

The ode also blurred distinctions between poet and essayist, as evidenced by Aaron Hill's unfinished *Gideon, or the Restoration of Israel* (1720; rev. 1749). At first glance, one may be inclined to regard Hill's *Gideon* as something other than a prosimetric ode. It is, Hill insists, a biblical epic—one that seems intended to rival not only Pope's *Iliad*, but also Pope's lengthy critical "Observations," which Hill emulates and counters in his "Reflections."[26] Cowley's *Davideis* was no doubt an influence. Yet the choice of verse form sets it apart from both Pope's and Cowley's epics. Hill tells us that "the Structure of my Verse . . . differs little from that which Mr. *Cowley*, toward the End of the last Century reduc'd into Practice, in Imitation of *Pindar*" (an innovation he would later praise in his

1726 ode "On Mr. Cowley's Introducing Pindaric Verse").[27] Hill likewise insists that the Hebrew poetry he wishes to emulate possesses the sublime qualities of the "*Lyric Ode*" (*Gideon* [1720], 25). Regardless of what we or Hill call this hybrid genre—Polonius, perhaps, would have called it the lyrical-epical-critical—it takes its inspiration from the prosimetric ode and pushes its features to the breaking point.[28]

Hill's notes overwhelm the poem and often swell to the length of short essays. For instance, one of the notes to the first book, ostensibly concerned with explaining Gideon's rising fortunes, turns into a more general mediation on the relationship between fortune and opportunity, in which Hill takes up the figures of Brutus, Cromwell, and Caesar (*Gideon* [1720], 42–43). The length of the note as it appears in Hill's final version of *Gideon* is comparable to one of Samuel Johnson's *Idler* essays. Hill was no stranger to essay writing: his next venture after *Gideon* was the journal *The Plain Dealer*, for which the notes to *Gideon* offered a convenient warm-up. The kinship between Hill's notes and the essay genre became more explicit when he published his revised *Gideon; or, The Patriot* in 1749. In the introduction to this edition, he describes the prose portions of the work as a self-contained, parallel work, rather than as a set of notes subordinate to the poem:

> The Notes to All the Books, will . . . be publish'd, by Themselves: and may be bound distinct from the Poetic Part: or be annex'd to Each Book relatively; making, so, *Two* Volumes; at Election of the Reader: who may also, in this Method, chuse to take, or leave, the *Notes*, at his own Pleasure.[29]

In keeping with this new approach, Hill dropped the enumeration of notes in the margins of the verse, severing the connection between verse and prose. The more essay-like quality of the notes in the 1749 *Gideon* is implicit in Hill's other prefatory remark: "As for the *Notes*, they are not merely of *poetical*, or *critical*, Intention: but consist, occasionally, of enlarg'd Discourses upon different Subjects, drawn from old and modern *History*; to elucidate and give Examples, to, *political* Deductions" and other topics (*Gideon* [1749], 8).

The notion of a kinship between the Pindaric ode and the modern essay may strike us as strange, yet eighteenth-century readers perceived that both forms of writing were predicated on the shared practice of digression. In the preface to the collected edition of *The Plain Dealer*, Hill remarks that

> the only *Rule* [of essay writing] that I know, (and it is generally well observed) is not only to go without, but to go against all *Order* and *Method* whatsoever. . . . The Honour of this Invention must still be ascribed to *Montaigne*, who first introduced that useful *Practice* of *Digression*.[30]

In *Rambler* 158, however, Samuel Johnson traces the invention of digression deeper into the classical past, noting that "the first authors of lyrick poetry . . . loosed their genius to its own course, passed from one sentiment to another without expressing the intermediate ideas, and roved at large over the ideal world with such lightness and agility, that their footsteps are scarcely to be traced." He then goes on to criticize the modern lyric and the modern essay on the same grounds:

> From this accidental peculiarity of the ancient writers the criticks deduce the rules of lyrick poetry, which they have set free from all the laws by which other compositions are confined, and allow to neglect the niceties of transition, to start into remote digressions, and to wander without restraint from one scene of imagery to another.
>
> A writer of later times has, by the vivacity of his essays, reconciled mankind to the same licentiousness in short dissertations; and he therefore who wants skill to form a plan, or diligence to pursue it, needs only entitle his performance an essay, to acquire the right of heaping together the collections of half his life without order, coherence, or propriety.[31]

Johnson can so effortlessly associate the modern ode and the modern essay because the "same licentiousness" obtains in both modes—not merely in the distant precedent of Cowley's Pindarics, but also in the more proximate example of contemporary emulators such as Hill.

For these reasons, the prosimetric ode was especially attractive to philosophers and divines. In their hands, it became an ideal vehicle for philosophical and theological speculation in which the verse can sometimes seem secondary to, or perhaps even an excuse for, the prose annotations. John Norris, rector of Bemerton and Malebranchian philosopher, offers a valuable example. His *Collection of Miscellanies* in verse and prose, first published in 1687, went through nine editions by 1730, and selections from Norris's religious verse continued to be reprinted in collections throughout the century. The *Collection* opens with a Pindaric ode, "The Passion of our B. Saviour," and includes a regular poem titled "The Elevation," both replete with Cowleyan annotations concerned with theological and philosophical matters.[32] The nature of the relationship between Norris's verse and prose annotations is best indicated by the frequency with which he uses the word "insinuate." "The thing intended in this whole stanza," he informs his readers, "is to insinuate the great facility and pleasure of the Divine life to one that is arrived to an habit of it." Elsewhere, he describes a line about Christ's mood in Gethsemane as "a good and proper insinuation of the excellency of our Blessed Lord's temper," and characterizes an idea as "not *directly* express'd, but only *insinuated* and *couch'd*, for the more elegancy of the thought" (56, 9, 4). Norris intends his verse to insinuate a theological or philosophical proposition whose "plain and *undisguised* meaning" he then unfolds in the notes (9).[33] The method, as Norris acknowledges, is allegorical. What is "done figuratively, under the Allegory" of the verse requires—or, perhaps more accurately, licenses—the prose, propositional disquisition we find in the notes (56).

When Norris acknowledges this division of labor in his preface, his use of gendered language suggests that he views the prose portions of the prosimetric ode as discursively superior to the verse: "I design here all the *Masculine sense* and *Argument* of a *Dissertation*, with the advantage of *Poetic Fineness*, Beauty and Spirit" (sig. a5r). In a pair of Pindaric odes in *Virtue and Science* (1695), one of Norris's imitators makes this gendered hierarchy even more explicit, insisting that in taking this Method, I had a due Regard to the *Devout Sex*, who take more delight in the *Tender* Expressions of Poetry, than in severe Precepts delivered in *Rougher* Prose; their *Genius* leading them to be more affected with what's *Quaint*, and to profit more by such Instructions as are usher'd in with Pleasure, and some kind of Gayity.[34]

At first glance, these comments recall the traditional view of poetry as a medicine of cherries that smuggles learning under the guise of pleasure, yet the prosimetric ode formally distinguishes the medicine from the cherries, revealing—rather than concealing—the discursive duplicity of the form.

The high watermark of the divine prosimetric ode is John Reynolds's *Death's Vision Represented in a Philosophical, Sacred Poem* (1709), which Reynolds revised and republished as *A View of Death: Or, The Soul's Departure from the World* (1725). This long physicotheological poem consists of twenty Pindaric stanzas (supported by "a copious Body of Explanatory Notes") in which Reynolds imagines the departing soul's flight heavenward and the knowledge of the universe, both scientific and theological, to which the soul would immediately gain access:

> Learn'd death! that in one hour informs me more
> Than all my years on earth before;
> Than all the academic aids could do;
> Than chronics, books, and contemplations too!
> Death! that exalts me strait to high'st degree!
> Commenc'd a more than *Newton* in abstruse philosophie![35]

This conceit of the departing soul's attaining knowledge perhaps takes its cue from Cowley's "The Extasie." But Reynolds's debt to Cowley is most visible in his learned and wide-ranging notes, which have left modern readers baffled. Marjorie Hope Nicolson, who remarks that Reynolds "showed more interest in his elaborate paraphernalia of scientific footnotes than in his text," views them as a distraction.[36] And when Roger Lonsdale included an excerpt of Reynolds's poem in *The New Oxford Book of Eighteenth-Century Verse*, he dropped the notes entirely.[37] Ignoring the notes, however, results in a partial understanding of the poem and the genre it represents, since Reynolds designs the two halves of his prosimetric ode to complement each other. Take, for instance, Reynolds's account of the mystery of the magnetic needle (the passage Lonsdale anthologized). The enlightened soul of the verse announces

> I see why the touch'd needle scents about,
> Till it has found the darling quarter out;
> And why, unconstant grown, it sometimes takes
> New-sprung amours, and its dear north forsakes;
> Why it at last (due honour to obtain)
> Repents its wandrings and returns again.
> (*A View of Death*, 33–34)

In the note to this passage, however, the benighted annotator continues to dwell in ignorance, listing phenomena we have yet to explain:

In reference to the magnetical needle there are these phænomena observable; 1. Its polarity; or direction towards the poles of the world, north and south; generally known. 2. Its variation; or declination from the direct polarity, either east or west. . . . 3. The variation of the variation; or the change that has been observed in the variation, at the same place, at different seasons. So Mr. *Boyle* reports, that in and about *London*, since the year 1580, the variation has been observed to decrease from 11 to 6, and then to 4 degrees, till, at last, there was scarce found any variations at all. . . . 4. The dipping; or inclination downwards. And here, the learned Mr. *Derham* seems to have made, and to have imparted to the *Royal Society*, a new discovery; *viz.* that, in its dipping, it describes a circle about the poles of the world; which is here ascribed to a sort of congratulation. But we must wait for a further account of that strange phænomenon. (*A View of Death*, 33n)

While the verse anticipates a solution revealed to the soul during its sublime flight, the note, dragging the reader down to the terrestrial

realm of the margin, parses and analyzes a philosophical problem yet
to be resolved. The relationship between these two parts—a glimpse of
poetic enlightenment clouded by the note's prosaic unknowing—dramatizes the thirst for knowledge that motivates the whole poem and its
valorization of death. In this fashion, Reynolds's work exemplifies the
prosimetric ode's analytic tendency, a quality central to Samuel Johnson's influential description and disapproval of the metaphysical poets
in his life of Cowley:

> Their attempts were always analytick; they broke every image
> into fragments: and could no more represent . . . the prospects
> of nature, or the scenes of life, than he, who dissects a sun-beam
> with a prism, can exhibit the wide effulgence of a summer noon.
> (*Lives*, 1:58)

Although Johnson limits his discussion of this school of poetry to
seventeenth-century poets, such as Cowley, Cleveland, and Donne, the
analytical prosimetric writings of Theobald, Hill, Norris, and Reynolds
exemplify Cowley's formal influence on the eighteenth century and raise
the possibility that Johnson, while writing the life of Cowley, had in mind
a living tradition of experimental writing inspired by this poet.

The story of the Pindaric ode's decline is well enough known that I
need not rehearse it here; one need only add that the use of notes played
a role in this decline. When Addison describes Cowley as "a mighty
Genius . . . / O're-run with Wit and lavish of his Thought," whose "fault
is only Wit in its Excess," this backhanded praise applies just as aptly to
Cowley's learned, prosaic digressions as to his metaphysical verse.[38] Likewise, Johnson seems to have in view both notes and verse when, following
Addison's lead, he finds in all Cowley's works "wit and learning unprof-
itably squandered" (*Lives*, 1:170), and criticizes the poet's inclination to
pursue "his thoughts to the last ramifications," whereby the reader's mind
is "turned . . . more upon that from which the illustration is drawn than
that to which it is applied" (*Lives*, 1:133). These digressions and the generic
law-breaking they facilitate are targeted for ridicule in Pope's *Dunciad*
amid a catalog of the kinds of writing inspired by the Goddess Dulness:

Here to her Chosen, all her works she shows;
Prose swell'd to verse, Verse loitring into prose;
How random Thoughts now meaning chance to find,
Now leave all memory of sense behind:
How Prologues into Prefaces decay,
And these to Notes are fritter'd quite away.[39]

For these canonical figures who have exerted a disproportionate influence over perceptions of eighteenth-century literary history, the generic licentiousness of Cowley's prosimetric ode was a fault. Yet we should not allow these influential critics to obscure the positive legacy of the prosimetric ode.

First, we should recognize the persistence and reach of the form itself, which led to ambitious works that blurred the boundary between poetry and scholarship. A century after Cowley inaugurated the genre, William Mason published his dramatic poem *Caractacus* (1759), which includes odes influenced by Thomas Gray's "The Bard" (1757), as well as a collection of learned "Illustrations" intended "to support and explain some passages in the Drama, that respect the manners of the Druids."[40] Mason's friend Gray was dismissive of such prosimetric habits and thought notes added to verse "signs of weakness and obscurity": "If a thing cannot be understood without them, it had better be not understood at all."[41] Yet when Gray was compelled to add notes to his difficult, allusive odes in 1768, he grudgingly revealed his debts to Cowley, who is cited more often than any other modern poet in "The Progress of Poesy."[42] The Cowleyan ode's persistence via Mason and Gray subsequently influenced a trio of Romantic-era prosimetric works: Frank Sayers's *Dramatic Sketches of the Ancient Northern Mythology* (1790?), a collection of masques and dramas made up of blank verse and odic choruses supported by explanatory notes on Nordic mythology; Robert Southey's *Thalaba the Destroyer* (1801), a prosimetric epic in irregular verse with copious, digressive notes reminiscent of Hill's *Gideon*; and Percy Bysshe Shelley's *Queen Mab: A Philosophical Poem with Notes* (1813).[43] Cowley by this point is long forgotten; the more proximate influences of Gray, Mason, and Ossian reign. But the prosimetric logic of these works is Cowleyan. A century and a half after the poet's death and long after he supposedly fell from favor ("Who now reads Cowley?" asks Pope in 1737), his prosimetric innovations endure.

In a more general sense, Cowley's generic innovation anticipates—and his emulators contribute to—the discursive fluidity and polyvocality characteristic of eighteenth-century verse. Many have argued that the verse of the period is nearer to "conversation"—what John Sitter calls a "multivoiced poetry"—than to the Romantic view of poetry (and especially the lyric) as confession overheard.[44] In this view, eighteenth-century poems often seek to digest distinct—at times conflicting—voices, perspectives, and content within a larger design. Cowley's prosimetric ode anticipates these aims, modeling compositional methods by which poets could put on, or appropriate, different voices—and, with them, forms of disciplinary authority—and thus participate in discourses seemingly far afield from poetry.[45] Such notable prosimetric works as Mark Akenside's *The Pleasures of Imagination* (1744); James Grainger's *The Sugar-Cane* (1764); and Erasmus Darwin's *Loves of Plants* (1789) and *The Botanic Garden* (1791) fall outside the bounds of this chapter because they are not written in Pindarics. Nonetheless, the generic hybridity and discursive fluidity of these and other works were made legible to eighteenth-century readers, in part, by the likes of Theobald, Hill, Norris, Reynolds, and others who fashioned Cowley's prosimetric ode into a distinctively porous, modern, and experimental genre.

CHAPTER FIVE

Black Comedy and Futility
Cowley's Notes to *Davideis*

Adam Rounce

D*avideis* (1656) has always seemed an odd work: an unfinished
biblical poem, fated to be published eleven years before *Paradise Lost*, and to always be very much in the shadow of the most
significant religious poem in English. Alongside the poem appeared its
copious endnotes, as if to suggest an inherent monumentality upon
publication. If so, it has never quite achieved such status, being seen
instead often as a curio that anticipates other things (Milton's work, the
representation of scripture via poetic transfiguration, an early example
of scholarly annotation of contemporary works in English). And this
curiosity has been increased by the endnotes, which add much to the
poem, but also open up opportunities for interpretation, rather than
fixing or confirming meanings in the main text. The endnotes have been
seen, variously, as fussy and overly detailed (an unconscious acknowledgment of the difficulties of trying to represent the divine in poetry, of
which the main text of *Davideis* is, for some readers, an object lesson); as
a compensation for or supplement to the poetry; a way station between
the exegesis of commentary and the later, more informal and anecdotal
style of footnote; and as an excessive display of learning that buries its
ostensible poetic referents, rather than enhancing them.[1] More recent
debates surround the ways in which Cowley uses the notes to refute allegory, and the more fantastical elements of scripture—it is hard to ignore
this side of the poem, where Cowley, the reader and scholar, tries, and

sometimes gives up trying, to rationalize the more implausible of the sacred truths of his narrative.[2]

The present account acknowledges such arguments, but also pays attention to the more personal side of Cowley's annotation. The notes are often funny in a dry, pawky, or sometimes near exasperated manner. They are self-conscious, witty, aware of the potential lumber-mill of pedantry, and of the near absurdity and futility of some scholarship, including Cowley's own. Although some notes start as an example of the fustian of excessive learning, they often leave the reader with a greater sense of the basic questions surrounding poetic creation, and the problems that Cowley faced. The notes call to mind other witty annotators in their humorous awareness of the futility of explanations, and in their repeated concessions to poetic license when all else fails. They show why *Davideis* is such an unusual poem, and how, in many ways, it could hardly be otherwise.

This essay will, therefore, offer something of an introduction to the playfulness of Cowley's annotation in *Davideis*; recent critical readings (of which there are perhaps more than might be expected, except that it is Cowley's odd fate to combine a venerable status with being perpetually overlooked) have considered the relationship between the theological and the naturalistic: the ways in which Cowley represents a biblical narrative with a quasi-scientific mode of thought, and how the poem's use of "disagreements between theological explanations" form "the basis for offering more naturalistic accounts" (Cole, 68). Equally, instead of allegory, Cowley "seeks to bridge the gap between the theological and metaphysical" (Cole, 66). Such accounts are useful, but sometimes seem too systematic for Cowley's more diffuse intentions: in what follows, I suggest that, while such patterns can sometimes be located, the notes can be seen as less comprehensive or designed, and more individual and quirky. After all, the very act of writing your own footnotes was something of a quirk, in 1656, and Cowley indulged in it in other works in his *Poems*, notably the *Pindarique Odes*; the note's allowance for reflection and afterthought seems to have suited Cowley's rather mercurial and involved poetic personality.[3]

Critics of annotation for its own sake have not perhaps been as numerous as would be expected: traditions—of philology, textual criticism, scriptural commentary, and so on—exist, of course, but there is little discussion of the peculiar nature of annotation of British literature (which, arguably, begins with Spenser at the end of the sixteenth century, and of which *Davideis* is such a good example), except in its most notable or notorious cases, such as eccentric eighteenth-century editions of Milton or Shakespeare; the variorums of Victorians; Pope's and Swift's satires on the pedantry of "modern" learning. It is not always easy to find agreement about such seemingly obvious ideas as there being a distance between the author writing the text, and the author annotating it, when they are the same person (that is, when their editorial role as annotator differs from that of their creative role as writer of the main text). The note is an "undefined fringe between text and paratext," according to Gerard Genette's ubiquitous collection of definitions and meditations on such related matters as prefaces, appendixes, and the like. He also has a useful remark on the nature of annotation by authors to their own works: "The basic function of the original authorial note is to serve as a supplement, sometimes a digression, very rarely a commentary."[4] This is helpful in indicating how the author's notes are often a way of adding information, or moving away from the text altogether, rather than a simple extension or recapitulation or paraphrase, as a way of clarifying it; notes may be presented as such clarifications, but they very often become instead digressive or supplementary. Genette is alive to the weird paradox whereby annotation can deflect, defend, or avoid things that the text may seem to discuss. Therefore, a note "is a fairly elusive and receding element" of the paratext. Some types of annotation provide "defensive commentary or autocriticism," and all represent "this indefiniteness and this slipperiness" about the "fringe between text and off-text" (342, 343). This gives some sense of the detached nature of commentary, where there is some sort of conscious gap between an annotator and his own text, howsoever paradoxical it may seem. It is, of course, a self-consciousness in large part because the author is commenting on his own performance.

Anthony Grafton's highly learned yet accessible introduction to the role of annotation in the evolution of history as a European academic discipline contains a brief summary of examples of self-annotation, where the "writer served as his own explicator":

> Dante and Petrarch wrote formal commentaries on segments of their own poetic production—a tradition which continued, through the erudite commentaries of Andreas Gryphius on his gruelingly learned six-hour tragedies, down to T. S. Eliot's notes on *The Waste Land*.[5]

Like Cowley's notes to *Davideis*, Eliot's notes, significantly shorter than the seventeenth-century poet and tragedian Gryphius's approach to annotations, which are an ordeal, are in part concerned with their own ambiguous purpose. They have, at times, a resigned tone, implying that spotting allusions and positing possible interpretations might actually be more of a hindrance than aid to the reader (something acknowledged by Eliot's later disputed suggestions about the notes being inserted chiefly to fill up the volume).[6] Furthermore, it might seem at first glance a little bold or even absurd to compare Cowley's endnotes to those of the recent novelist David Foster Wallace, whose annotations of his novels, stories, and essays became celebrated for their hipster ironies and laid-back witticisms, but the comparison is fruitful. Wallace defended annotation as a way to "make the primary text an easier read," while "allowing a discursive, authorial intrusive style," whereby, since wit becomes an extension of (or diversion from) the creative imagination behind the main text, a personality can flourish, and where the notes do not attempt to offer absolute knowledge, but instead offer up sometimes rueful acknowledgment of their insufficiency.[7] These type of notes do not fix the meanings of passages, but rather discuss why such finite knowledge is impossible, both in their own text, and in the larger sublunary world to which they relate, on some level. The relevance of this to *Davideis* will hopefully become clearer after some examples of the latter, where Cowley is happy to admit both his, and our, larger ignorance, the potential inefficacy of his poetic project, and, in unusually plainspoken fashion, the eccentricities of his creative decisions, undertaken often to follow traditions, sometimes to break them, and sometimes, in an oddly contemporary manner, purely to resist convention, or to stave off tedium.

Two relevant views from a century after Cowley's poem help frame the debate about what annotation is meant to accomplish. In the "Life of Cowley," Samuel Johnson, not really assured that the ambitions of the poem could be achieved, to judge from the evidence of what is extant, described how "if the continuation of the *Davideis* can be missed, it is for the learning that had been diffused over it, and the notes in which it had been explained" (*Lives*, 1:165). The notes are more valuable than the poetry, in what they offer, and act as something of a compensation for its aesthetic shortcomings. The annotation in this sense demonstrates Cowley's rich intellectual abilities, and offer an incidental, and apparently congenial, form of learning.

Thomas Gray, a less sympathetic contemporary of Johnson's, and a recurrent critic of his own works and the public idea of authorship that accompanied them, on being asked to annotate the obscurities in his Pindaric odes upon their publication in 1757, seemingly was troubled by how annotation drew attention both to the ignorance of readers and his own failure to make his meaning clear: his complicated reaction was compressed into the rather cutting comment, in his *Poems* of 1768, "When the Author first published this and the following Ode, he was advised, even by his Friends, to subjoin some few explanatory Notes; but had too much respect for the understanding of his Readers to take that liberty."[8] Gray's suspicious view is that the superficial flourish of learning displayed through authorial notes may only conceal a fundamental difficulty—that the need to annotate so extensively indicates a weakness in the construction of the poetry, and a failure to express its ideas properly through its own content and form. The self-conscious and self-critical Gray was acutely aware of such factors, but another tradition, arguably more generous, rewards the reader with extra information: more recently, William Empson defended adding notes to highly abstract poems, like his own, as a form of politeness—it would be rude, and exclusive, to expect any reader to share a highly specialized form of knowledge that the author might possess.[9]

There are, indeed, times when what Cowley is trying to explain is obscure, to say the least, and not made less so by his annotation, yet there are also many occasions when the notes create something of a micro-narrative or learned trail that is more interesting than the poetic text in which it originates, even if it sometimes leads nowhere. There are a couple of times where Gray's point seems very apposite, but there is also evidence to support Johnson's position, in that the notes, in their perusal of odd byways of learning, radiate a certain charm that diverts the reader from the poem itself.

The most simple of Cowley's endnotes in *Davideis* are functional, acting as glosses, either where some scriptural element or obscure quality needs to be acknowledged, or stressed. When David's potential nuptials with Saul's daughter Michal, for instance, are near, "He curst the stops of form and state, which lay / In this last *stage* like *Scandals* in his way." (3:104).[10] "*Scandals*" in this context, the note tells us, are "in the sense of the *New Testament*," meaning "*Stumbling blocks*," or "Stops in a mans way, at which he may fall, however they retard his course" (3:120). The New Testament reference is supported by *OED* 1b., "an occasion of unbelief or moral lapse; a stumbling-block," citing, amongst others, Galatians 5:11: "Then is the scandal of the crosse euacuated." The note explains and justifies the somewhat esoteric usage.

But look a few lines up, and the previous note requires a discrimination that is not linguistic: the context of note 60 is that, to win the hand of Michal, Saul demands that David kill a hundred Philistines, and, as a dowry, provides their foreskins as somewhat unedifying evidence. This huge task is not a problem, as he excels himself: "A double *Dowre*, two hundred foreskins brought / Of choice *Philistian* Knights with whom he fought" (3:104). This requires rather different annotation to engage with its meaning. Cowley, for neither the first nor the last time, confronts what appears to a modern reader an exaggeration that might as well be a metaphor, but has to decide whether to regard it as a figurative device, or to accept it literally. He chooses the latter, and takes up the task of explaining it, focusing upon the motive (Saul wants to kill David off through the impossible challenge), rather than the considerable difficulties of accepting the story:

> If it might have been allowed *David* to carry with him as many Souldiers as he pleased, and so make an inroad into the *Philistines* Countrey, and kill any hundred men he could meet with, this had been a small *Dowre* for a Princess, and would not have exposed

David to that hazard for which *Saul* chose this manner of *Joyn-ture*. I therefore believe, that he was to kill them all with his own hands. (3:120)

That is to say, paradoxically, the unlikeliness of the deed makes it more plausible—David is more likely to have personally killed two hundred warriors and brought back their foreskins because Saul wanted to set him a near-impossible task that would destroy him. It is an interesting type of logic that uses the narrative itself to confront its own unrealism, and thus take it on its own hyperbolic terms; at other points, Cowley would instead find the claims made too bold or outlandish, even by this standard.

Even this brief juxtaposition, of definition and interpretation, gives some indication of what the notes to the poem have to encompass. As well as such theological areas as typology, and the significance of figures and symbols to other scriptural sources and appearances, there are repeated debates around the nature of Cowley's presentation of religious figures and symbols, as his representation of his materials turns into interpretation, whenever there are ambiguities (which is often). The notes, therefore, continually debate the success or otherwise of Cowley's attempt at religious epic, comparing the often odd and inconsistent sources with what he then turns into poetry. These debates illustrate the difficulty of what Cowley was trying to accomplish, in presenting a religiously sanctioned source through his own modern scholarly and poetic filter.

An apparently innocuous example is in 2 Samuel 5:6–8, where David heads off the Jebusites and recaptures Jerusalem. From the King James Version:

6 And the king and his men went to Jerusalem unto the Jebusites, the inhabitants of the land: which spake unto David, saying, Except thou take away the blind and the lame, thou shalt not come in hither: thinking, David cannot come in hither.

7 Nevertheless David took the strong hold of Zion: the same is the city of David.

8 And David said on that day, Whosoever getteth up to the gutter, and smiteth the Jebusites, and the lame and the blind that are hated of David's soul, he shall be chief and captain. Wherefore they said, The blind and the lame shall not come into the house.

The lame and blind here represent a sort of symbolic or prophetic barrier to the taking of the city: the Jebusites seem to mean something along the lines of when Birnam Wood comes to Dunsinane, that is, "You will only conquer us when you remove all the lame and blind too." This is how Cowley renders it:

> The *Blind* and *Lame* th'undoubted wall defend,
> And no *new* wounds or dangers apprehend.
> The busie *image* of great *Joab* there
> Disdains the mock, and teaches them to fear.
> He climbs the *airy* walls, leaps raging down,
> New-minted shapes of slaughter fill the town.
> They curse the guards their mirth and bravery chose;
> All of them now are slain, or made like *those*. (2:55)

The blind and lame here are actually guarding the walls, rather than being a symbol of the city's defiance (a futile one, as Joab, David's nephew and commander of the army, scales the walls and kills them all). It is no reflection on the blind or lame to argue that they may not be the most efficient defenders of the city, and that it seems odd to place them, of all the Jebusite army, on the battlements. Cowley has a note:

> Unless thou take away the *Lame* and the *Blind*, thou shalt not come in hither, thinking *David* cannot come in hither, 2 *Sam.* 5. 6. There are some other interpretations of the place, then that which I here give; as that the *Idols* of the *Jebusites* were meant by the *Lame* and the *Blind*. But this carries no probability. Thinking *David* cannot come hither; is a plain proof that they did it in scorn of *David*, and confidence of the extraordinary strength of the place; which without question was very great, or else it could

not have held out so many hundred years since the entrance of
the *Israelites* into the land, in the very midst of them. (2:72)

Here Cowley makes some effort to explain his own reading, but he is a
little tentative, and, while mentioning other possibilities, doesn't really
defend his own: 2 Samuel, for all its ambiguities, does not suggest that
the lame and blind are more than an exhortation, or that they actually
man the barricades—why should they? They are not the elite guard, but
rather a diffuse threat or goad to David. Cowley takes David's commands
to the troops to scurry up the battlements and take the lame and blind
prisoner rather literally, as he does the whole scene. It is an intriguing
case of what to do when the base narrative offers ambiguous detail
that the poet must try to put into a pattern, even one that seems rather
inflexible.

It is no surprise that Cowley's defenses of this sort of transfiguration
of the Bible are sometimes tenuous, and depend upon his dramatizing
the figurative and the typological, even when he cannot directly admit
that this is so. There are, conversely, some points where the notes become
somewhat exasperated at what they are expected to believe and represent.
When, for instance, Saul's conflict with the Philistines leads the latter to
confront him, "The Philistines gathered themselves together to fight with
Israel, thirty thousand chariots, and six thousand horsemen, and people as
the sand which *is* on the sea shore in multitude" (1 Samuel 13:5). Cowley
renders this accurately: "Like fields of *Corn* their armed Squadrons stand; /
As thick and numberless they hide the land," but baulks at the numbers
of chariots: "Here with worse noise three thousand *Chariots* pass / With
plates of Iron bound, or louder Brass" (4:137). He expands on this decision
to cut 90 percent of the apparent chariots in the note:

The Text says, *Thirty thousand Chariots*; which is too many for
six thousand *Horse*. I have not the confidence to say *Thirty thousand* in *Verse*. *Grotius* believes it should be read Three Thousand.
Figures were often mistaken in old *Manuscripts*, and this may be
suspected in several places of our *Bibles*, without any abatement
of the reverence we ow to Scripture. (4:153)

Cowley here carefully absolves the potential obscurity and confusion of his sources from any charge of impiety, hence his invoking the authority of Hugo Grotius's recent *Annotations* of the Old and New Testaments (published in the 1640s). The problem here is that numbers are often vehicles for hyperbole—a host being like grains of sand is one thing, but a more tangible equation of 30,000 chariots and only 6,000 horsemen, making each horseman have to control five of them at the same time, seems excessive and rather heavy handed, as military tactics go (it would be odd to organize your calvary so that they would find it almost impossible to fight). Therefore, 3,000 is a safer bet, even if it is a conjectural emendation, given the history of mistaken numbers in the Bible, as Cowley mentions, where a figure, approximate or no, was used to indicate "a lot."

Much of Cowley's work in the notes is to try and explain similar things, where his original materials are possibly corrupted, or anyway fantastical, legendary, or allegorical to such an extent as to call the relation between actual detail and poetic license into question. In the vision of David in book 2, part of the long account of futurity of Israel involves a brief description of the war between Abijah (of David's line) and Jeroboam: "Ne're saw the aged *Sun* so cruel fight, / Scarce saw he *this*, but hid his bashful light." The reason for the sun hiding was that "*Nebats* curst son [Jeroboam] fled with not half his men" (2:57). In the note, Cowley questions the numbers, again, which are indeed large: Abijah's army is four hundred thousand strong, and Jeroboam's eight hundred thousand (2 Chronicles 13:3). Of the latter, five hundred thousand really were slain (13:17); Cowley is rather skeptical:

> The story of this great battel between *Abijah* and *Jeroboam* is one of the strangest and humanely most hard to believe, almost in the whole Old Testament, that out of a Kingdom, not half so big as *England*, five hundred thousand chosen and valiant men should be slain in one battel; and of this not so much, as any notice taken in *Abijahs* or *Jeroboams* lives in the first of *Kings*. It addes much to the wonder, that this defeat should draw no other consequence after it but *Abijahs* recovery of two or three Towns. (2:74)

The notable point here is that Cowley sees the battle as impossible to believe, not just because of the huge size of the loss of life relative to population, but also because it does not even get a mention in the descriptions of Abijah and Jeroboam in the actual chronological narrative (1 Kings 15). He is incredulous that something so enormously destructive could pass with so little apparent notice in other reports, when it must have influenced so many things. Therefore, he implies, it must be doubtful, not just because it sounds unrealistic and exaggerated, to him and to us (the proportion of casualties being more akin, alas, to the wars of the twentieth century, with modern technology), but in terms of standards of veracity of historical evidence, or its absence. It is one of the places where Cowley, respectful toward the origin stories of his narrative, is nevertheless prepared to use the notes to question the details, when they fail to correspond with a contemporary sense of what could be called verisimilitude or likelihood. In the tone of his remarks, as elsewhere, he notices the more fanciful aspects of the claims made. In this respect, the notes are something of a more forensic questioning of the poetic materials: Cowley is prepared to suggest in the poem that five hundred thousand lives were lost in an otherwise completely obscure battle (and it would seem churlish and digressive to argue about it in that part of his text), but he can then undermine the idea in the annotation quite effectively, whilst showing a welcome sense of perspective: the reader who wishes to can believe in the literal truth of scripture, howsoever strange, whereas the more skeptical can go along with Cowley's note, and consider it either a metaphor for the great loss of the battle, or a kind of shorthand not meant to be taken literally. In this way, the notes both reinforce the impression of the cross-referenced biblical sources of *Davideis*, whilst simultaneously viewing them through a modern filter.

The scriptural discussion shows Cowley's ambivalence toward the material that very much results from his awareness of competing ideas and traditions. This is also a large part of the notes' charm: at points, Cowley attempts to record the implausibility of what is being claimed poetically, or, indeed, throw up his hands and concede that facts and science are ill-served by allegory, and that the stories of the Old Testament should not be mistaken for anything resembling realism; the narrative might have a certain resonance that is rooted in some facts, but the more rococo details can still be treated with skepticism. This is, of course, part of a larger seventeenth-century debate about the relationship between science and history, but carried out on a more intimate and less specialized level of discussion. Cowley instead aims at the conversational, and pitches the oddities of these stories and their specifics to the curious, rather than the knowledgeable, reader. He thus raises questions that are apparently commonplace, but seemingly often passed over and rarely asked, and not really intended, anyway, to be fully answered. How large is Hell, for instance?

> No bound controls th'unwearied space, but *Hell*
> *Endless* as those dire *pains* that in it dwell.
> Here no dear glimpse of the *Suns* lovely face,
> Strikes through the *Solid* darkness of the place. (1:6)

It is not a question often asked of a metaphoric, allegorical space, but Cowley does not shy away, his curiosity piqued:

> This must be taken in a Poetical sense; for else, making *Hell* to
> be in the *Center* of the Earth, it is far from infinitely large, or
> deep; yet, on my conscience, where ere it be, it is not so strait,
> as that *Crowding* and sweating should be one of the *Torments* of
> it, as is pleasantly fancied by *Bellarmin*. *Lessius* in his Book *de
> Morib. Divinis*, as if he had been there to *survey* it, determines the
> *Diameter* to be just a *Dutch mile*. But *Ribera*, upon (and out of the
> *Apocalypse)* allows *Pluto* a little more elbow-room, and extends it
> to 1600 furlongs, that is 200 Italian miles. *Virgil* (as good a Divine
> for this matter as any of them both) says it is twice as deep as the
> distance betwixt heaven and earth. (1:27)

Here the literalism of three Jesuit authorities, Robert Bellarmine, Leonard Lessius, and Francis Ribera, is turned into something of a joke, with Cowley's beloved Virgil (as he then illustrates by quoting from the journey to the underworld in *Aeneid*, book 6) being as likely to guess right as any of them; the humor comes from a sense that the hyperbole of allegory is too amorphous for such attempts at precision and specificity, which makes them almost bathetic. The idea of Hell in the center of the earth can only be infinite with much damage to reason, just as with the related idea that a more limited space would mean crowding and sweating, a very ridiculous punishment (the damned would have other things to worry about, after all). Such notes show Cowley's recognition that there is a limit to what scholarship can achieve, other than piling up citations to no real moment, and that in such cases it has to concede to poetic license, with endless hell becoming, in effect, darkness visible.

It is the informal register of such notes that conveys a rather winning intimacy—Cowley is quite happy to roll his eyes in the notes along with the reader at the more fabular elements that he renders into verse relatively effectively. The annotation and poetry therefore enter into a sort of dialogue, allowing Cowley to comment on his own poetic practice, and on the attendant difficulties of dramatizing the literal in the biblical and the classical, even where it must be read as figurative by a modern reader. Cowley's unguarded and outspoken self-reflections do sometimes lead to digression, and its familiar offsprings, anecdote and non sequitur. The following allegory of Love is an example:

> In thy large state, *Life* gives the next degree,
> Where *Sense*, and *Good Apparent* places thee;
> But thy chief *Palace* is *Mans Heart* alone,
> Here are thy *Triumphs*, and full glories shown,
> Handsome *Desires*, and *Rest* about thee flee,
> *Union, Inhærence, Zeal*, and *Extasie*. (2:47)

The first sentence of the note sticks to the story, and offers a paraphrase, but after that, it very quickly becomes about something else entirely:

> The *Object* of the *Sensitive Appetite* is not that which is *truly good*,
> but that which *Appears* to be *Good*. There is great caution to be
> used in English in the placing of *Adjectives* (as here) after their
> *Substantives*. I think when they constitute specifical *differences* of
> the *Substantive*, they *follow* best; for then they are to it like *Cogno-*
> *mina*, or *Surnames* to *Names*, and we must not say, the *Great*

> *Pompey*, or the *Happy Sylla*, but *Pompey the Great*, and *Sylla the Happy*. (2:65)

This has started to wander quite far off point, and it continues to go even further out:

> Sometimes even in other cases the *Epithete* is put last very grace-fully, of which a good *ear* must be the *Judge* for ought I know, without any *Rule*. I choose rather to say *Light Divine*, and *Command Divine*, then *Divine Light*, and *Divine Command*. (2:65)

The note that began as a precise description of the meaning of the first two lines then goes on to debate with itself the potential rules for the placing of epithets, concluding ("for ought I know") that this is really informal and to do with subjective judgment, rather than prescriptive. The impatient reader who could, quite feasibly, ask Cowley why he brought it up in the first place if he doesn't have any particular conclusion to draw, would be justified; conversely, it is rather refreshing to be addressed in such a familiar way, without the usual presumed consequence and authority of editors, and the note is no less interesting for being inconclusive: there is something leveling about a poetic practice that can step out of itself and admit that it does not always precisely understand all poetic rules, and suggest that, on occasion, there might not be any, other than custom. The process aims at glossing but becomes a sharing that breaks down the fourth wall. Finally admitting that a good ear works as well as anything in determining where to place epithets, Cowley displays charm and intimacy as an annotator, and reveals why he sidesteps the usual charge of pedantry or a fustian excess of detail, given the personality of his annotation, with regard to tone and approach.

There are also related moments of non-apology for poetic practice, where the note does not concede anything, but instead confronts the reader's ignorance and confirms the poet's aims, even if they haven't been achieved. Take the following long line, describing Heaven:

> Here *peaceful Flames* swell up the sacred place,
> Nor can the glory contain it self in th'endless space.

> For there no twilight of the *Suns* dull ray,
> Glimmers upon the pure and native day. (1:11)

A modern description of the tone of Cowley's apologia in the note to these lines might well be "passive-aggressive":

> I am sorry that it is necessary to admonish the most part of *Readers*, that it is not by *negligence* that this verse is so loose, long, and, as it were, *Vast*; it is to paint in the number the nature of the thing which it describes, which I would have observed in divers other places of this *Poem*, that else will pass for very careless verses: as before, *And over-runs the neighb'ring fields with violent course.* In the second Book, *Down a præcipice, deep, down he casts them all*—and, *And fell adown his shoulders with loose care.* In the 3. *Brass was his Helmet, his Boots brass, and ore his breast a thick plate of strong brass he wore.* In the 4. *Like some fair Pine ore-looking all th'ignobler Wood*; and, *Some from the Rocks cast themselves down headlong*; and many more: but it is enough to instance in a few. The thing is, that the disposition of words and numbers should be such, as that out of the order and sound of them, the things themselves may be represented. (1:32–33)

The note tells the reader off: the line is not negligent, but a perfect encapsulation of the vast sublime it draws: "The disposition of words and numbers should be such, as that out of the order and sound of them, the things themselves may be represented." The poetry, therefore, paints the nature of the thing itself, and represents it by order and sound. Too few poets of any culture notice this, says Cowley (Virgil of course excepted, he notes).

This annotation anticipates later ideas of the sound being the echo to the sense, including Blake's rather circular defense of his prosody in *Jerusalem* ("The terrific numbers are reserved for the terrific parts," and so on) and Johnson's earlier lampoon of the idea in the figure of Dick Minim.[11] The cynic could argue, like Gray, that a poetic effect that has to be justified by a note is not a successful one, as we have to take the poet's word for it. In this vein, there are other places where the commentary attempts to explain unusual poetic choices, sometimes successfully, sometimes less so. Near the start of the poem, the Devil's conversation with Envy and the speech of the latter are both harbingers of Miltonic allegories to come, and a chance for Cowley to fill in the gaps in Genesis, rather gratuitously in this instance:

> By Me *Cain* offer'd up his *Brothers* gore,
> A *Sacrifice* far worse then that before;
> I saw him sling the *stone*, as if he meant,
> At once his *Murder*, and his *Monument*. (1:8)

In the notes, Cowley tells the reader, hardly controversially, that "*Cain* was the first and greatest example of *Envy* in this world; who slew his *Brother*, because his Sacrifice was more acceptable to God then his own." It is "hard to guess what it was in *Cains Sacrifice* that displeased *God*," so

> we must therefore be content to be ignorant of the cause; since it hath pleas'd God not to declare it; neither is it declared in what manner he slew his *Brother:* And therefore I had the Liberty to choose that which I thought most probable; which is, that he knockt him on the head with some great stone, which was one of the first ordinary and most natural weapons of *Anger*. (1:29)

Not many readers would necessarily quibble with this, or the concomitant that in the absence of a description of a weapon, Cowley was compelled to think up the most likely, but the subsequent claim, "that this stone was big enough to be the *Monument* or *Tomb-stone* of *Abel*, is not so *Hyperbolical*," is a bit harder to swallow, even as Cowley goes on to cite the supporting examples of Turnus, in Virgil, taken in turn from the *Iliad*, and also from *Metamorphoses* (1:29). All the classical sources are used to back up Cowley's Old Testament dramatization, showing how the poet combines such sources freely in his own mind as a natural confluence of Western religious and poetic history; Milton, no doubt, would use the example to veer off from his inspiring but unholy pagan forebears. But the intellectual side here is not as significant as the strange judgment in Cowley's poetic image and defense of it in the note: the effect of the dire and wicked crime of Cain is diffused through the idea of the murder weapon also being his brother's tombstone, which seems to aim for a sort of grim reinforcement of poetic injustice, but overeggs the pudding; there is something superfluous in expecting the stone to double up as a marker, nor is it clear why this would be the case anyway (one cannot imagine the first humans after Eden needing particularly to conserve the supply of rocks). Rather like discussion about how crowded it would be in the underworld, this seems such a minor and irrelevant detail as almost to produce bathos, rather than awe.

In cases like this, notes can be a way of filling in poetic gaps, or supplementing the poetry, a way of doing what it cannot. But they sometimes also reveal other attendant difficulties that would otherwise have been passed over (as does, possibly, the overabundance of notes in proportion to a fragmentary, unfinished poem). Yet the advantage of the conversational mode Cowley adopts in the endnotes is that it also allows him to explain his creative decisions and critical conclusions by an indirect route, or back door. These are marked by a sometimes rueful honesty, that also takes in the need to avoid tedium, and the desire to keep the reader on his side, especially when this involves abridgment or avoidance of longueurs undertaken for no good reason. At these moments, the notes are often sympathetic, with Cowley showing a sort of contractual understanding with the reader, akin to the later Sternean self-reflexive awareness of the potential for boredom in even such high-minded materials:

> In this *Enumeration* of the chief *Persons* who came to assist *David*, I choose to name but a few. The *Greek* and *Latine Poets* being in my opinion too large upon this kind of subject, especially *Homer*, in enumerating the *Grecian* Fleet and Army; where he makes a long list of *Names* and *Numbers*, just as they would stand in the *Roll* of a *Muster-Master*, without any delightful and various descriptions of the persons; or at least very few such. Which *Lucan* (methinks) avoids viciously by an excess the other way. (3:108)

This somewhat irreverent truthfulness is more appealing than the performance of stilted epic conventions for their own sake, including perfunctory lists of worthies, titles, dominions, and the like. In this sense, and in others, Cowley's notes anticipate much later poetic annotation in English in a liberating way: his annotations are subjective, sometimes irreverent, rarely pompous, and all too aware of the limits of any ultimate authority, in terms of both poetry and prose. The finality and comprehensive claims of much scholarship are often a mirage, and the notes acknowledge this, stressing also the distance between creativity and interpretation, a distance the notes cannot always bridge. As Cowley declares in one note, "For this liberty of inserting an *Ode* into an *Heroick Poem*, I have no authority or example; and therefore like men who venture upon a new coast, I must run the hazard of it. We must sometimes be bold to innovate" (1:37). The boldness is somewhat undermined by its self-consciousness, but the way in which Cowley declares his lack of precedence is refreshing, showing an openness to criticism and a sense of his own potential limitations that was often the exception in annotation, rather than the rule. One test of reading annotation is to convey the feeling that the writer is on the side of the readers, and there ultimately for their edification and enjoyment, rather than merely to supply information for its own sake. In this respect, primarily because of their quirks of personality and awareness of the strangeness of dramatizing such a story and tradition into poetry, Cowley's annotations to *Davideis* pass admirably, and remain unique in this large, but often unmemorable genre.

CHAPTER SIX

"More Famous by His Pen than by His Sword"

Weaponizing the Classics in Abraham Cowley's *The Civil War*

Caroline Spearing

Here *Learning* and th'Arts met; as much they fear'd,
As when the *Huns* of old and *Goths* appear'd.

What should they doe? unapt themselves to fight,
They promised noble pens the Acts to write.

—Abraham Cowley, *The Civil War*, 1:229–32.[1]

Written at breakneck speed from Charles I's headquarters at Oxford as the momentous events of 1643 unfolded, the three books of Cowley's unfinished epic *The Civil War* have typically been read—not least by the poet himself—as yet another victim of the parliamentary ascendancy starting in the autumn of that year. In his "Preface" to his *Poems* of 1656, Cowley claimed to have burned the manuscript, citing the absurdity of making "*Lawrels* for the *Conquered*" (*Poems* [1656], sig. a4r). Twentieth-century critics tended to the view that Cowley's was a wise decision: his biographer, Arthur Nethercot, judged the work "pedestrian" and even "flatulent"; for David Trotter, it represented "a deeply flawed undertaking."[2] Others have identified a lack of nuance deriving from the poet's entrenched ideological position; an unattractive "bitterness, vindictiveness, and bloodthirstiness"; a generic failure to fuse epic and polemic.[3] More recent criticism, however, has tended to look to the poem's strengths: Philip Hardie has drawn attention to Cowley's remarkable generic experimentation and innovation, while Henry Power and Edward Paleit have asked, in the light of Cowley's debt to the unfinished epics of Virgil and Lucan, whether the poet might, in fact, have left *The Civil War* in a deliberately unfinished state.[4]

It is this latter strand of criticism that I shall develop here. The unmistakable allegiance owed by *The Civil War* to Virgil's *Aeneid* and Lucan's *Bellum Civile* should not be permitted to obscure the radically innovative nature of Cowley's undertaking in writing an epic narrative that not only unfolds in real time, but also, crucially, has a quite literally polemic (Greek πολεμος, "war") purpose. Moreover, the aggressively political character of this polemic can be shown to destabilize the view of Cowley—promulgated by the poet himself as well as by his first biographer, Thomas Sprat—as a poet of retirement and retreat, dragged unwillingly into public life by his powerful friends and by his own sense of civic duty.

Cowley in 1643

When the Civil War broke out, his affection to the Kings Cause drew him to *Oxford*, as soon as it began to be the chief seat of the Royal Party. In that University he prosecuted the same Studies with a like success. Nor in the mean time was he wanting to his duty in the War it self, for he was present and in service in several of the Kings Journeys and Expeditions.

—Thomas Sprat, "An Account of the Life and Writings of Mr. Abraham Cowley" (sig. A2v)

Now though I was here engaged in ways most contrary to the Original design of my life, that is, into much company, and no small business, and into a daily sight of Greatness, both Militant and Triumphant (for that was the state then of the *English* and *French* Courts) yet all this was so far from altering my Opinion, that it onely added the confirmation of Reason to that which was before but Natural Inclination.

—Abraham Cowley, "Of My self"[5]

Modern readers of Cowley have access to a remarkably rounded portrayal of the poet's character, thoughts, and desires. He himself wrote extensive introductions to his *Poems* of 1656 and, in Latin, to the *Plantarum Libri duo* of 1662, in which he writes with apparent disarming frankness of his aims and intentions for the works and of the circumstances of their composition.[6] His "Several Discourses by way of Essays, in Verse and Prose," dating from his years of retirement in the English country town of Chertsey and published posthumously in 1668, provides a series of personal meditations and reflections, including "Of Solitude," "Of Obscurity," and, tantalizingly, "Of My self." Moreover, his friend and literary executor, Thomas Sprat, published his "Account of the Life and Writings of Mr. Abraham Cowley," which forms the preface of the 1668 volume, and wrote the Latin version appended to the *Poemata Latina* of the same year, providing one of the first literary biographies in the English language.[7]

The Cowley that emerges from these sources is a modest, bookish, private individual, affectionate and loyal to a few close friends, reticent to the point of ineptitude in grand company, dragged into momentous events by his own sense of duty, all the while longing to be back in his garden with his books.

> He had indeed a perfect natural goodness, which neither the uncertainties of his condition, nor the largeness of his wit could pervert. . . . Nothing vain or fantastical, nothing flattering or insolent appeared in his humour. He had a great integrity, and plainness of Manners; which he preserv'd to the last, though much of his time was spent in a Nation, and way of life, that is not very famous for sincerity. But the truth of his heart was above the corruption of ill examples: And therefore the sight of them rather confirm'd him in the contrary Virtues. (Sprat, "Account," sig. d2r)

This picture has been challenged in recent years, above all by Paul Davis and Jane Darcy, who have looked unsparingly at Cowley's bitter resentment at being denied the promised court sinecure of the master of the Savoy Hospital and have argued that the pose of retirement was essentially a case of sour grapes. They also point out how important it was to Sprat to cover his own dubious activities during the Interregnum by emphasizing the unswerving nature of his friend Cowley's loyalty.[8] I have argued elsewhere that even this revisionist position can be critiqued: Cowley's final master-piece, the *Plantarum Libri Sex* (1668), shows him engaging deeply with questions of government, politics, and society, and suggests that his retire-ment should rather be viewed as a Stoic withdrawal from the noise of the world in order to ponder its difficulties.[9] It is my contention here that we should view *The Civil War* not as a failure or a false start, but as a distinct step in the development of a fiercely ambitious poet, one whose desire for actively participating in the overlapping worlds of literature, court, and politics developed early and endured to the end of his life.

Cowley published his first book of poetry at the age of fifteen, during his time as a king's scholar at Westminster School. Cowley's father had been a stationer, and it is tempting to speculate that the volume may owe something to the family's preexisting contacts in the London book trade. The first edition of *Poetical Blossomes*, which appeared in 1633 but which may well contain poems written even earlier, consists of two long narrative poems, two elegies, "A Dreame of Elysium," and dedicatory poems to the dean of Westminster and to Cowley's headmaster, Lambert Osbaldeston. The frontispiece shows a somewhat pinch-faced youth, with a heavy, straight fringe, and quotes a poem by his schoolfellow, Benjamin Masters, which asserts that "for ought I can see / *Cowley* may yongest son of *Phoebus* bee."[10] The title-page bears the inscription *fit surculus Arbor*—"the sapling becomes a tree"—an image with multiple resonances. It represents an early statement of the poet's ambition: not only will the fragile blossoms of the juvenilia develop into ripe fruit, but the sapling on which they are borne will also become a mature tree. It resonates with Cowley's claim in "Of My self" that his early love of the poets "stampt first, or rather engraved these Characters in me, . . . like Letters cut into the Bark of a young Tree, with which the Tree still grow[s] proportionably" ("Of My self," Cowley, *Verses Written*, 144).

During his time at Cambridge, Cowley continued to work toward a career as a court poet. As the posthumous and seventh child of a stationer, he needed to earn a living, and the minor fellowship he obtained at Trinity in 1640 should be regarded as much as a source of income as an opportunity to devote himself to scholarship. Such as is known of his activity during this period shows him cultivating the great and good, and, above all, the world of the court: he contributed Latin poems to university anthologies celebrating the birth of royal children and Charles I's less than glorious return from Scotland in 1641; he is known to have made the acquaintance of the courtier, Sir Kenelm Digby, and the painter, Sir Anthony Van Dyck (whose death in 1641 he commemorated in an elegy). In March 1641/42, he was commissioned to write a comedy, *The Guardian*, to entertain the eleven-year-old Prince Charles when he visited Cambridge on his way to York. Cowley also formed possibly the most significant friendship of his life: with George Villiers, second Duke of Buckingham, foster-brother of Charles II, courtier, politician, and rake. Although Buckingham was a decade younger than Cowley, their bond was to last through the upheavals of the succeeding years. Cowley was best man at Buckingham's controversial wedding in 1657 to Mary Fairfax, heiress to Cromwell's general (and Marvell's former pupil); Cowley's magnificent memorial in Westminster Abbey was erected at Buckingham's expense. Moreover, it appears that Cowley's efforts to procure Buckingham a meeting with Cromwell in 1654 incurred the lasting mistrust of the king (see Nethercot, *Cowley*, 146).

The purpose of this biographical excursus is to argue that, when Cowley's Royalist sympathies forced him out of Cambridge in late 1642 or early 1643, we need not take at face value Sprat's account of an unworldly *scholar* reluctantly packing up his books and papers, but rather we could see a young man excitedly launching himself into a career that could bring his already-proven poetic ability into direct contact with those in the seat of power. "What shall I do to be forever known / And make the *Age to come* my own?," he asked in "The Motto" (*Miscellanies*, 1), probably composed during his early Cambridge years (Nethercot, *Cowley*, 48). In 1642/43, "*Fames Trumpet*" summoned him, and he prepared to cut through "Unpast *Alpes* . . . And march, the *Muses Hannibal.*"

The Civil War as Polemic Epic

Her Words were Bullets, and her Breath was Flame.
—*The Civil War*, 2:416

The English Civil Wars were the first major armed conflict to which the written—and, above all, the printed—word made a substantial contribution. Two generations earlier, Spenser's Errour, vomiting a grotesque medley of stinking frogs, toads, books, and papers (*The Faerie Queene*, 1:20), had allegorized the role of text in the conflicts of the Reformation; by the 1640s, facilitated by the collapse of censorship in 1641, a steady stream of newsbooks, pamphlets, prophecies, ballads, and broadsides waged a propaganda war on both sides, exaggerating or downplaying victories and defeats, and sharing heavily sensationalized reports of enemy atrocities.[11] This war of words was further underpinned by the early Stuart tradition of what Thomas Cogswell has called a "guerrilla war in manuscript," satirical squibs from court poets, including such Cavalier luminaries as Suckling, Denham, Carew, and Cowley's friend and later business partner, Sir William Davenant.[12]

Cowley, the stationer's son with, by now, lengthy familiarity with the London book trade, is fully aware of the power of the written word. "Then onely in *Bookes* the *learn'd* could mis'ery see," he writes of the halcyon days of the personal rule of Charles I (1:85); rebellion's "Words were Bullets" (2:416); the catalog of heretics that opens book 3 includes "Goodmans, and firy Knoxes his brood, the men / Of bloody Inks, Ravillacs with their Pen" (3:63–64) (Norbrook, 85). "Beware next, *Plymmouth*," he warns the rebellious city of Devon: "for if future thinges,"

> Nere faile my prophesing *Muse*, in what shee sings,
> Thy conquest soone fame from my pen shall git. (2:353–55)

Cowley worries that his poetic ability will not be up to the task of commemorating the Royalist fallen. "Would my Verse were nobler for your sake!," he laments (3:462). Conversely, he knows that by passing over the enemy he can consign them to oblivion: "But with them let their Names forever dy; / Too vile, and base for well-writ Infamy" (3:453–54). No matter that the middle-class Cowley, unlike the aristocratic Cavalier poets Suckling and Carew, was "unapt [himself] to fight": the Muse's Hannibal would wield his "noble pen" under the banner of Learning and the Arts (1:231). And it is, of course, the pen that gives up the ghost in the closing lines of the poem, when the poet's grief for the dead Falkland replaces ink with tears.[13]

Nonetheless, this war of the pen is undermined and complicated by the nature of its subject matter, a civil war in which—as the Roman poet Lucan (AD 39–65) observed in the proem to his *Bellum Civile*—there can be no victor. Cowley's opening lines establish the transgressive and abhorrent character of civil war, as well as the classical lens through which he observes it:

> What rage does *England* from it self divide
> More then Seas doe from all the world beside?
> From every part the roaring *Canon* play;
> From every part *blood* roares as loud as they
> [. . .]
> Alas, what *Triumph* can this vict'ory shew
> That dyes us red in *blood* and *blushes* too!
> How can we wish that *Conquest*, which bestowes
> *Cypresse*, not *Bayes* upon the conqu'ering browes! (1:1–4, 9–12)

The opening couplet clearly refers to the opening of Lucan's *Bellum Civile*:

> What fury, Countreymen, what madness could
> Moove you to feast your foes with Roman blood?
> And choose such warres, as could no triumphs yield.[14]

Coupled with it is Virgil's allusion in the first *Eclogue*, a poem that refers to the land confiscations of civil war Italy in the 40s BC, to the distant Britons, "divided from the whole world" (65).[15] Line 5 picks up Lucan's reference to the impossibility of a ceremonial triumph after civil war (*Bellum Civile*, 1:11): there can be no grounds for celebration in defeating one's fellow citizens. The laurel (or bay) of victory gives way to the cypress of mourning (11–12). But as well as being sacred to Apollo in his role as slayer of the monster Python, the laurel is also associated with the god in his role as patron of poetry.[16] Cowley as poet must don the cypress of funerary elegy.[17]

Virtually every account of *The Civil War* has commented on its divided, fractured, fragmented quality. James Loxley notes the impossibility of reconciling Cowley's polemical aims with what he calls "the authoritative idiom of historical epic"; David Trotter sees an "irresolvable antagonism between modes" that prevents the work from cohering into a satisfactory epic whole; for Maggie Kilgour, Cowley's opposition between the forces of unity (the king) and those of division (Parliament) creates a fissure in the poem itself, generating a narrative of "unending fragmentation and loss."[18] But this divided quality need not be seen as evidence of failure. Power tellingly observes that the image of division in the opening lines both anticipates the various "truncations and erasures" of the poem and provides a striking image of the alienation of civil war (Power, 151). When the laurel is added to the discourse of madness and the divided self, the poet himself is brought into play: just as winning a civil war is an impossibility, so is writing about it. This reading is strengthened towards the end of book 1, in the account of the southwestern campaigns of Sir Ralph Hopton:

> Mirac'ulous man! How would I sing thy Praise
> Had any *Muse* crown'd *me* with halfe the *Bayes*
> *Conquest* has given to *thee*, and next thy name,
> Should *Barkley, Slaning, Digby* presse to fame,
> *Godolphin* thee, thee *Greenvill* I'd rehearse,
> But *teares* breake off my verse. (1:425–30)

Even at this point in the war, when Royalist victories justified optimism among the king's party, Cowley's discourse is one of failure. Tears—in one of the half lines designed to evoke the unfinished hemistichs of the *Aeneid*—prevent the poet from writing of the deaths of the poet Sidney Godolphin (b. 1610) and the great general Sir Bevil Grenville, but he also lacks even the capacity to do justice to successes. Moreover, Cowley has already told us that there are no laurels in civil war. The line breaks off in tears of frustration as well as grief, simultaneously exposing the illusory nature of victory and the inadequacies of poetry. It is on this division in

The Civil War that I shall focus for the remainder of this chapter: between a rigidly polarized, partisan polemic on the one hand, and, on the other, a more reflective, elegiac discourse of grief and loss in which the mythological figure of Orpheus plays a key part.

The Civil War and Classical Epic

As we have seen, Cowley announces his debt to Lucan in the first two words of *The Civil War*. While the opening Virgilian allusion is to the pastoral *Eclogues*, the world of the *Aeneid* follows swiftly with the echo in the conquest of the "farthest West" (15) of Aeneas's voyage to "Hesperia," the "western land," and the mention of Cyprus, the birthplace of Aeneas's mother, Venus (22). The proem ends with another conflation of Lucan and Virgil: like Lucan's Caesar, Charles is lightning in battle; in an image recalling the fire that plays harmlessly around Ascanius's temples in *Aeneid*, 2, he is "Calme in *Peace*, calme as a *Lambent* flame" (1:78–79, Lucan, *Bellum Civile*, 151–57; Virgil, *Aeneid*, 2:682–84: "tactuque innoxia mollis/lambere flamma comas," "a soft flame, harmless to the touch, licked his hair").

What Cowley achieves by his use of classical epic is not a foregone conclusion: the extent to which early English writers were immersed in Latin and Greek literature, especially in Virgil, led to a broad range of often highly sophisticated engagements with the classical tradition. David Quint's influential identification of a teleological Virgilian "epic of victory" contrasting with a more circular Lucanian narrative of opposition and defeat has informed readings of *The Civil War* that argue that Cowley's projected Virgilian epic of Royalist triumph collapsed when the tide turned in the enemy's favor after the Battle of Newbury in September 1643.[19] And, of course, Cowley himself claims that he abandoned the work when a narrative of Royalist victory became impossible: "The succeeding *misfortunes* of the *party* stopt the *work*; for it is so uncustomary, as to become almost *ridiculous*, to make *Lawrels* for the *Conquered*" ("Preface," *Poems* [1656], sig. a4r). The association of Virgil with the king's party is further supported by the spate of Royalist translations and editions of Virgil from the 1640s and 1650s, by writers such as John Ogilby (1649), Richard Fanshawe (1652), and John Denham (1656).

The first English translation of the entirety of Lucan's *Bellum Civile* was published in 1627 by the republican Thomas May, and until recently Lucan was associated more generally with seventeenth-century English republicanism.[20] However, this neat polarity, associating Virgil with Royalists and Lucan with republicans, has been increasingly challenged: Payne Fisher's Cromwellian Latin epic *Marston-Moor* (1650) shows how Virgilian intertextuality was not exclusive to Royalists; Edward Paleit has argued that aesthetic and stylistic responses to Lucan were as important for writers as political issues.[21] Lucan's Pompey, as both a republican and a representative of legitimate government, carried highly ambivalent political resonances in the English Civil War, while, as has been often observed, Virgil's apparently imperialistic *Aeneid* bears a strong subtext of internecine conflict—one that was widely recognized in England.[22]

Cowley later referred to his poem as "*three Books of the Civil War it self*" (*Poems*, sig. a4r), postulating an equivalent between action and its representation that further emphasizes the importance of the war of the pen. Unlike Virgil's narrative that led to an inexorable, glorious culmination, Cowley's poem relied on the texture and substance of the narrative itself, which provided a stirring partisan spin to events as they unfolded— a spin that would be markedly different from the murky and morally ambiguous Lucanian universe. Cowley uses classical epic in order to find appropriate diction for the heroizing of his allies, and the denigration of his enemies. The *Aeneid* and the *Bellum Civile* also provide a partial solution to the representational problems posed by civil war, a conflict that provided laurels neither for its generals nor for its poets.

Loxley, in his perceptive discussion of *The Civil War*, notes the work's polemic function and its kinship with the more ephemeral genres of the newsbook and the verse miscellany (86–88). Loxley rightly identifies the poem's deployment of the language of epic in order to insert the events of the present into a Royalist narrative of English history and to generate an illusion of distance between the poem and the events it describes, which will, in turn, add to its polemical force. However, running counter to the discourse of classical epic is a lyric and elegiac mode that complicates this triumphalist narrative.

The Civil War's Heroes

Cowley's battle narratives draw extensively on the last four, "Iliadic," books of the *Aeneid*—above all, in their focus on the exploits of individual warriors, the courage and heroism of their successes, and the pathos of their deaths. The valiant Charles Cavendish, younger son of the Earl of Devonshire, "*Hector* in his *Hands*, and *Paris* in his *Face*" (2:140), is slain at the siege of Gainsborough and lamented with the image of a fallen flower whose classical pedigree can be traced beyond Virgil to Catullus, and ultimately to Sappho:

> Like some fair *Flower*, which *Morne* saw freshly gay,
> In the feilds [*sic*] generall ruine mowne away.
> The *Hyacinth*, or purple *Violet*,
> Just languishing, his coloured *Light* just set.
> Ill mixt it lies amidst th'ignobler *Grasse*;
> The country *daughters* sigh as by'it they passe. (2:151–56)

In *Aeneid*, book 11, the fallen body of the young warrior Pallas is compared to the flower of a "soft violet or drooping hyacinth," cut from its stem by a young girl's thumbnail (68–69); in book 9, another young hero, Euryalus, meets his death like a purple flower cut by the plough or the drooping head of a poppy weighed down by a rain shower (435–37). Catullus uses the image of a flower on the edge of a meadow cut down by the passing plough to convey his heedless destruction by his mistress Lesbia (11:19–21).

Cowley's use of the image shows a careful harvesting of detail from his classical predecessors: the purple color borrowed from the Euryalus simile emphasizes the youth's nobility, and "his coloured *Light* just set" renders beautifully Virgil's evocation of the plucked flower at the precise moment when its color begins to ebb, "cui neque fulgor adhuc nec dum sua forma recessit" ("whose radiance nor beauty has yet thus far receded," *Aeneid*, 11:70). The hyacinth, with its epithet "languishing," a literal translation of Virgil's "languentis," invokes Apollo's beloved, the youth Hyacinthus. In Virgil, it suggests Euryalus's role as beloved of his older companion, Nisus; in Cowley, it provides a delicate reminder of Cavendish's Paris-like good looks. Catullus has his flower merely touched ("tactus") by the plough, "ultimi prati" ("on the edge of a meadow"); Cowley's is more violently "mowne," while the "field," as well as simply translating Catullus's "prati," stands, too, for the battlefield on which Cavendish dies. The rustic straw ("*agrestis*," a word that similarly carries connotations of an uncouth lack of polish), which forms Pallas's pyre (*Aeneid*, 11:67), is replicated in the "ignoble grass" where Cavendish lies, though in Cowley, the grass serves as a metaphor for fallen comrades of lower birth. Cowley also retains the erotic quality of the classical metaphor, but while Pallas's flower falls victim to the unthinking violence of a young girl, and Catullus's is casualty of female indifference, Cavendish's actual death is an impersonal "mowing," and the eroticism lies in his lament by the country girls whom he will never get to charm with his beauty.

By locating Cavendish's death in the intertextual space of classical literature, Cowley causes him to be numbered among the fallen youth of epic, endowing him with both a heroic grandeur and the particular pathos afforded Virgil's lost adolescents—not only Pallas and Euryalus, but also Pallas's victim, Lausus, his killer, Turnus, the warrior maiden, Camilla, and Augustus's nephew, Marcellus, whose elegy marks the end of the first half of the poem (*Aeneid*, 6:863–86). Throughout the descriptions of battle, Cowley can be seen deploying the idiom of classical literature and, above all, of Virgil, both to heroize his fellow Royalists and to convert the ugly chaos of civil war into a polished literary product. This is achieved by means of the device, that Virgil adopts from Homer, of introducing and dispatching an individual warrior within a few lines, often with the addition of biographical details that enhance the pathos of his end.

One of the most substantial such vignettes is the account of the death of the French aristocrat Vincent, marquis de le Vieuville, who had joined the king's army after coming to England on a diplomatic mission.[23] Cowley here follows the account of the Royalist newsbook *Mercurius Aulicus* (September 19, 1643, p. 38, cited by Pritchard) in depicting him as slaughtered after being taken prisoner.[24]

> With him charg'd in the matchlesse Digby too;
> And Vivevile, but with fates of different hew
> [. . .]
> They force their passage through an Host, and strow

The way with groaning Rebells as they goe;
Onely young Vieuville whilst hee well did tread
The dangerous path to Fame theise Heroes led,
Opprest by Numbers, and ill Starres, was ta'ne,
Revil'ed, and mockt, and in coole Malice slaine.
Soe when the Canniballs on some stranger ceaze,
(The only race more barbarous then theise)
They dance about their Pris'oner, and around,
Their shouts, and laughters, and wild Musicks sound.
[. . .]
Gallant young man! Well worth a gentlier doome,
Then by base hands to fall soe farre from home!
How has thy fate transgrest thy friends intent!
And sent thee, ah, much farther then they ment!
Thy wretched parents Hope, whilst they should Mourne;
And marke in vain all Winds for thy returne. (3:227–28,
    233–42, 245–50)

In its outline, the story recalls Virgil's Nisus and Euryalus, a pair of warriors who slash their way through the enemy before the capture of the younger (though Virgil's account is of a night raid through an enemy host sunk in drunken sleep). The episode ends with the lament of Euryalus's aged mother (*Aeneid*, 9:473–502), echoed in Vieuville's "wretched parents" (249). But, as with the description of the fall of Cavendish, Cowley casts his net beyond a single Virgilian passage. The trope of the young warrior falling far from home is a particular feature of Homer's *Iliad*, adopted by Virgil in his account of Antores, whose dying thoughts return to his Greek homeland (*Aeneid*, 10:782).[25] Vieuville's "wretched parents" recall one of the *Iliad's* most poignant moments, when the aged Priam, attempting to ransom the body of his son Hector from Achilles, reminds the Greek warrior of his own father, hoping one day to see his son return from Troy—a moment that the reader knows will never arrive (*Iliad*, 24:486–92).

Other moments are epic in color and tone rather than in their allusions to specific classical passages. Cowley writes of the Earl of Sunderland, who was "snatcht away" from the light of sun and from his "brighter Wife" (3:466–48); of the Earl of Northampton, who continues fighting after his horse is shot from underneath him, eventually cut down by the enemy and falling like a "tottering *Oake*" (2:52); of "fearless *Lindsey*" and "bold *Aubigny*," who was killed at Edgehill (1:281–82). Throughout, Cowley is fully aware of the epic poet's responsibility to ensure that such heroes are appropriately remembered—and of the challenge inherent in the task. "Would my Verse were nobler for your sake!" (3:462), Cowley apostrophizes the colonels Fielding and Morgan, casualties of the Battle of Newbury (Pritchard, 175).

It is these valiant individuals who are the epic heroes of the poem, rather than the king himself. Charles's speech before Newbury (3:277–28), his most extended action in the work, certainly draws on Pompey's speech at *Bellum Civile*, 3:315–26, ending with an invocation of the Church of England that echoes Pompey's of Rome (Paleit, 297). Cowley replaces Pompey's appeal to national identity with one that is sectarian and ideological: as Norbrook points out, it is the insistence on the monolithic authority of the Church, and its earthly representative the king, that reveals the vulnerability of the Royalist cause.[26]

In the account of the Battle of Edgehill, Charles acts as a static and numinous presence of awe-inspiring countenance:

> In his great looks what cheerfull anger shone!
> *Sad warre* and joyfull *Triumph* mixt in one.
> In the same beames of his *Majesticke* Eye,
> His owne men *life*, his Foes their *Death* espie. (1:253–56)

The passage evokes the stylized world of court masque, as does the later scene of Charles's reunion with Henrietta Maria (1:491–508), with its bevy of Cupids scattering oriental perfumes (MacLean, *Time's Witness*, 199–202). The Charles of *The Civil War* is the majestic, mysterious, and symbol-freighted Stuart monarch, enshrined in the Rubens painting of his father, James I, on the ceiling of the Banqueting House, not the martial hero of epic action.

Vilifying the Opposition

Low, wretched Names, unfit for noble Verse
—*The Civil War*, 3:383–84

Cowley elevates his allies by using the language and tropes of ancient classical epic, inscribing them into the heroic literary tradition. In contrast to his epic predecessors, and in keeping with his work's polemic purpose, he does not grant moments of pathos to the fallen enemy. Often Cowley presents his opponents in aggressively contemporary and satirical terms, which emphasizes their separation from the world of heroic epic:

> The greedy Tradesmen scorne their Idol Gaine,
> And send forth their glad Servants to bee slaine.
> The bald and gray-hair'ed Gownemen quite forsooke
> Their sleepy Furrs, black Shoes, and City looke,
> All ore in Iron and Leather clad they come;
> Poore Men that trembled earst at Finsburies Drumme!
> (3:51–56)

However, the grotesque nature of enemy deaths provides a passport to the world of epic. Grisly ends tend to be associated with Lucan, but the tradition of dark humor stretches all the way back to the *Iliad*, where teeth are knocked out by the blow of a sword (*Iliad*, 16:345–51); eyeballs fall out of their sockets (*Iliad*, 13:614–19); a heart continues beating to try to dislodge the spear that has pierced it (*Iliad*, 13:441–44).[27] In the *Aeneid*, a severed hand twitches (*Aeneid*, 10:395–56); a warrior is choked with blood from a wound in the throat (*Aeneid*, 7:531–34); a headless trunk is left belching out gore (*Aeneid*, 9:332–33).

Cowley enthusiastically adopts this mode for his catalog of the parliamentarian dead at Newbury (*The Civil War*, 3:383–454). Stane the butcher's skull is cleft by a poleaxe, the bisected halves hanging down on either side (3:402–403); Towse the dyer is simultaneously stabbed through the chest and shot through the head (3:419–20); Blore the tailor is shot through the mouth by a bullet that singes his brain (3:449–50). Unlike his classical predecessors, however, Cowley reserves these grisly deaths for the enemy: the indiscriminately grim carnage of Greco-Roman epic warfare gives way to a humiliation of the enemy that has its roots in the violent mockery of the lower-class troublemaker Thersites in *Iliad*, 2:212–70. The tone is similar in the parody of the epic catalog of Dissenters in *The Civil War*, 3:59–185, where the metrically virtuosic piling-up of increasingly outlandish sects descends into a kind of satirical gibberish:

> Besides th'Apostolicks, and Encratites,
> Angelicalls, Jovinians, Hieracites.
> Paulists, Priscillians, Origenians,
> Cerinthians, and Nicolaitans.
> Wicleffians, Hussites, and the Zwinglian crew,
> Hemerobaptists, and Sebaptists too.
> Weigelians, Vorstians, and Suencfeldians;
> With hundred more ill Names of Puritans. (3:175–82)

"Ill names"—while Cowley's "noble pen" could linger over inscribing his Royalist comrades in the epic tradition, the parliamentarians are wholly alien to and unworthy of the genre.[28] This is repeatedly stressed: theirs are "low, wretched names, unfit for noble Verse" (3:384); "Too vile, and base for well-writ Infamy" (3:454); "Damn'd, and infam'ed for fighting *ill soe well!*" (2:136). While Charles is given a lengthy speech on the eve of the Battle of Newbury (3:277–28), the parliamentary commander, the Earl of Essex, significantly, can barely string a sentence together:

> On th'other side th'Essexian Rebell strove,
> His fainting Troopes with powrelesse words to move;
> His Speech was dull and tædious; for him made
> By some great Deacon of the Preaching trade.
> Of Tyr'anny and Pop'ery much hee told;
> An hundred Declaration Lies of old;
> Unhappy Man; even their ill Phrase hee tooke,
> And helpt it nether with his Toung nor Looke.
> But with long stops the livelesse sentence broke;
> Noe Muse nor Grace was neere him when hee spoke. (3:329–38)

This failure of the enemy to generate or merit words reflects the opposition Cowley sees at the heart of the conflict: between civilization and barbarism, aristocrat and artisan, ancient and modern, order and chaos.[29] A true, classically educated aristocrat will be able to construct and deliver a powerful speech: by failing to do so, Essex lowers himself to the status of the "low, wretched Names" he commands.

Moreover, whereas "*Learning* and th'Arts" stood alongside Charles's army at Edgehill (1:229), Essex has the assistance of "Noe Muse nor Grace." Oxford becomes both a Royalist bastion and a fortress against

> *Religious Vandalls.* . . .
> All *Bookes* (they know) the chiefe *Malignants* are.
> In vaine they silence every Age before;
> For *Pens* of times to come will wound them more. (1:350–53)[30]

This insistent association of classical scholarship with Royalism and the aristocracy was by no means an accurate reflection of contemporary English society, thanks to the widespread presence of grammar schools and the remarkable uniformity of the humanist classical curriculum they followed.[31] It is, therefore, striking that Cowley chose to frame the conflict in these terms.

Cowley privileges the classical over the modern in describing battles, where the unprecedented horrors enabled by newly invented explosives are realized by his use of a Lucanian idiom. For a society raised to see war as the means for the expression of noble masculinity, the reality of the English Civil War proved difficult to absorb. Diane Purkiss has written powerfully of the challenge presented to the humanist tradition of war as an arena for statesmanship and citizenship by the destruction, dismemberment, and mutilation caused by artillery and gunfire, and by the uncanny speed with which it was effected.[32] Lucan's grotesque and gruesome episodes provide Cowley with the language and idiom for depicting, and hence assimilating, the incongruous horrors enacted in the familiar settings of the English provincial landscape and townscape. In his description of the siege of Lichfield, Cowley recalls Lucan's storming of Dyrrachium, not least in the detail of hands severed as they clutch the battlements (*Bellum Civile*, 6:175–76):

> Some whilst the walls (bold men!) they'attempt to scale,
> Drop downe by'a leaden storme of deadly haile.
> Some with huge stones are crusht to dust beneath,
> And from their hasty *Tombes* receive their *Death.*
> Some leave their parted hands on th'highest wall,
> The joynts hold fast a while, then quake, and fall. (2:107–12)[33]

The wall is finally breached with a land mine, the first to be used in England:

> With a dire noyse the earth and wall is rent,
> High into aire th'unwilling Stones are sent.
> Twice all about, the ground did tremble there,
> First with the violent *shock*, and next with *Feare.*
> The wicked *Guards* thought t'had some *earthquake* binne,
> Their Soules confest the guilt of *Korahs* Sinne. (2:117–22)[34]

Elsewhere we see the Royalist sword pitched against parliamentarian firearms in accordance with the schematic binaries of the work:

> The violent *Sword* outdid their *Muskets* ire,
> It struck the bones, and there gave dreadfull Fire.
> Wee scorn'd their *Thunder*, and the reeking *Blade*
> A thicker Smoake then all their *Canon* made. (1:449–52)

The noble, aristocratic sword of classical epic is contrasted against the upstart musket and cannon, while, in an image worthy of Lucan himself, the reader is invited to see the steam arising from freshly spilled blood as denser even than that of artillery fire.

Falkland, Orpheus, and the Unwritability of Civil War

> The trowbled Muse fell shapelesse into aire,
> Instead of Inck dropt from my Pen a Teare.
> —*The Civil War*, 3:547–48

Thus far I have concentrated on *The Civil War* as polemic, one that attempts to frame a narrative of the conflict in terms of a sharply polarized opposition between good—monarchist, Anglican, traditionalist, humanist, Virgilian, aristocratic swordsmen—and evil—seditious, schismatic, modernist, philistine, Lucanian, artisanal musket men. In the closing section of this chapter, I shall turn to the "other voice"—that which, as we saw earlier, recognizes the anomalous and transgressive nature of civil war and of its literature. It is this voice that ends the work, as the poet weighs the material and topographical gains of battle against the immensity of the loss of a man of Falkland's intellect and humanity: "Wee gain'd a Feild [*sic*], and lost in him a World" (3:568).[35]

Cowley introduces his elegy for Falkland with a strong evocation of the lament for Orpheus in book 11 of Ovid's *Metamorphoses*.

> Ah Godlike Falkland! Thee each Hill and Vale,
> Thee all the Trees, and Fields, and Floods bewayle,
> Thee all the Graces wept, and Muses all;
> Amoung the rest thus mine bemoan'd thy Fall. (3:525–28)

A few lines later, when a wind comes from Newbury sighing out Falkland's name,

> Falkland, meethoughts, the Hills all Eccho'ed round,
> Falkland, meethoughts, each Bird did sadly sound. (3:543–44).

Compare Ovid:

> For you, Orpheus, wept the mournful birds, the throng of wild beasts, the hard rocks, the woods which had often followed your songs; the tree, shorn of its foliage with its leaves laid aside, grieved; they say the rivers swelled with their own tears, and the water-nymphs put on linen robes edged with black, and the dryads' hair was disheveled. (*Metamorphoses*, 11:44–49; my translation)

In Greek mythology, Orpheus is the first lyric poet, and comes to embody the power of poetry. Through myths of him charming animals, trees, stones, and even the gods of the Underworld with his song, he represents the civilizing and rational impetus; his dismemberment at the hands of a maddened band of Thracian women demonstrates the limitations of poetry, the arts, and, by extension, scholarship.[36] For Cowley, grappling with issues of representing a conflict in which he perceived the entire humanist and classical tradition to be under attack, Orpheus provided a useful focus for his concerns.

The myth first appears in book 1 of *The Civil War*, when Cowley narrates the popular fury that led to the impeachment and execution of the king's unpopular minister, the Earl of Strafford, in 1640–41:

> In sencelesse Clamours and confused Noyse,
> We lost that rare and yet unconquered *voice.*
> So when the sacred *Thracian Lyre* was drown'd
> In the *Bistonian Woemens* mixed Sound,
> The wondering *stones*, that came before to heare,
> Forgot themselves and turn'd his *Murderers* there. (1:143–48)

Cowley alludes to the episode in Ovid (*Metamorphoses*, 11:15–19) when the Thracian bacchants, frustrated by the refusal of trees and stones to act as weapons, drown out Orpheus's song with their own cacophony, breaking his hold over the natural world. Barbarian chaos overwhelms civilized and sacred order, as Rebecca Rush has pointed out, severely threatening the power of poetry to withstand the forces of wanton destruction (120–22).

When Cowley returns to Orpheus in his elegy for Falkland, he has already appropriated the Greek bard to his own purposes. Moreover, Lucius Cary, Viscount Falkland (ca. 1610–43), supplied a ready contemporary proxy for Orpheus. One of the most admired personalities of the age, Cary was an enlightened intellectual whose estate at Great Tew in Oxfordshire was home to an eclectic circle that included clerics, statesmen, and writers, and whose promotion of tolerance and peace was in marked contrast to the increasingly polarized discourse of the period.[37] Enlisting on the side of the king when war broke out, but increasingly disillusioned at the progress of the war, he was killed at Newbury in 1643, riding to certain death at a gap in a hedge commanded by enemy musket men. Although Sprat makes Cowley a member of the Great Tew circle, and Cowley wrote an ode for Falkland on the occasion of his departure for Scotland in 1639, how well the two men actually knew one another is not clear, given that it was only in 1642 or 1643 that Cowley moved into the orbit of Great Tew with his relocation to Oxford.

> Though he was then very young, he had the entire friendship of my Lord *Falkland*. . . . That affection was contracted by the agreement of their Learning and Manners. For . . . we have often heard Mr. *Cowley* admire him, not only for the profoundness of his knowledge, . . . but more especially for those qualities which he himself more regarded, for his generosity of mind, and his neglect of the vain pursuit of humane greatness. ("Account," sig. A2v–3r)

Praised in "To the Lord Falkland" as a "great *Prince of Knowledge*" (*Poems* [1656], *Miscellanies*, 4), Falkland embodied the culture and scholarship that Cowley considered to be threatened by the conflict: he was "a Man, whose Knowledge did containe, / All that the Apple promis'd us in vaine" (3:563–64). "Here," he continues, "wee beat up Ignorance by degrees / From Trenches, Hedges, Works, and Fastnesses" (3:581–82). The struggle with ignorance recalls Orpheus's dismemberment by the barbarian Thracian women, and the discordant clamor with which they drown out his song (Ovid, *Metamorphoses*, 11:15–19). Here, though, Cowley anticipates success for the forces of culture, albeit in a painfully slow process that he contrasts with the celestial "Spires of lofty Science" where Falkland's soul now finds itself (3:583–84). This remarkable metaphor posits a cosmic battle of heavenly forces of learning and scholarship against a brute terrestrial ignorance.

In an intertextual sleight of hand, Cowley also embeds Falkland further in the classical lyric tradition, this time in Pindar by way of Ben Jonson. Fifteen years previously, Jonson had written "To the Immortal Memory and Friendship of That Noble Pair, Sir Lucius Cary And Sir Henry Morison," one of the earliest attempts at a Pindaric ode in English, in which Cary's friend, Morison,

> leaped the present age,
> Possessed with holy rage
> To see that bright eternal day. (ll. 79–81)[38]

Cowley had long been viewed as a poet in the Jonsonian tradition, and he was to go on to write in the Jonsonian-Pindaric mode.[39] Jonson's image of the Dioscuri recurs near the beginning of *The Civil War* (1:189–92), imparting a potentially Jonsonian flavor at this early stage of the work. Moreover, when Jonson talks of "priests and poets" ("To the Immortal Memory," 82), he effectively translates the Latin "vates," the poet-seer, which both describes Orpheus's function and is evoked by Cowley's image of the heavenly "spires of Science" (Mann, *Trials of Orpheus*, 11–12). The allusion seems secure: as Philip Hardie suggests, Cowley ends on a note of "Pindaric triumph" ("Generic Dialogue," 78).

We have arrived at a very different conclusion from those who read in the ending of *The Civil War* an admission of failure. I have argued throughout this chapter that the poem contains two distinct voices, that of epic and that of elegy, and that the elegiac, rather than appearing with the death of Falkland, is present throughout. Power has argued that the poem's incompleteness, in its reflection of the unfinished state of the *Aeneid* and the *Bellum Civile*, itself indicates Cowley's conception of the writing of civil war. It is my contention here that the presence of Orpheus at the beginning and end of the poem argues for the work as a fully realized whole. *The Civil War* is an exploration of the discourse proper to the representation of internecine conflict, setting a partisan polemic-epic voice against the eirenic and elegiac. When Falkland-Orpheus's soul ascends to heaven in Pindaric triumph, the victory is a metapoetic one, as elegy displaces epic as the only appropriate way of representing the reality of civil conflict.

CHAPTER SEVEN

Cowley's *Essays*
Martial and the Ironies of Retirement

Michael Edson

I once had an academic interview that opened with this icebreaker: "You must have a lot to say about Cowley." Perhaps never before, and surely not since, has Abraham Cowley headlined an MLA interview. To be fair, writing a dissertation on the poetry of rural retirement set me up for this, so perhaps this opening shouldn't have been entirely unexpected. At any rate, Cowley was not central to my project, and I had little to say. The interview did not go well. In the years after, I've often laughed at my neglecting Cowley, who is remembered (when he is remembered at all) as an advocate for rural retreat. Since then, too, I've thought more about Cowley, thanks in part to this book. When the late Mark Pedreira, who planned this collection, asked me to contribute, I replied as I should have a decade earlier: "I have much to say about Cowley." But what to say?

My doctoral project underplayed Cowley because his chief work on retirement, "Several Discourses, by way of Essays in Verse and Prose" (1668), felt different from the many other long eighteenth-century writings rejecting urban noise and courtly dependence for a peaceful country life.[1] I couldn't explain the incongruity then, but I can now, and I will argue here for *Essays* as something less than a solemn vindication of classical *otium* or a stern warning about the emptiness of urban fame and ambition. This is not to deny Cowley's influence on later, earnest celebrations of rural retirement. Reprinted continuously over the decades, *Essays* looms large in such retirement guides as George Wright's *Retired Pleasures*

(1787) and Ely Bates's *Rural Philosophy* (1803). Cowley's fingerprints are also all over the hundreds of overearnest poems in eighteenth-century miscellanies, periodicals, and occasional collections under titles like "The Happy Life," "Solitude," and "The Choice," some of them by bricklayers (Robert Tatersal), weavers (John Bancks), and cookmaids (Elizabeth Hands), for whom skipping a day of work, let alone retiring to the country, was never a choice.[2] It is precisely in this tendency, to become more shrill and uncompromising about the necessity of retirement the more unavailable it is, however, that Cowley differs from those he influenced. No doubt Cowley prates too much in *Essays* about his own virtue in seeking retirement, and did manage to retire after many struggles, first at Barn Elms (1663–65), near London, and later, at Chertsey, in Surrey (1665–67). Yet the failure of Cowley's retreats to meet his expectations when he finally secured them, leads him, I will argue, to laugh at his own overinvestment in the retirement fantasy drawn from classical poetry. Unlike so many, Cowley had the privilege to retire and leisure to question his own fantasies.

Seeing *Essays* as playfully, even irreverently, reflecting on the retirement poet persona Cowley had studiously cultivated from youth challenges the dominant view of *Essays* as a grave philosophic exercise. Mainly written after Cowley's move to Chertsey in 1665 and published posthumously, *Essays* as a whole functions much as Philip Major has characterized the final essay in the volume, "Of My self": *Essays* "finesses" for Cowley "a continuum of youthful and middle-aged" commitment to the ethic of retirement, downplaying his political activities and poetic ambitions.[3] All of the eleven essays in the 1668 volume—notably, "Of My self" and "The Garden," the latter addressed to Cowley's friend John Evelyn— voice a genuine belief in the virtuous happiness to be gained through moderate living on a quiet farm with books and friends nearby. Yet self-ridicule is confession by another means, and throughout *Essays* we encounter "a variety of tones, manners, and voices," allowing self-congratulation at times to shade into self-mockery.[4] For this reason, I think *Essays* involves as much role-playing as confession and is, therefore, lighter and funnier than nearly everyone has noticed. Irony, as Dustin Griffin notes, often goes overlooked for its working like a "dimmer switch," with a spectrum of effects that do not neatly reduce to "'I mean the opposite of what I say.'"[5] As I will show, the irony in *Essays* fluctuates from "I almost mean

this" and "I sometimes mean this," to "I wish I still meant this." Cowley
is genuinely attached to rural retreat, but he also is skeptical about that
attachment and its consequences. What is ironic and not depends ultimately more on the reader than on anything *in* a piece of writing, yes, but I
will nevertheless identify places in *Essays* where I think Cowley, revealing
that he takes himself too seriously, invites readers to laugh at his own
over-righteous love of retirement. Accordingly, many claims to follow will
contradict Paul Davis, who regards *Essays* as dour and self-congratulatory.
I instead find humor in Cowley's humorlessness, and wit in his apparent
imperviousness to wit.[6] And where Davis sees Cowley's "self-divisions"
about retirement as unacknowledged, I see him addressing his conflicts
through humor and irony (124).

One hint that Cowley fools around is his use of the Roman poet
Martial (AD 41?–102?). Although *Essays* contains eight Martial epigrams,
the most poems of any Latin writer included, scholars have overlooked
Martial's prominence. Ignoring Cowley's interest in Martial, I think,
leads to mistaking at times Cowley's tone and attitude. Martial traded in
irony and self-mockery, and he claimed to regret his retirement in Spain.
He is, therefore, a strange poet to prioritize if Cowley deals solely in
solemn counsels, without second thoughts. Approached with Martial in
mind, some of Cowley's alleged self-panegyric in *Essays* look instead like
Martialian self-subversion. Cowley wants to think and say the best about
retirement, but he also knows this isn't true and makes fun of himself for
wanting to ignore the fact. Recognizing this self-ridicule reveals something important about retirement. While scholars often see retirement as
an actual removal from society and politics, much of the mockery in his
Essays targets such literalism, a literalism sometimes distorting Cowley's
own thinking. Fantasizing about retirement entails an orientation toward
the world, a refusal to be absorbed by politics, media, and markets, even as
we remain in that world. Actually retreating to the country brings one no
closer to such independence, as Cowley learned firsthand.

Most readers have found little to laugh at in *Essays*. It was Cowley's biog-
rapher, Thomas Sprat (1636–1713) of the Royal Society, who first saw
Essays as deadly serious. In his "Account" of Cowley's life, Sprat hailed
Essays as the "unfeigned Image of [Cowley's] Soul" and "a real Character

of . . . [Cowley's] thoughts upon the point of his Retirement" ("Account," sig. d1v). As scholars have noted, Sprat spun Cowley's retreat to the country, prompted by his failure to gain preferment under Charles II, particularly the mastership of the Savoy Hospital, as a virtuous embrace of withdrawal.[7] Sprat naturally wanted to spare his friend suspicions of feigning or half-heartedness: in retiring, Cowley was making a virtue out of financial necessity, even if his income was not as "narrow" as he and Sprat made out.[8] Alexander Pope carried Sprat's view forward, praising *Essays* for its confessional qualities—"I love the language of [Cowley's] heart."[9] Richard Hurd, who issued an edition of Cowley's works in 1772, further emphasized the candor of his *Essays*: Cowley "writes of himself with good faith."[10] Even Samuel Johnson, ever skeptical about the morality of retreat, thought the "wish for retirement" in *Essays* "undissembled" (*Lives*, 1:195). While critic Jane Darcy has called attention to how both Sprat and scholars into the twentieth century assume Cowley's "moral earnestness," this recognition has done little in fact to dispel the assumption.[11] The only recent shift has been that such seriousness is now often viewed as too secure in its own high-mindedness. While David Hopkins detects irony in Cowley's paraphrase of Horace's *Satires* 2.6 ("The Country-Mouse"), he also sees Cowley as "several notches higher up the scale of earnestness and solemnity from . . . Horace," with *Essays* displaying "a uniform commitment and earnestness" that make reading "a slightly monotonous experience" (63, 86). For Paul Davis, the translations in *Essays* "lay bare" Cowley's "interior landscape" while subjecting readers to his "sanctimonious" and "self-righteous" views about retirement (114, 98).

That so many have insisted on the earnestness of *Essays* should raise red flags. No one felt a similar need to reiterate, say, that Cowley meant what he said in *Davideis* (1656), or that he sincerely served Queen Henrietta Maria in exile during the Interregnum. Such insistence feels a bit defensive, a response, I think, to a key tension in *Essays*: Cowley touts the abstract ideal of retirement in the vague, glowing ways familiar from classical poetry, yet what little we hear of his actual retirements at Barn Elms and Chertsey belies the fustian. Dashed expectations first appear in "The Garden," where, after "abandoning all ambitions and hopes in this World, and . . . retiring from the noise of all business and almost company,"

Cowley laments that he remains "st[u]ck still in the Inn of a hired House and Garden, among Weeds and Rubbish" (*Essays*, 168). The "hired House" is likely the Porch House in Chertsey, twenty miles up the Thames from London, where Cowley sought his second retirement after his first retreat, to Barn Elms, an outlying London neighborhood, displeased him. "Neither Barn Elms nor Chertsey was far enough from London" to match the classical standards of retirement, Major suggests (*Royalists*, 218). In his essay "The dangers of an Honest Man in much Company," Cowley admits that his own hopes, fed by classical poetry, are partly to blame: "I thought when I went first to dwell in the Country, that without doubt I should have met there with the simplicity of the old Poetical Golden Age." But, he discovered, "I was still in Old *England*, and not in *Arcadia*" (*Essays*, 203). While Cowley's nod to his naïveté is wry, the tone is of grief—less at the impossibility of the poetic fantasy than at the failure of reality to conform to that ideal. As Cowley's May 1665 letter to Sprat reveals, Chertsey had even more drawbacks:

> The first night that I came hither I caught so great a cold, with a defluxion of rheum, as made me keep my chamber ten days. And, two after, had such a bruise on my ribs with a fall, that I am yet unable to move or turn myself in my bed. This is my personal fortune here to begin with. And, besides, I can get no money from my tenants, and have my meadow's eaten up every night by cattle put in by my neighbours. What this signifies, or may come to in time, God knows; if it be ominous, it can end in nothing less than hanging?[12]

In a private letter, Cowley confesses his miseries and quips that death would be their logical culmination. As a public document, "Of My self" instead puts on a brave face and minimizes these sufferings, though Cowley's dismay remains clear: "I met presently not onely with many little encumbrances and impediments, but with so much sickness . . . as would have spoiled the happiness of an Emperour" (*Essays*, 220). Still, something doesn't add up: why would Cowley continue to urge and idealize retirement in *Essays* when his own two retreats were so second-rate?

The clash between dream and reality in *Essays* at first appears to reinforce Cowley's commitment. When the hoped-for patronage fails to materialize, Cowley tells us, "I did not quit the Design which I had resolved on, [but] I cast my self into it . . . without making capitulations, or taking counsel of Fortune" (*Essays*, 220). Far from debunking retirement as a myth, the straitened conditions at Chertsey therefore confirm Cowley's devotion to retreat, a devotion brooking neither delay nor financial planning. Yet the fervency of this commitment also looks misplaced or affected. What rational person would continue to urge retirement without qualification after such disappointment? Perhaps for this reason at least one past scholar, A. W. Ward, detects something forced or fake in *Essays*. Writing in Henry Craik's 1894 *English Prose, Selections*, Ward identifies the prose-verse mixture in Cowley's *Essays* as "giv[ing] to both something of the sprightly insincerity of the *vaudeville*."[13] Ward's claim is extraordinary given the consensus on the sincerity of *Essays*, but I think he is on to something. Retirement writings are always affected: the farm is never as idyllic, nor the city as corrupt, as writers imagine. That many urban poets urged the benefits of retirement also doesn't make such writing feel any less inauthentic. Cowley tried and found the retirement fantasy wanting, making his praise for it in *Essays* even more strained. He could have said nothing of Chertsey, but his complaints suggest some second-guessing of his choice, if not some wry amusement at his continued allegiance to his dream after two failed attempts at realizing it. In other words, he warmly endorses a life he implies he should be cooling to, and this tension perhaps recalls for Ward the disingenuousness of vaudeville. At the least, Cowley's mentioning Chertsey indicates he went too far in literalizing his fantasy—too far, that is, for one lacking the £500 a year he estimates in "Of Greatness" to be the ideal income for retreat (183).

Ward's logic in linking the "vaudeville" quality of *Essays* to its mixing of verse and prose becomes clearer when we put Ward's statement in conversation with Tom Mason's "Abraham Cowley's Amiability," the only previous article I know to question the supposed solemnity of *Essays*. "Cowley's tone is seldom purely grave, or seldom grave for long," Mason argues, "and his force of thinking often issues in a strange species of joke."[14] Mason finds one such "half-suppressed half-joke" in Cowley's remark in "Of My self" that he was "made a Poet . . . as a Child is made a Eunuch" after reading Spenser in his youth ("Amiability," 208, *Essays*, 218). Carrying some awkward implications—poets are emasculated, poetic production replaces reproduction, Spenser did the snipping—the incongruous comparison is, Mason notes, a joke at the expense of "the profession of poetry" and probably also, I would add, of Cowley's bachelorhood (200). Such humor also informs the structure of *Essays*, where Cowley "incongruously" mixes verse and prose, per Mason, "to achieve gaiety" (195). Ward may be thinking of similar incongruities: while Cowley's prose is more restrained, the poems—both the translated ones and Cowley's own—rhapsodize over retirement. Cowley's translations are more idealizing than their Latin originals, as I will discuss later, and that many of the translations are reprinted from his 1663 *Verses Written on Several Occasions* suggests some distance between the Cowley writing *Essays* from Chertsey and the Cowley who translated the poems before having tried out retirement himself. This occasional tension between verse and prose makes *Essays* feel, again, a bit insincere: we encounter an exaggerated type, whom Mason terms "Cowley the poet," distinguished by his poems on retirement, and this poet differs for Mason from "the real Cowley" in the prose (197).

I'm less sure that poet and person can be so easily separated, or that Cowley's prose is a more reliable guide to his true feelings than the poetry. Even in his letter to Sprat, he could be looking to shock, to make things at Chertsey out to be worse than they are. He could be putting on a mask in *Essays*, too, exaggerating his misery (would marauding cows "spoil the happiness" of an emperor?) to heighten further the contrasts with his fantasy. Such contrasts make it hard fully to trust anything Cowley has to say about retirement. Still, I agree with Mason that Cowley plays a role or type, with this persona most noticeable in the supposedly confessional "Of My self," where he connects his retirement to poetry: "It was the immature and immoderate love of them [poets] which stampt first, or rather engraved these Characters [his love for retirement] in me" (*Essays*, 218). The Cowley of 1665–67 may shake his head at his continued clinging post-Chertsey to the "retirement poet" character—a role he assumed as early as his "boyish" retirement poem, "A Vote" (1636)—but he apparently remains too invested to scrap it. He can't not celebrate retirement because it is his persona: panting for retirement is just what, for Cowley, a poet does.

Both Sprat and Cowley himself recognized this uncompromising, unhealthy attachment to the retirement fantasy. Consider Sprat's account of Cowley's motives for going to Barn Elms:

He was now weary of the vexations and formalities of an active condition. He had been perplexed with a long compliance to Foreign Manners. He was satiated with the Arts of Court: which sort of life, though his virtu had made innocent to him, yet nothing could make it quiet. These were the reasons that moved him to forego all Public Employments, and to follow the violent inclination of his own mind, which in the greatest throng of his former business, had still called upon him, and represented to him the true delights of solitary Studies, of temperate Pleasures, and of a moderate Revenue. ("Account," sig. a2v)

Sprat's referring to Cowley's desire for retirement as "a violent inclination" criticizes Cowley's zealousness for retreat, not the idea of retirement per se. This charge of impulsiveness returns when Sprat later condemns Cowley's fascination with retirement directly: "If any thing ought to have been chang'd in his Temper, and Disposition: It was his earnest Affection for Obscurity and Retirement" ("Account," sig. e1r). In casting Cowley's retreat as something forced by temperament and circumstance, and not freely chosen, Sprat in fact follows Cowley's own lead. Abandoning the emphasis early in *Essays* on retirement as a principled choice, Cowley's "Of My self," as Alan De Gooyer notes, frames his retirement as answering some irresistible "affections" (6–7), which Cowley attributes to "an immoderate love" of poetry. In its intensity, his poetry-inspired desire for a retreat compares to greed: "I NEVER had any other desire so strong, and so like to Covetousness as that one which I have had always, that I might be master at last of a small house and large garden" (*Essays*, 168). This implicitly disapproving self-description again sits oddly with his energetic urging of retirement, leading readers again to suspect what they already detected in the tension elsewhere in *Essays* between Cowley's fantasies and Chertsey's realities: in his investment in retirement and the retired poet identity he goes a little bit overboard. If retirement, as *Essays* defines it, is a life of moderation, then the desire for retreat nevertheless can become immoderate, and such intemperance shows in Cowley's continued embrace of the "retirement poet" role after the alleged deprivations in Surrey.

That Cowley presents himself as cleaving immoderately to his retirement persona explains why some early readers doubted his hewing to the ideals voiced in *Essays*. Disputing Sprat's official story of Cowley catching his fatal illness working his fields, an end Virgil would approve, Pope told Joseph Spence that Cowley had died of a fever after getting drunk and sleeping outdoors.[15] Similarly, the politician Arthur Onslow (1691–1768) opined that Cowley at Chertsey was none of the "oeconomist or strict philosopher" of retirement he fashioned himself as in *Essays*, rather enjoying "his friends and bottle there."[16] Such rumors show skepticism about the severity or discipline of his retreat, of his heeding his own exhortations to quiet moderation. Despite judging Cowley's desire "undissembled," Johnson suspected Cowley's praise for retreat was divorced from the realities of his retirement, a discrepancy that Johnson saw also reflected in Cowley's retiring to Chertsey, less than a day's ride from London, instead of to America, as he had proposed in the "Preface" to his 1656 *Poems*: "My desire has been for some years . . . to retire my self to some of our *American Plantations*, . . . to forsake this world for ever, with all the *vanities* and *Vexations* of it."[17] Of Cowley's change in plans, Johnson remarks archly:

> Cowley certainly retired; first to Barn-elms, and afterwards to Chertsey, in Surrey. He seems, however, to have lost part of his dread of the *hum of men*. He thought himself now safe enough from intrusion, without the defence of mountains and oceans; and, instead of seeking shelter in America, wisely went only so far from the bustle of life as that he might easily find his way back, when solitude should grow tedious. (*Lives*, 198)

In suggesting Cowley settled near London lest a more remote retirement prove too excruciating, Johnson poses the question raised against all moralists with rigid platforms: do they live up to their professed principles? Such skepticism was justified: retreating from London to Barn Elms in 1663 would be like "retreating" from midtown Manhattan to

Chinatown today. Cowley's retreats involved little sacrifice. Even Sprat, who asserted Cowley's deep sincerity, leaves open Cowley's being both himself and not when he declares *Essays* as revealing the "real Character of . . . [Cowley's] thoughts" ("Account," sig. d1v). "Character" bridges authenticity and forgery, signifying not only "the moral and mental qualities which distinguish an individual" (*OED*, 9a), but also the "part played by an actor" (*OED*, 14a). As Sprat implies, sincere though Cowley is, he may still play a role, a role played for so long that he has become the very character: the poet–partisan of retirement, the character he organizes his life around in "Of My self." Deciding when Cowley means it and when he fakes it, or separating his real self from his character, then, is impossible. Better instead to attend to places in *Essays* where he laughs at the caricature he had embraced.

So far I have argued that, while celebrating the retirement ideal central to his identity, Cowley also humorously exposes his excessive attachment to this ideal. His promoting retreat in *Essays* is not disingenuous, but he does distance himself from his own ideas; as Shane Herron has observed, "Not everything in ironic representations is disavowed," and this certainly applies to Cowley.[18] The overlooked self-distancing or self-mockery emerges from inconsistencies and contradictions in *Essays*—and not just between Cowley's poetic fantasies and his actual retreat. Mockery also arises from the friction between his sources and his presentation of those sources. For Scott Black, *Essays* reads like a commonplace book, with snippets from Montaigne, Seneca, and the Bible running into Cowley's own remarks, which, in turn, frame Cowley's translations of the Latin retirement classics (Horace's *Epode* 2, Virgil's *Georgics* 2, Claudian's "Old Man of Verona," etc.).[19] Knowing where Cowley's views end, and his sources begin, is, as a result, often unclear. Cowley also adjusts his translations, dropping, for example, the end of Horace's *Epode* 2 and the first half or so of Horace's *Satires* 2.6 (Davis, 140). Omission and paraphrase assimilate these authorities to Cowley's perspective. Despite this, distinguishing what Cowley presents other writers as saying from what these writers actually said is central to appreciating the subtle, intermittent self-satire throughout *Essays*.

Departures from the originals would have been evident to early readers. Most of what Cowley translates from Horace, Virgil, and Martial was in 1668 already familiar to anyone educated; as Davis rightly observes, many of "Cowley's readers might already have copied [previous translations] into their commonplace books" (119). These readers were not the Latin-less working-class poets who imitated Cowley in the eighteenth century. His *Essays* includes many untranslated Latin tags, suggesting he expected his initial readers to be familiar with the Latin classics. Where the 1668 volume omits the original Latin, Hurd's 1772 edition includes it, indicating that Hurd also thought that Cowley expected bilingual readers who could compare his translations with the originals. Cowley also counts on familiarity with non-Latin writers. When discussing Machiavelli in "Of Liberty," Cowley gestures at his audience's knowledge "(as most of you may well remember)" (*Essays*, 111). The informed reader he constructs is also a skeptical reader. In "Of Solitude," for instance, Cowley anticipates an objection to his claim that worldly success demands sacrificing honesty: "But you may say, . . . yet there are narrow, thorney, and little-trodden paths too, through which some men finde a passage by vertuous industry" (*Essays*, 113). Similar hypothetical objections appear throughout. The merits of the active versus the retired life were much debated at the time, so perhaps the imagined naysayer in *Essays* is Cowley admitting that his views would not go unchallenged.[20] In any case, by embedding a knowing interlocutor who challenges Cowley's own statements, he invites his actual readers to do the same thing.

What were knowledgeable readers supposed to see? In Cowley's dropping of the final lines to Horace's *Epode* 2, for example, where the poem's paean to retirement is revealed as the swift-forgotten fancy of Alfius, an urban moneylender, they may have seen nothing amiss. Other previous imitations, including Ben Jonson's "To Sir Robert Wroth" (1616), also left off Horace's ironic ending. However, since Cowley also omits material from nearly all the sources he brings into *Essays*, *Epode* 2's fate might acquire a different significance amid the other departures from source-texts. As Davis discusses, Cowley also omits allusions in his sources to the laboriousness of farm work, as he does when translating the famous "O fortunatos nimium" section of Virgil's *Georgics* 2, one of six translations reprinted in *Essays* from Cowley's 1663 collection, the others being

Horace's *Odes* 3.16, *Epodes* 2.6, and *Epistles* 1.10, as well as Claudian's "Old Man of Verona," and Martial's *Epigrams* 10.96 (98–101). What might these omissions together imply? Davis and Hopkins have examined Cowley's translations of Horace and Virgil in detail, so I will say no more about them individually here. But what we should notice is how these omissions, viewed collectively, illustrate something else beyond merely the liberties taken in paraphrastic translation, especially considering, as I will discuss below, Cowley's frequent mis-citations of his sources as well. His omissions and mis-citations should instead be seen as part of a recurrent problem of distortion, which, I'd propose, knowing readers of *Essays* were meant to notice.

The immediate takeaway from Cowley's adjusting of his sources is that the idealizations of the rural life in previous writings were never idealizing enough for him. He always had to make retirement better, more perfect, by denying any difficulties or drawbacks hinted at in the longer tradition of retirement writing. Cowley, for instance, quotes Montaigne twice in *Essays* (in "Of Solitude" and "Of Greatness")—in both passages, as Davis puts it, "humorlessly root[ing] out Montaigne's ironies" and showing himself utterly "impervious to Montaigne's eloquence and wit" (102). Worse, in the first of the two passages Cowley misrepresents Montaigne's retirement:

> Since we cannot attain to Greatness, (saies the *Sieur de Montagn*) let's have our revenge by railing at it: this he spoke but in Jest. I believe he desired it no more than I do, and had less reason, for he enjoyed so plentiful and honourable a fortune in a most excellent Country, *as allowed him all the real conveniences of it, sep[a]rated and purged from the Incommodities.* (*Essays*, 178; my emphasis)

On the contrary, Montaigne encountered constant "incommodities" when sequestered in his tower in Dordogne (103).[21] Reading *Essays* as dour and pompous, Davis views such distortions as accidents of Cowley's vehement passion for retirement. For Davis, Cowley's convictions "override" whatever in his sources doesn't square with his own wishful thinking.

But this is only half of the story. For one, no amount of enthusiasm could blind Cowley to so blatant a misrepresentation; if he knew

Montaigne well enough to quote him, presumably from memory, he also knew that Montaigne's retirement sometimes fell short of the ideal. For two, even if Cowley knowingly misrepresented, he couldn't have thought it would go unnoticed; the informed audience he anticipates would probably know Montaigne and recall that his retirement was often interrupted by visitors. And if Cowley was serious, then he lied to a knowledgeable set of readers, which seems unlikely insofar as it would discredit his argument for retirement in their eyes. My reading, therefore, differs from Davis's. If Cowley allows his vehemence for retirement to rewrite Montaigne, then Cowley knows this and jokes at his own expense. Ever the retirement poet, he says only the best things about retirement, but he also laughs at his indulging in such self-delusions. His "overriding" Montaigne is comic self-subversion, aimed not at retirement but at the absurd magnitude the retirement fantasy had taken in his life, an absurdity that Chertsey had revealed to him. In running roughshod over Montaigne, Cowley calls attention to his zeal for retirement, which even he at times finds ridiculous. In other words, he does with Montaigne what he does with Chertsey. In that case, Cowley implies his denial or self-delusion by filling *Essays* with poetic idealizations contradicting his realities at Chertsey. Here, with Montaigne, Cowley again exposes his denialism to mockery, this time by foregrounding his suppressing of negative accounts of retirement by other writers. The humor in *Essays* arises from his use of obvious falsehoods to send up his own tendency to deny or distort whatever detracts from his views.

To learn more about these strategies of self-deflation, let's consider two other passages that Davis also discusses. The first example is the epigraph to "Of Obscurity." It reads, "*Nam neque Divitibus contingunt gaudia solis, / nec vixit male, qui natus moriensque Fefellit* " ("For joys fall not to the rich alone, and he has not lived amiss who from birth to death has passed unknown"), and has the citation, "Hor. Epistle 1.18" (136).[22] "Cowley has misremembered Horace: the lines he quotes are from *Epistles* 1.17 not 18," Davis comments (104), regarding this error as further evidence of Cowley's enthusiasm for retirement trumping concerns with accuracy. Cowley seems to have often quoted from memory—many small instances of misquotation in *Essays* indicate as much—but it is hard to believe an expert Latinist like Cowley would confuse two epistles so different.[23] Moreover, if he mislabeled the epigraph purposefully, he again would only have damaged his credibility with knowing readers who would notice the inaccuracy. I think this is more self-subversion: he wants in his enthusiasm for retreat to deny the perspective in 1.17 but he also realizes and exposes such tendentiousness to ridicule. *Epistles* 1.18 lauds retirement, whereas *Epistles* 1.17 defends moderate worldly involvement, and by connecting the two epistles through an "erroneous" citation, Cowley challenges his own over-enthusiastic distinctions elsewhere in *Essays* between retreat and engagement. As Cowley knew, Chertsey was owed to worldly action: it was a gift from his patron, George Villiers, second Duke of Buckingham, and, indirectly, from Queen Henrietta Maria, in thanks for Cowley's service as cryptographer and spy.[24] Moreover, *Epistles* 1.17 lauds Aristippus, whose love of solitude is not so extreme as to exclude all society, while reproving Diogenes, whose purity of commitment to retreat isolates him. The mis-citation thus links the fantasy of retirement in 1.18 to the isolating fanaticism in 1.17, hinting that Cowley, like Diogenes, took things a little far. Through the mis-citation Cowley again mockingly acknowledges his own uncompromising fantasies of retreat.

The second passage involves a quotation in "Of Agriculture." "What I have further to say of the Country Life shall be borrowed from the Poets, who were always the most faithful and affectionate friends to it," Cowley writes at one point (*Essays*, 148). A quotation from Ovid's *Ex Ponto* 1.3 follows, which reads: "Nescio qua Natale solum dulcedine Musas / Ducit & immemores non sinit esse sui" ("By what sweet charm I know not the native land draws all men nor allows them to forget her").[25] "No classical poet comes less readily to mind as an advocate of country life and rural values than Ovid," Davis observes, pointing out that Ovid's quotation in fact refers to Rome, which Cowley conveniently fails to mention (105–106). Davis argues for Cowley again falling prey to his own zealousness, assimilating Ovid's urban nostalgia to his own "high-minded affection for country life" (106). I agree that Cowley lets his immoderate attachment get the better of him, though he is again more self-aware than Davis allows. To introduce a quotation informed readers would know refers to Rome with the sentence, "Poets . . . were alwayes the most faithful and affec-tionate friends" to country life, must be a joke, in part because Cowley is right: city poets were always warm in their praises of pastoral ease. Cowley would know, too, as he praised retirement while hunting for patronage at Windsor. While Davis reads Ovid's presence as Cowley hinting that his own retirement sometimes felt like "exile" (106), this reading strikes me as too literal-minded, with Davis, like Sprat, seeing *Essays* as more confessional than it is. If Cowley implies that his retirement feels like an Ovidian exile, then he again pokes fun at his own exaggerated self-importance and self-pity: thinking that Chertsey's bovine hassles are equal to Ovid's Black Sea banishment is ludicrous. Once again, readers are invited to laugh at Cowley's eagerness to assimilate materials that challenge the very ideals their assimilation would serve.

Viewed singly, these three passages look merely erroneous, which is how Davis regards them. Taken together, however, I believe they are ironic. Cowley would not make such mistakes or indulge so many self-defeating falsehoods. The irony becomes even clearer when we place such willful omissions and outright distortions on a larger spectrum of misrepresentation that includes Cowley's translations in *Essays* as well. His persona's habits of misrepresentation—in fact, in citation, and, as I will argue momentarily, in translation—imply that in his zeal for retirement he has lost touch with reality, leading him to denial and falsification. This twisting of anything challenging his idealism extends to the facts of his own life. As Major notes, Cowley's claims of lifelong commitment to retirement in "Of My self" ignore the ambition displayed in "The Motto" (1656): "Sure I *Fames Trumpet* hear; [. . .] / Unpast *Alpes* stop me, but I'll cut through all, / And march, the *Muses Hannibal*" (*Essays*, 221).[26] His presentation of his goals after the Restoration seems equally distorted or falsified: "I never . . . proposed to my self any other advantage from His Majesties Happy Restoration, but the getting into some moderately convenient Retreat in the Country" (*Essays*, 220). The persona in this latter statement deceives neither himself nor his readers. This comment is both so clearly false—Cowley's angling for the Savoy was public information—and so absolute ("I never") that it screams irony, as Cowley saying the opposite of the truth and expecting all to notice.[27] By casting the joke as an ironic denial, he also broadens the satiric target. Cowley isn't just mocking himself for mulling opportunities beyond retirement; he is also mocking himself for denying or wanting to deny he was mulling them over.

Another way of viewing Cowley's method of self-mockery is not as blatant falsehood, but as extreme exaggeration. Poetic praise of rural retirement was always disproportionate to the unromantic realities of the countryside, as I stated previously, and Cowley's "retirement poet" persona in *Essays* overrates, for gentle comic effect, both retirement and his virtue in pursuing it. Sometimes Cowley's exaggeration takes the customary overstatement of such poetry into the realm of caricature. We've already seen something of this with Cowley's eunuch conceit, which is self-deprecating precisely because the implied finality of it—becoming a poet is like being castrated—is absurdly exaggerated. Other strange, over-the-top comparisons abound in *Essays*, and though they haven't been read by previous scholars as cheeky or flippant, I think they can and should be read that way. In "Of Solitude," Cowley declares, for example, that those unused to deep thinking will fall prey in retirement to their passions. For these individuals, retirement becomes "like the punishment of Parricides among the *Romans*, to be sow'd into a Bag with an Ape, a Dog, and a Serpent" (*Essays*, 132). Surely retirement was not so terrible for anyone! Whether one laughs out loud at this particular bit of bombast, the exaggeration combines with similarly extreme statements in *Essays* to make Cowley's persona often seem silly and extravagant. In another instance from "Of Solitude," Cowley proclaims that Scipio Africanus's supposed adage, "*Nunquam minus solus, quam cum solus* ["never less alone, than when alone"], is now become a very vulgar saying. Every Man and almost every Boy for these seventeen hundred years, has had it in his mouth" (*Essays*, 129). The phrase is surely not in every mouth, since only boys from well-off families attended school and university and learned to speak Latin through rounds of debate and oral examination based on such ancient maxims. Cowley's untranslated Latin points to the exaggeration behind his "vulgarization" charge. Whatever his own feelings, the hyperbole makes his poet persona sound a bit paranoid, certain of things changing for the worst.

The humor in some passages is easily missed. But Cowley's self-mockery is not always faint. In "Of Agriculture," for example, when his persona urges that the heirs to landed estates learn the arts of cultivation, he criticizes the over-reliance on classical sources: "The business of these Professors should not be . . . onely to read Pompous and

Superficial Lectures out of *Virgils Georgickes, Pliny, Varro,* or *Columella,*
but to instruct their Pupils" in real methods based on "solid and experimental Knowledge." Cowley satirizes a common educational approach, as
Major observes, but Cowley also satirizes his own reliance on the classics (*Royalists,* 212). Cowley himself spends only four pages on modern
methods before he announces, "What I have further to say of the Country
Life, shall be borrowed from the Poets" (*Essays,* 148), and then spends the
next twelve-and-a-half pages of "Of Agriculture" quoting or paraphrasing
poets who praised the country life (and also some, like Ovid, who did
not).The self-contradiction is too obvious to be accidental. Cowley, too,
cites Varro in the sentence preceding his complaint about "Superficial
Lectures out of . . . *Varro,* or *Columella*" (*Essays,* 148), and then goes on to
cite Columella three times, the only times Columella appears in the entire
volume. This is Cowley making fun of his retirement-poet persona. Nor
is the laughter directed only at his *Essays.* In his earlier *Proposition for the
Advancement of Experimental Philosophy* (1661), where he had proposed
an "Apprenticeship" in natural science through the Royal Society, Cowley
urged students be taught authors "who treat . . . Nature," including, "Varro,
Cato, Columella, Pliny, . . . Virgil's Georgicks, Grotius, Nemesianus, [and]
Manilius" (*Essays,* 39–40). If Cowley thought that Latin texts could have
practical uses, he also at times questioned that practicality. He thus uses
"Of Agriculture" to mock how the classics and classical fantasies had
supplanted hard realities and practical concerns.

Many other humorous or ironic passages could be discussed. At one
moment in "Of Agriculture," Cowley seems to aim for laughs by denying
the obvious in an apparent allusion to Oliver Cromwell.[28] There is also a
point later in the same essay where Cowley argues for rural virtuousness
on the basis that the "first Men" of the Bible were husbandmen, shrug-
ging off the inconvenient fact of Cain being, by the way, also a murderer,
offering the ridiculous sophistry that after Abel's killing, Cain immediately gave up tilling for a new career in construction.[29] But a more
important question needs asking: if Cowley is so ironic, why has no one
noticed it before? First, no one has questioned Sprat's credulous framing
of *Essays* as deeply confessional, a presumed seriousness that has become,
except in Ward's and Mason's cases, the premise for all later readings.
Even if he recognized Cowley's playfulness, Sprat had to deny it. Cowley's

Royalism and reconciliation with Cromwell made his retreat fodder for malicious inferences across the political spectrum, as a proof of disloyalty or cowardice. Davis agrees: Cowley's retirement for Sprat "could not be a laughing matter" (Davis, 113). In order to protect him, those close to Cowley and most attuned to his humor would also be those least likely to point it out. Perhaps early readers kept quiet, too, because they also felt targeted by the satire: if they came looking to indulge their own fantasies of retirement while reading about Cowley's, they were exposed to Cowley's irony as well. Moreover, since some of Cowley's humor also depends on outlandish conceits (poets as eunuchs), the impatience in the following century with "metaphysical wit" also inadvertently reinforced the volume's reputation for solemnity.[30] Eighteenth-century readers like Johnson who regarded such conceits as a cheap drollery were too busy ridiculing Cowley to notice he ridiculed himself. Ultimately, however, the greatest obstacle to appreciating the playfulness of *Essays* today may be scholars' own discomfort with humor. Light, noncommittal writing is all too often regarded as trivial and unworthy, especially at present, when moral earnestness and political commitment define both what and how we read in literary studies. No surprise, then, that Cowley's sly jokes and irony continue to be mistaken for self-congratulatory sermonizing.

One parallel to the kind of mistaken (humorless) reception I'm proposing for Cowley's *Essays* is that of Jonathan Swift's *Verses on the Death of Dr. Swift* (1731–32, 1739), which was regarded as serious until Barry Slepian pointed out its ironies in 1963. Even Pope thought that Swift meant what he said and accused him of erroneous self-praise, though to modern eyes the praise is too excessive and the errors too obvious to be anything but self-deprecation.[31] If Pope could miss the jokes of a friend and known satirist, then Sprat could surely have missed his friend's self-ridicule or could have been sure readers would miss it: Cowley was not known for satire and irony, so readers weren't looking for jokes. I know that claims for the overlooked irony in works long-regarded as earnest can go terribly wrong—as when David Vieth infamously argued Dryden's Anne Killigrew ode (1685) was satirizing, rather than celebrating, its subject.[32] My claim for Cowley is more like Slepian's than Vieth's, however, and not only because Cowley, like Swift, mocks someone who (or whose friends and family) wouldn't object: himself. Cowley also had a clear precedent for endorsing something he sometimes doubted or laughed at himself for believing. In a letter to Cowley from March 1667, John Evelyn apologizes for taking the side of worldliness in his *Publick Employment and an Active Life Prefer'd to Solitude* (1667):

> You had reason to be astonish'd at the presumption . . . that I, who have so highly celebrated Recesse, and envied it in others, should become an Advocate for the Enemie. . . . I conjure you to believe that I am still of the same mind, and that there is no Person alive who dos [*sic*] more honor and breathe after the life and repose . . . [I] have [praised] publique Employment . . . in so weake a style, compar'd to my Antagonists, as by that alone, it will appeare, I neither was, nor could be serious; and I hope you believe I speake my very soule to you.[33]

While scholars acknowledge this letter, no one seems to take seriously Evelyn's assurance that he feigned when he argued for the superior virtue of political and economic activity.[34] Writing from Sayes Court, Deptford, Evelyn might defer to his retired friend's feelings, but that Evelyn himself also kept a part-time retirement at Wotton, Surrey, suggests he was at least half serious when he says he wasn't being serious. It is hard to imagine in our own time of aggressive authenticity that one could write a whole book arguing for what one didn't believe, yet that seems to be what Evelyn did. Both Evelyn and Cowley would have been familiar with arguing *in utramque partem*, on both sides of a question, from grammar school exercises, and Cowley read *Active Life Prefer'd to Solitude* in 1667, so he had models for pitching what he simultaneously doubted or disagreed with.[35] Though Cowley's *Essays* takes the opposite tactic—far from "weak," his urging of retirement is so fierce as also to raise doubts about his commitment to the ideas expressed—Evelyn's arguing both sides further supports my approaching Cowley's *Essays* as having similar moments of ironic or half-hearted endorsement.

In addition to Evelyn, Cowley after 1665 was reading another writer known for looking at his own dreams and commitments skeptically: the Latin poet Martial. *Essays* contains eight Martial translations: *Epigrams*

1.55, 2.53, and 2.68 are attached to the first essay, "Of Liberty"; *Epigrams* 4.5 is included in the eighth essay, "The Dangers of an Honest Man in Much Company"; *Epigrams* 2.90 and 5.58 are attached to the tenth essay, "The Dangers of Procrastination"; and *Epigrams* 10.47 and 10.96 to the eleventh essay, "Of My self."[36] While scholars emphasize the debt *Essays* owes to Horace, the included translations of Martial outnumber those of Horace, with Martial, not Horace, also getting the first and last word in the volume.[37] Moreover, only one of the eight Martial epigrams—10.96, first published in Cowley's 1663 *Verses Written on Several Occasions*—is reprinted. Counting 10.96, Cowley had only published two translations of Martial before moving to Chertsey in 1665, the second being *Epigrams* 5.20, which appeared in his 1656 *Miscellanies*.[38] By contrast, three of the five Horace selections in *Essays*—*Satires* 2.6, *Epistles* 1.10, *Odes* 3.16— are reprints from 1663 and may have been translated earlier, implying Martial's new relevance to Cowley at Chertsey, where all the component parts of *Essays*, except "The Dangers of Procrastination," were written.

Little of Cowley's correspondence survives, but one of the six letters discovered by Allan Pritchard documents Martial's ascendency for Cowley at this time.[39] The recipient of the October 18, 1661 Cowley letter was his Trinity College friend, Martin Clifford, also secretary to Cowley's patron, Buckingham. The salutation reads, "Dear Fuscus," an allusion to Horace's *Epistles* 1.10, which is addressed to Horace's friend Aristius Fuscus and is one of the translations reprinted in *Essays*. In another letter possibly from 1663, Cowley playfully likens himself and Clifford to the mice from Horace's *Satires* 2.6: "I am now a Mouse of yᵉ wiser kind, & long very much to entertain you of yᵉ other, wᵗʰ cheese and apples."[40] As this suggests, Horace's poetry offered Cowley a template for his own self-presentation. But Martial gave a model, too. Immediately following Cowley's salutation is a strange aside, "I hope the compellation [i.e., appellation] will a little puzzle you" (Pritchard, 260). Cowley expects Clifford to be confused about Fuscus or wishes to point out multiple identities by predicting Clifford's confusion. There is another Fuscus: Cornelius Fuscus, the addressee of Martial's *Epigrams* 1.54 and 6.76, the prefect of the Praetorian Guard and protector of Martial's patron, Emperor Domitian. Horace's Fuscus fits Clifford well enough: Horace invites Aristius Fuscus down to the country, just as Cowley asks Clifford to visit him. Hailing

Clifford as Cornelius Fuscus fits, too, and adds a mock-grandiose compliment—both to Clifford, the secretary made bodyguard, and to Cowley's patron, Buckingham, who is promoted to emperor. The close of the letter confirms Cowley as moving between Horatian and Martialian templates. Declaring that his current "indisposition will not suffer mee to wait upon him [Buckingham] at present nor thee, Jucundissime Martialis," Cowley asks again for Clifford to visit him (Pritchard, 261). Taken from *Epigrams* 10.47, Martial's famous epigram on retirement, included in *Essays*, the phrase "jucundissime martialis" ("most delightful Martialis") assimilates Clifford to Martial's addressee in that poem, his friend Julius Martialis, a retired lawyer. Scholars who focus on Cowley's debt to Horace overlook Martial as a competing model for Cowley's poet persona.

Why Cowley's interest in Martial has been ignored is unclear. Perhaps the discomfort with conceits that made critics overlook Cowley's humor generally also led them to overlook Martial specifically. As Joseph Addison confirms, Martial was seen in later years as having the same false, "mixed" wit that Cowley specialized in, a wit associated with what was later called "metaphysical poetry":

> As *true Wit* consists in the Resemblance of Ideas, and *false Wit* in the Resemblance of Words, . . . there is another kind of Wit which consists partly in the Resemblance of Ideas, and partly in the Resemblance of Words; which for Distinction Sake I shall call *mixt Wit*. This Kind of Wit is that which abounds in *Cowley*, more than in any Author that ever wrote. . . . If we look into the *Latin* Writers, we find none of this mixt wit in *Virgil*, *Lucretius*, or *Catullus*; very little in *Horace*, but a great deal of it in *Ovid*, and scarce any thing else in *Martial*.[41]

Why Cowley turned to Martial in the mid-1660s is far clearer. Both Horace and Martial offered Cowley precedents for the "retirement poet" type he eagerly conformed himself to, but Martial apparently offered parallels that Horace did not. Of course, we know little of Marcus Valerius Martialis's life except from his poetry, and these poetic self-representations cannot be trusted, making it more accurate, probably, to say that Cowley saw self-parallels in Martial's persona or personae, rather than in the real, historical Martial. Like Cowley, this "Martial" never married, and, as Cowley did in France and London, Martial spent his life in Rome hunting for patronage. Like Cowley, too, Martial, knew firsthand the problems of preferment amid changing regimes. Where Horace always had Augustus's favor, Martial, thanks to his compliments to Domitian, became suspect to Domitian's successors, Nerva and Trajan, a fate Cowley could appreciate, his accommodation to Cromwell putting him out of favor later with Charles II. If one compares two writers at a high enough level of abstraction, one is bound to see similarities, but of course Cowley and Martial are not alike in many ways. Yet their similarities are more than superficial and would likely have been visible to Cowley himself. When Martial retired, at Bilbilis in Spain, it came with the help from a benefactress, Marcella, much as Cowley also retired, with assistance, in part, from a woman, Henrietta Maria. Most important, Martial found that Bilbilis did not live up to his claimed lifelong retirement dream, much as Cowley found Chertsey inadequate. Martial voices regrets, real or feigned, in the preface to his *Epigrams* 12, which was written from Spain:

> I miss the ears of the community to which I had grown accustomed. It is like pleading a case in a strange court. For if there is anything to please in my little books, the audience dictated it. The subtlety of judgments, the inspiration of the themes, the libraries, the theaters, the gatherings where pleasure is a student without realizing it, . . . all those things which in my fastidiousness I forsook, I now regret as though they had deserted me.[42]

Martial blamed his "fastidiousness," his refusal to compromise on any aspect of his retirement fantasy, for rushing him into real-life disappointment. Whether Cowley knew Martial's regretful comment is uncertain, but the epigrams subverting Martial's own fantasies were sufficiently well known to offer Cowley a model for poking fun at his own dreams.[43] By bringing Martial into *Essays*, Cowley could gesture at his own disenchantment—with retirement, yet more so with his own over-fastidious embrace of it—without voicing his doubts directly. One is tempted to see Martial's persona as an avatar of Cowley's, and Cowley probably saw something of his own persona in Martial. Given the letter to Clifford, however, the only thing short of speculation to say is that Martial helped Cowley represent the conflicts in his own attitude about retirement.

Martial's prominence in *Essays* is not good news for anyone wanting to read it as consistently earnest, however. A common vehicle for neo-Latin satire in Britain in the 1600s, the epigram form was associated with mockery, and including epigrams specifically by Martial only heightened these associations.[44] If Cowley used Martial to frame his own conflicted views about retirement, then this framing entailed a wry recognition, as Martial's poetry did, of his own over-investment in the retirement ideal. A tool for flattering patrons, the epigram for Martial was for saying what you didn't believe or didn't always mean; as Niall Livingston and Gideon Nisbet observe, Martial "writes in a genre that is easy not to take seriously, and Martial himself is at pains to tell us not to."[45] For all their flashes of seriousness—if seriousness is what to call it—Martial's epigrams are exercises in role-playing and self-subversion, much as I think Cowley's *Essays* often is, too. Martial's going to Spain indicates some sincerity, perhaps, but his epigrams specifically celebrating rural retreat teem with "humorous inconsistencies," "often qualified," too, via juxtaposition with other epigrams reveling in the same urban debauchery that retirement claims to reject.[46] As all this about Martial also confirms, my reading so far in this chapter has assumed Martial as a model, even a muse, for Cowley, especially when sending up his own retirement-poet persona in *Essays*. Cowley's persistent self-subversion is clear in the volume even before we consider his including eight translations of Martial, inclusions that only invite readers to look even more closely for irony in places in the *Essays* that might seem at first in earnest.

This is not to say that Martial doesn't receive the same treatment in *Essays* as the other Latin poets. In translating Martial, Cowley again suppresses whatever in the original threatens his persona's idealism. Martial's irony attracted Cowley, but Cowley also apparently couldn't resist the opportunity to subvert his own self-delusion by calling attention to his own efforts to erase Martial's ironies. For example, Martial tends to describe his wished-for retreat as humble, so humble, in fact, that there is an ironic hint that it barely needs or deserves wishing for, as in *Epigrams* 2.90: "Me focus et nigros non indignantia fumos / tecta iuvant et fons vivus et herba rudis" ("My pleasure is a hearth, and a roof that does not resent black smoke, and a running stream, and fresh grass") (*Epigrams*, 1:186–87). Cowley will have none of this: the house in his translation has no smoke and the outdoor setting is grander:

> My humble thoughts no glittering roofs require,
> Or Rooms that shine with ought but constant Fire.
> [. . .]
> Pleasures abroad, the sport of Nature yeilds [*sic*]
> Her living Fountains, and her smiling Fields. (*Essays*, 215)

Cowley's changes to *Epigrams* 2.53 are more elaborate. In the original, the addressee, Maximus, is outed as a liar: "Vis fieri liber? mentiris, Maxime, non vis: / sed fieri si vis, hac ratione potes" ("You want to become a free man? You lie, Maximus; you don't want. But if you do, this is how you can") (*Epigrams*, 1:164–65). Other seventeenth-century translators of Martial—Thomas May, Robert Fletcher, Henry Killigrew—retain the focus on falsehood.[47] By contrast, Cowley's version reads: "Would you be Free? 'Tis your chief wish, you say, / Come on; I'le shew thee, Friend, the certain way" (*Essays*, 123). Even if "you say" carries residual skepticism, Cowley downplays the possibility of anyone falsely wishing for retirement. He alters the ending as well. Martial's "haec tibi si vis est, si mentis tanta potestas, liberior Partho vivere rege potes" ("If you have strength and willpower enough for that [i.e., a small house with a low ceiling], you can live more free than the king of Parthia") becomes "If in thy Mind such power and greatness be, / The *Persian* King's a Slave compar'd with Thee" (*Epigrams*, 1:164–65, *Essays*, 123). For Martial, the king was free and the retiree freer; for Cowley's poet persona, quick to overvalue retreat, freedom resides in retirement alone. Moreover, if the shift from "Parthian" to "Persian" is more than misremembering, then Cowley sidelines Martial's emphasis on freedom (as the "kings of kings," the Parthians were freer than other kings) to point instead the contrast between retreat and luxury (the Persians are sensualists in the Latin tradition). Cowley's idealism is obvious.

Removing inconvenient material from an earnest poem (like Virgil's *Georgics*) is one thing; removing irony from poems (like Martial's) ironizing the poet's overzealous pursuit of retirement is something else. Such efforts themselves become evidence of Cowley's own zeal, of his trying too hard, too frantically, to get Martial on message. Cowley's handling of *Epigrams* 10.47 offers an example. The original opens like this: "Vitam quae faciant beatoriem, / iucundissime Martialis, haec sunt" ("Most delightful Martialis, the elements of a happy life are as follows") (*Epigrams*, 2:358–59). Then Martial rattles off the necessary components:

> money not worked for but inherited; land not unproductive; a
> fire all the year round; lawsuits never, a gown rarely worn, a mind
> at peace; a gentleman's strength, a healthy body; guilelessness not
> naïve, friends of like degree, easy company, a table without frills;
> a night not drunken but free of cares; a marriage bed not austere
> and yet modest; sleep to make the dark hours short; wish to be
> what you are, wish nothing better; don't fear your last day, nor yet
> pray for it. (*Epigrams*, 2:359–61)[48]

Before attending to the list, let's consider Cowley's version of the opener:

> SINCE, dearest Friend, 'tis your desire to see
> A true Receipt of Happiness from Me;
> These are the chief Ingredients . . . (*Essays*, 221)

The original does not indicate the addressee's preference; it leaves open Martial's possible lack of interest (and why would the historical Martialis, already retired, be interested?). By contrast, Cowley's speaker insists on Martial's desire to know his recipe for happiness, the speaker coming off (at least for those recalling the noncommittal original) as presupposing this desire and giving unsolicited advice. Cowley's speaker is similarly officious elsewhere, too. Where the original 1.55 begins, "Vota tui breviter si vis cognoscere Marci . . . / hoc petit" ("If you wish to know in brief your friend Marcus's dearest wish, this is what he wants"), for example, Cowley drops the conditional and thus the speaker's sensitivity to his addressee's wishes: "Well then, Sir, you shall know how far extend / The Prayers and Hopes of your Poetick Friend" (*Epigrams*, 1:80–81, *Essays*, 122). Cowley's speaker is going to tell you whether you asked or not. Cowley's opener to 2.53—"Come on; I'le shew thee, Friend, the certain way" (*Essays*, 123)— also casts the speaker as too fixated on his subject to attend to his addressee:

Maximus's truthfulness needn't be questioned because the speaker can't imagine Maximus thinks differently from himself. By stressing the 10.47 addressee's desire to hear the "receipt," Cowley thus heightens the self-absorption already apparent in his versions of 1.55 and 2.53. Informed readers comparing Cowley's 1.55, 2.53, and 10.47 to Martial's originals would probably notice this egotism. As with so many of the poets quoted or translated in *Essays*, Martial comes to sound a lot like Cowley's own persona, though the assimilation in perspective is not to Cowley's advantage. The speaker's disregard for his audience implies Cowley's disregard for his own readers, suggesting, in turn, that *Essays*, at times, like Cowley's version of 10.47, is the monologue of a fanatic or enthusiast.

The self-subversion continues in the "true Receipt" portion of Cowley's 10.47. None of the contemporary translators—Fletcher, Thomas Randolph, Richard Fanshawe—used anything like Cowley's "receipt," a word apparently wrong-footing some readers.[49] Hurd takes issue in 1772: "This unlucky notion of—a receipt—has much debased the following imitation. But the author, I supposed, felt his inability to express, in our language, the concise elegance of the original and therefore hoped to supply this defect by what the courtesy of his time was ready to accept under the name, of wit and humor" (273n). Blaming such a usage on the usual suspect, "metaphysical wit," Hurd apparently feels that "receipt" piggybacks on the original's irony and further cheapens the retirement ideal. In his original 10.47, as in his original 2.53, Martial uses itemization to deflate his pretensions: the poem's checklist quality makes retirement seem more demanding yet also more banal than Cowley's wishful thinking allows. Cowley further dissipates the mystique of retirement by likening it to something cooked up, like a pie, by rote or by recipe. Moreover, where the *arguta brevitas* of Martial's original thirteen lines made his remarks look so offhand, so perfunctory, as to seem facetious, Cowley's 10.47, as happens with some of his other Martial translations as well, expands, having thirty-one lines.[50] For those familiar with the original, Cowley's longer 10.47 seems less flippant only because it now feels a little bloated, the speaker's urging of retirement coming off in turn as self-indulgent or self-important. One might even say that Cowley's changes to these epigrams enact in translation the same excess and self-absorption in the retirement fantasy that the epigrams satirically depict. If Martial ironizes his own fantasies, Cowley pokes fun at himself in his heavy-handed efforts to de-ironize Martial.

By shifting the classical framework for understanding *Essays* from Horace to Martial, I have aimed in this chapter to argue for the overlooked irony and humor in Cowley's reflections on his own schemes of retirement. I'm not saying that all, or even most, of *Essays* is tongue-in-cheek. But there is enough self-subverting humor, or what looks to be self-subverting humor, that we should question the old view of the *Essays* as solemn and self-righteous. Irony lies in the eye of the beholder, and perhaps none of what I've pointed out as ironic or humorous in *Essays* will be obvious enough to convince some that Cowley mocks his own over-enthusiastic embrace of the retirement fantasy. But I would argue that we both can and should see Cowley as laughing at himself, and not only because doing so counters the modern assumption that past writers were as earnestly committed to their own ideas as scholars are to various causes today. Admitting that Cowley may subvert his own enthusiasm also helps us see retirement in potentially new ways.

In ridiculing his own investment in classical ideals, Cowley also questions the literalism of writing on retirement. The notion of retirement as an actual place, and of virtue and happiness as depending on a literal abandoning of the court and city, suffuses classical poetry, as it does the many eighteenth-century poems inspired by *Essays*. The writers of such poems, especially the working-class poets like Tatersal, Bancks, and Hands, would have likely missed much of the irony, given that seeing it requires, above all, minute knowledge of Cowley's sources, especially of the Latin he translates, available to Cowley's earliest, more highly educated readers. And what Cowley ridicules in *Essays* is, most basically, the idea that these poets tend to endorse: that refusing or resisting certain economic and social values associated with towns and courts is best achieved by literally leaving towns and courts. As Cowley surely realized, what makes his commitment to retirement so extreme is this literalism; otherwise, he would never have ended up in Chertsey, which was more a market town than an isolated retreat. He hints at this in "The Dangers of an Honest Man in Much Company": "Happy are they . . . who have not onely quitted the Metropolis, but can abstain from ever seeing the next Market Town"

(*Essays*, 204). His phrasing recalls the clichéd opening of many a retirement panegyric, including Cowley's own "The Garden"—"Happy art Thou . . . / In Books and Gardens thou hast [been] plac'd" (*Essays*, 170). This similarity serves only to point out the difference in perspective. Cowley qualifies the traditional retirement fantasy with his recognition after 1665 that leaving the metropolis does not insulate one from politics and business. Literalists ignore that one cannot fully escape thoughts of and desires for political and social involvement. Worldly cares showed up at suburban Barn Elms, as they did later in the "market town" of Chertsey, as they did for Martial in his far remoter retreat at Bilbilis. No doubt these cares and pressures would have also appeared a third time if Cowley had lived long enough to relocate to an even more isolated place, perhaps even to America, where he had once contemplated retiring. At bottom, Cowley asks: why take classical poetry at its word? Why keep thinking of retirement as a real, physical place?

The alternative to the literalist view, as Cowley implies, is to fantasize about retirement—to talk, write, and read about it—amidst political and economic activity. This is what Cowley did before Barn Elms, and this is what Martial did (mockingly) before Bilbilis. Note the telling shift in the above passage from literal removal ("quit . . . the Metropolis") to moral or intellectual reorientation ("abstain from . . . the Market Town"). Keeping one's mind from being wholly absorbed by political and economic concerns is the goal of retirement, and this requires mental abstention, a reorienting of one's attention and aspirations. Leaving London was the easy part. That Cowley supplemented his move to Chertsey with writing about retirement in *Essays* indicates physical retirement wasn't enough, and that preserving one's independence amid social and economic concerns lay in fact with finding something to wish for beyond them. Cowley's inviting readers to laugh at some of his own statements in *Essays* serves much the same goal: to expose the untruth of most writing about retirement, something Cowley himself grasped too late. This is not to say that writing about retirement from an urban perch isn't good. To the contrary, Cowley sets up readers to see that dreaming about retirement, and enumerating its virtues in writing, are valuable and are what retirement truly involves. As with social media today, where many exaggerated posts and tweets less reflect sincere beliefs than a poster's commitment to a cause or identity, so the fictions of retirement also confirm their authors' resistance to certain trends or forces more so than any real beliefs or intentions. Attention and desire are reoriented from worldly things in healthful ways in simply wishing for retirement. Those most absorbed in politics, as Cowley was before 1660, or those with the least agency to retire, like the working-class poets mentioned previously, are most likely to talk up retirement. Seen this way, perhaps the eighteenth-century laboring poets without Latin I've already mentioned didn't, in fact, miss Cowley's irony after all; rather, in earnestly urging retreats they themselves could not have, they grasped exactly the point of the irony in the *Essays*. Of course, a privileged few did realize the retirement dream and, like folks today who act on fanciful (as well as extreme and conspiratorial) internet posts, perhaps not all rued the consequences of doing so. But I do think many in the long eighteenth century did not believe for a minute that retirement, if possible, would live up to the written fantasies about it. Cowley uses his own experience at Chertsey to remind us of this.

That Cowley knew quite well that his own retirement didn't live up to his own fantasies becomes apparent from what we know of his activities while writing *Essays*. Surviving letters show Cowley, as Caroline Spearing indicates, continuing to inquire, from retirement, about national events; he asks, for example, if Clifford has heard the outcome of a battle in the Second Anglo-Dutch War in June 1666.[51] Cowley was also much in London. When he couldn't find a book, he wrote to Evelyn asking if he could borrow Evelyn's copy, directing him to "send it to my brothers hous [sic] . . . in King's Yard," presumably the Royal Naval Dockyard at Deptford.[52] Unless his brother Thomas was soon planning to head up to Chertsey, Cowley apparently visited London frequently enough that it was more convenient to pick up the book himself than to have it delivered. And when not in London, Cowley invited others to join him. In 1663, Cowley invites Clifford, alone or with Thomas Paulden and Thomas Sprat, to visit Barn Elms.[53] Fantasies of retreat often included socializing with a select few, but Cowley seems a little desperate to trade the quiet contemplation valorized in *Essays* for socializing. In a letter of December 1666, Cowley writes to Clifford: "If you will come hither, here I will stay, if not, I have a mind to go to London, . . . for I am little affraid of yᵉ Country impertinencies here, of being Invited, & forced to invite others."[54] Besides again plotting to leave London, Cowley presents the metropolis as sheltering him from social "impertinencies." In his first essay, "Of Liberty," Cowley touts the countryside as an escape from the rounds of visits associated with courtly patron-client systems, with "impertinencies" appearing four times in reference to courtly visitors (*Essays*, 108–24). But, as this letter shows, Cowley knew that such visits were not at all specific to court.

Do these examples of Cowley visiting London and compromising on his retirement ideals mean he was a hypocrite or liar? Yes, but only if we persist in reading *Essays*, as many critics following Sprat have, as a sincere statement of principles. If we instead grant the occasional humor and self-irony in *Essays*, we realize that Cowley was writing about retirement in pompous ways to compensate for his not living up to his own idealizations of both retirement and of the retired poet persona he had constructed for himself. Cowley's frequenting London after 1660 shows that much of what he says in *Essays* he probably didn't mean, at least some of the time, and that there was nothing wrong with this. Celebrating retreat was always a space for saying what you didn't fully believe or act upon. Cowley recognized this and could laugh at himself for it, something that made him different from so many later writers on retirement. This is what I should have said about Cowley during that interview long ago. Thank you, Mark, for giving me the opportunity to say it here.

CHAPTER EIGHT

Abraham Cowley's *Six Books of Plants* and the Diversification of Textual Authority

Katarzyna Lecky

A s his fellow founding members of the Royal Society turned their attention to systemizing and classifying botanical knowledge as a scientific field, Abraham Cowley instead valorized the enjoyment of flora in a descriptive poem, *Plantarum Libri duo* in 1662. Another version, edited by Thomas Sprat, *Plantarum Libri Sex* was published posthumously as part of *Poema Latina* in 1668. In 1689, *The Second and Third Parts of the Works of Mr Abraham Cowley* appeared, the third part containing his *Six Books of Plants*, translated from the Latin into English by some of the Restoration's most preeminent poets.[1] In the first lines of book 1, the narrator promises to "sing" of "Life's lowest, but far greatest Sphere," the vegetable world:

> For, with delight
> Each gentle Plant me kindly does invite.
> My self to slavish Method I'll not tye,
> But, like the Bee, where-e'er I please, will flie;
> Where I the glorious hopes of Honey see,
> Or the free Wing of fancy carries me.[2]

At the outset of a work that translates the burgeoning science of botany into a literary language, the poet offers a mode of understanding nature that elevates delight over edification, imagination over reason, and earthiness over transcendence.[3] Taking inspiration from Horace, in which the classical author described himself as a wandering bee creating verses out of little flowers, Cowley refashions the inductive Baconian method of botanical knowledge embraced by the Royal Society into an experiential poetics of vegetable joy.[4]

This chapter shows how the poesis of the English *Six Books* became an enduring model of plant knowledge for expanding audiences in the century following the society's institutionalization of botany as a life science. The 1689 translation of the *Plantarum* into the *Six Books of Plants*, which made Cowley's work accessible to those without Latin, offered ordinary readers a mode of understanding flora that valued aesthetic appreciation over clinical assessment, and enjoyment over edification.

Although his approach has much in common with the printed herbals (manuals cataloging the medicinal benefits of plants) popular in Europe, he diverges from his largely pragmatic predecessors by combining the experimental expertise of the naturalist (which Cowley gained from his study of practical herbalism) with the transformative spirit of Ovidian poetics.[5] The result is a text that continued to be printed in new editions and reissued over the course of the eighteenth century, even as the publication of herbals generally fell out of fashion. This chapter focuses on the Englished *Plantarum*'s paratextual elements, such as epistles to readers and dedicatory verses framing how to read both the poet and his work, to ask why Cowley's poem captured the imagination of broad and diverse publics even as poetic latinity yielded to "scientific" prose. In her excellent study of the original Latin text, Caroline Spearing urges that the *Plantarum* "be read at least in part as a political meditation, . . . a Royalist production of the late Interregnum."[6] I argue that Cowley's work, at least in its 1689 translation, which drops many of the scientific footnotes in the Latin original, offers an alternate mode of textual authority outside of the literary, political, and scientific writings shaped by post-Restoration culture. Cowley opens a creative space at a remove from this culture, a refuge for those alienated by the increasing consolidation and institutionalization of knowledge systems. His book creates not an exile of those marginal to the late seventeenth-century intellectual culture, but rather a poetic mode that disrupts all systemic understanding with its delight in a botanical world characterized by entanglements and growth—a world in which usefulness succumbs to the inutile pleasure of experiencing the disordered, weedy matter of common English nature.

Cowley's career gave him an expansive view of those places where intellectual capital and sovereign control came together, while forcing him to take paths to alternative authorial landscapes. A precocious writer who published his first book of poetry at the age of fifteen, he was frequently lauded by his contemporaries as one of the greatest authors of the seventeenth century. His career straddled the Civil Wars and the Interregnum, bringing him into the circle of some of the most powerful individuals steering the tumultuous course of the nation as it moved from monarchy, to commonwealth, back to monarchy. Nonetheless, Cowley's aspirations ultimately ended in disappointment rather than preferment after he returned to England from Paris along with the exiled English monarchy and its court. Rather than being rewarded for his service to the Stuarts, including his role as a royal spy, for which he was imprisoned, Cowley was passed over in the flurry of pensions and sinecures granted by the newly installed Charles II, inducing him to retire, first to Barn Elms, then to Chertsey, where he remained until his death (possibly by catching a chill while helping his laborers with the harvest) in 1667. His exclusion from the Restoration court was offset by his association with the naturalists who would found the Royal Society in 1660, and who made him one of its original members (although he never paid dues).[7] Royal recognition of his poetic efforts never arrived; nor did it arrive posthumously, since Charles appointed Dryden as England's first official poet laureate within a year of Cowley's death.

Thomas Sprat, Cowley's first biographer as well as the first historian of the Royal Society, explains how the poet embraced the experimental philosophy of herbalism practiced by seventeenth-century naturalists such as John Gerard, John Parkinson, William Coles, and other seminal figures of pre-Linnaean botany.[8] Sprat explains that this new profession was a diversion:

> The occasion of his chusing the subject of his Six Books of Plants, was this; when he returned into *England*, he was advised to dissemble the main intention of his coming over, under the

disguise of applying himself to some settled Profession. And that of Physic was thought most proper. ("Account," sig. c2r–v)

Sprat continues with a description of Cowley's course of study: "Having furnish'd himself with Books of that Nature, he retir'd into a fruitful part of *Kent*, where every Field and Wood might shew him the real Figures of those Plants of which he read" (sig. c2v). The poet followed the Baconian method of the seventeenth-century naturalist virtuoso, but veered away from the expected profession that should have followed it: "He speedily Master'd that part of the Art of Medicine. But then, . . . instead of employing his Skill for practice and profit, he presently digested it into that form which we behold" (sig. c2v). Cowley, who graduated from Oxford with a degree in medicine, applied experimental practice to his verse in ways that made Baconian induction the province of the poet rather than of the medicinal herbalist; instead of using botanical knowledge to effect physical cures for the reading public, Cowley deployed poetry. Robert Hinman claims that Cowley adopted Bacon's division of "learning into history, poetry, and philosophy," and translated it into a distinct field of empirical and materialist poetics: "Since good poetry ought to be concrete, any impulse toward concern with things rather than abstractions was a service to poetry."[9] Cowley used the methods and materials of the naturalist to create a form of cultural health dependent on access to a vegetable landscape whose wild entanglements are beautified by a versifier rather than dissected by a physician.

The incongruities and disappointments marking Cowley's career emerge in the *Plantarum* in his fascination with the errant, multifaceted, and eccentric field of plant study. His 1662 Latin preface was included in the English translation of 1689; in it, Cowley declares he included footnotes citing herbals to expand the sphere of botanical literati to a broader audience:

I have added short Notes, not for ostentation of Learning (whereof there is no occasion here offered; for what is more easie, than to turn over one or two Herbalists?) but because that beside Physicians (whom I pretend not to instruct, but divert) there are few so well vers'd in the History of Plants, as to be acquainted with the

Names of them all. It is a part of Philosophy that lies out of the common Road of Learning; to such persons I was to supply the place of a Lexicon. (sig. b1v)

This passage shows the poet thinking about his verse herbal as a "place" of knowledge-making, which he builds by appropriating a discourse normally deployed to "instruct" the cognoscenti further. Cowley "divert[s]" this field of knowledge from professional expertise to reorient plants instead as "easie" or accessible forms of literary authority that are exploratory and keyed to appreciation rather than practicality. This aesthetic combines the utility of medicinal flora with an Ovidian structure wherein the agency of plants is superior to the agency of people. While gardener, poet, or virtuoso can attempt to control the plants, it is the plants themselves who express joy, suffering, and self-worth by acknowledging their experience as well as their rootedness in a literary history characterized by interspecies entanglements. At once speaking selves and exemplary species, these metamorphic, metonymic vegetable beings form dynamic communities structured by debate, divergence, and dissent, communities that would include the humblest weed as well as the noblest tree.

Cowley's lexicon invites those outside of the governmental, literary, and scientific worlds into a space "that lies out of the common Road of Learning" about plants. As it turns away from a straightforward outlook and interpretation, the *Plantarum* diversifies; as it diverges from organizing institutions and intellectual systems, it randomizes. It resists the social consolidation of knowledge by imagining a distinctively poetic authority able to refashion its exclusion into a tapestry woven out of organic plant and human matter. The *Plantarum* crafts this authority at the intersections of artistic and scientific descriptions of nature, even as the two modes start to drift apart in the late seventeenth century, anticipating the modern schisms dividing scientific study from artistic representation. Victoria Moul argues,

This is a work intended to be memorable for scientific as well as literary reasons, and it is also a thorough demonstration of the seventeenth-century conviction of the unity of knowledge: poetic and scientific authority complement one another, and belong together. ("Transformation," 223)

If this were indeed the poet's intention, then it diverged significantly from the Royal Society's simultaneous drive to establish discursive prose as the vehicle of naturalist knowledge, and the lexical correlative to the charts, engravings, and tables that Robert Hooke (the author of the 1665 *Micrographia*, the book that established the study of microscopy) lauded as offering a "plaine simple, cleer and uncompounded Representation of the Object to the sense."[10] In a nation struggling to unify in the immediate aftermath of civil strife and intestine violence, Cowley's virtuosity as both a poet and a naturalist allows him to germinate a vegetable poetics that unifies disparity of thought by including voices tangential to official structures of power in producing knowledge.

Cowley's support of writers peripheral to the classically masculine canon is exemplified in his influential praise of his poetic contemporary Katherine Philips.[11] In the *Plantarum*, the voices that dominate Cowley's syncretic site of poetic authority are often feminine: the speaking plants reflect on their simultaneous centrality to (as objects) and exclusion from (as agents) botanical knowledge generated by medical practitioners, Royal Society naturalists, and classical writers alike. The poet inverts this social hierarchy; for instance, Spearing notes that at the beginning of the second book, "Cowley dismisses his male audience: he is celebrating the Roman rite of the Bona Dea, from which men were rigorously excluded" (46). Victoria Moul states, "These female speaking plants are both very Ovidian (female subjects of metamorphosis and the victims of sexual violence) and also very un-Ovidian in their eloquence, their scientific knowledge (remember, these ideas about menstruation are presented as a learned debate in an entirely female company), and their medicinal utility" ("Transformation," 232). Moul argues that Cowley's verse herbal appropriates while undercutting the basic constitution of Ovidian poetics:

> The female plants not only survive their transformations with their voices intact, but they wield and express the power to prevent exactly the sorts of calamities from which they have suffered: seduction or rape, various difficulties of gestation and birth, and even pregnancy itself. ("Transformation," 234)

These female plants, excluded from the province of the masculine intellectual tradition, manage to heal themselves. Furthermore, the *Plantarum's* simples speak with a composite voice that identifies with the varietal, the species, or the family rather than with the individual, ensuring that care of the self cannot be separated from care for the silenced and diminished—as Elaine Miller observes, it "is difficult if not impossible . . . to identify a plant as an individual: where does it begin and where does it end? What part of it is 'it,' and what part its offspring?"[12] Cowley's plant world explicitly includes women, but it can also reach beyond gender in fashioning a poetic authority radically outside of the male-dictated, codified social boundaries of authority.

The purpose behind this poetic voice begins to emerge in Cowley's defense of poetry in his preface. The poet explains that his botanical verses "are offer'd as small pills made up of sundry herbs," and insists that during the process of this medicine-making, he has not attempted to impose any authorial order to his compositions, but has instead taken them "as they came to Hand" (sig. b1r–v). The plants themselves embody a form of vitalism that places human and nonhuman creative acts into symbiosis, which the text then dramatizes in the series of personified flowers who recount their happy Ovidian metamorphoses from hunted humanity into powerful flora filled with virtues. Cowley also emphasizes the sacred nature of plants by challenging perceptions of herbalism as a lowly craft. He imagines detractors of the *Plantarum* saying, "You are fastn'd to the ground with your Herbs, and cannot soar as formerly to the Clouds," and responds with an encomium to herbs as "wonderful Works of Providence, not to be far distant from a sacred Poem. Nothing can be found more admirable in Nature than the Virtues of several Plants" (sig. b2v). Cowley defines his herbal as a material artifact suffused with the soul of vegetable nature, while establishing, especially in the first two books on herbs, an ethics of humility that undercuts authority by finding it distributed among the low-growing and the overlooked.

The weedy orientation of Cowley's work, which embraces the native agency of plants more than the cultivating prowess of the poet, mirrors the methodology of the men who would soon define the emerging field of botany in England. Douglas Chambers states, "By the middle of the 1650s,

... the future founders of the Royal Society were beginning to form the nucleus of what later became the Georgicall Committee within the society, a committee concerned with reforms in agriculture and horticulture."[13] In their publications in the early 1660s, John Beale, John Evelyn, Samuel Hartlib, and other members of the Georgicall Committee created a methodology for improving the nation by incorporating a workaday georgic, borrowed from Virgil.[14] Chambers addresses in particular Beale's call for a "georgic arcadia, ... Virgil translated into England, the golden age restored in a farmer's field" through its attention to not just ordinary (as opposed to elite, highly ornamented) gardens, but also unbounded, "wild" landscapes (181). The simple rusticity of this mode of cultivation was aligned with the return to a national Edenic existence: it was "an argument about how Elysium (and paradise) might be 'translated onto the landscape of England'" (184). For instance, Evelyn's *Sylva* was a product of this intellectual foment: "Published in 1664, it both reflected the Virgilian and empirical debates that preceded it and offered a new myth of patriotic husbandry to a country seeking to heal the wounds of division" (183). Ultimately, in their writings, "It is ethics not economics that govern agriculture and horticulture: principles firmly grounded in the *Georgics*" (187). In practice, however, the studies of the horticulturalists among the Royal Society became increasingly "preoccupied with mathematical and physical questions" in ways that veered from the emphasis on practicality promoted by the Georgicall Committee (188). Consequently, Chambers notes, "The resources that might have relieved the poor by reforming the agricultural economy (the very principles still being reiterated by Beale in the 1680s) were instead squandered on vain speculation and abstract science" (188). Their ideal of a wild, weedy, perpetual nation cultivated with a light touch was well meaning, but the realities endorsed by the Royal Society publications kept botany in the abstract, the realm of the small group of virtuosi rather than of the many who would have benefited from its ground-level deployment.

In response, Cowley uses a variety of plants, developing the tools of the naturalist to generate an alternate language of inclusive botanical ethics that resists these abstractions. He ensures the solidity of his project by including copious notes referring to some of the major European printed herbals of his day, building his verse on practical botanical knowledge.[15]

The poet claims that relying on both naturalism and medicine allows him to home in on the specificities of what was since classical antiquity a privileged landscape. The 1689 English translation of "The Author's Preface" begins, "Considering the incredible Veneration which the best Poets always had for Gardens, Fields, and Woods, . . . I wondered what evil Planet was so malicious to the Breed of Plants, as to permit none of the inspired Tribe to celebrate their Beauty and admirable Virtues" (sig. b1r). The author challenges the poetic tendency to dwell on the vague generalities of the natural environment by instead stressing the importance of exploring the specific flora that cover it and give it life. Rather than being regarded as simply a backdrop, plants should be viewed as significant, each adding its unique qualities to the "Gardens, Fields, and Woods" that are the classical sources of much poetic production. This "copious Field of Matter," Cowley assures, "would yield" the willing writer "a plentiful return of Fruit," since "each particular, besides its pleasant History (the extent whereof every body, or to speak more truly, no body, can sufficiently understand) . . . contains the whole Fabrick of humane Frame, and a compleat Body of Physick" (sig. b1r). The poet defines plants as the basis for three different courses of study: the first is naturalism, the third medicine, and—sandwiched between the two—poetry, which connects the origins and the ends of these plants emphasizing how vegetable life maps "the whole Fabrick of humane Frame." Poetry about vegetable matter is simultaneously a philosophy about the matter of the human, which draws on, yet escapes, both historical and practical discourses about either plants or people.

Cowley distinguishes between his botanical method and the methods of the naturalist and the physician: "Because Poets are sometimes allowed to make Fictions, and some have too excessively abused that Liberty, Trust is so wholly denied to us. . . . I was therefore willing to cite proper Witnesses, that is, such as writ in loose and free Prose, which compared with Verse, bears the Authority of an Oath" (sig. b1v). By basing his work on herbalists, Cowley offers a defense against accusations that his verse herbal is untrustworthy—because it's poetry: as Joanna Picciotto states, "He wants to adapt poetry to the ends of magnifying truth" (388). This stance, contrasted with the experimental manipulations of Royal Society naturalists, frames Cowley's text as a form of experiential knowledge production guided by the vegetable world rather than by human desires. Cowley also separates his labor from that of the physician who classifies various plants according to their medicinal benefits. Since "there being none amongst them which contain'd not plenty of Juice, if it were drawn out according to Art," they all equally (if diversely) serve his artistic project: "The Method which I judged most genuine and proper for this Work, was not to press out their Liquor crude in a simple enumeration, but as it were in a Lymbeck, by the gentle heat of Poetry, to distil and extract their Spirits" (sig. b1v). Finally, Cowley refuses "to put them together which had affinity in Nature, that might create a disgust for want of Variety"; instead, he has "connected those of the most different Qualities, that their contrary Colours, being mixt, might the better set off each other" (sig. b1r). The poet does not seek either medical benefit or natural order from the vegetable world; rather, plants are material to inspire him, as occasions inspire a poet, or nature inspires a landscape painter.[16] Cowley sees poetry as an answer to the various types of human machinations threatening a true understanding of plants; it is a discourse with the potential for working through an everyday politics that decenters the anthropomorphic as it reveals deeper truths of what constitutes life.

Although Cowley demonstrates himself to be well versed in the standard, scientific naturalist strains of plant work, he defines his own labor as distinct. He separates his poetry from both medical and academic discourses by avoiding those ways of talking about plants in verse and placing them into notes, while differentiating his writing as undertaken "for the sake of the very Plants themselves" (sig. b1r). Claire Preston has argued that seventeenth-century scientific discourse depended on rhetorical devices we now associate with the literary: "The humanist curriculum, with its huge emphasis on the rhetorical as the mother art, preconditioned and shaped the conduct of early modern science."[17] Here, the author frees poetry from its entanglements with the pragmatic or medicinal as well as from what is now thought of as scientific language. Cowley grants scientific language only a tangential place in his work, well outside the bounds of his own territory of literary expertise. Cowley departs from the taxonomies of the naturalist and the practicalities of the physician, thereby placing plant life outside of human systems of organization.

Cowley, accordingly, begins his poem of speaking plants by dividing uncultivated from cultivated plants: he promises to "sing" of

> Such as in Deserts live, whom, unconfin'd,
> None but the simple Laws of Nature bind;
> And those, who growing tame by human care,
> The well-bred Citizens of Gardens are. (1)

In his distinction, the poet showcases the human actions separating the wild from the sown; as Mauro Ambrosoli observes, "There is no botanical difference between cultivated species and weeds. It is man who . . . labels plants as suitable for food or ornament or merely as weeds."[18] At the outset of his epic poem, the apian narrator stakes out his chosen territory in the jumble of wild landscapes:

> My self to slavish Method I'll not tye,
> But, like the Bee, where-e'r I please, will flie;
> Where I the glorious hopes of Honey see,
> Or the free Wing of Fancy carries me.
> Here no fine Garden-Emblems shall reside,
> In well-made Beds to prostitute their Pride:
> But we right Nature, who her Gifts bestows,
> Unlimited (nor the vast Treasure knows)
> And various plenty of the pathless Woods
> Will follow. (1–2)

The poet here aligns himself with the native and untended, dismissing the "Citizens of Gardens" in the same way he rejects the life of human society in his *Essays*.[19] It is not so much a vision of physical withdrawal from the sites of human power as it is an embrace of an "other" world, one not guided by human interventions into nature, but rather teeming with unconstrained vegetable life. Here, pleasure is linked to the unchecked freedom of plant growth, with the human narrator illuminating this limitless world of flora. Cowley establishes the organicity of his form of literary authority, while foregrounding its receptive, almost passive orientation to the world from which it draws its materials.

Cowley's writerly disposition challenges authorial modes that link textual production to human agency over nature; moreover, his rejection of garden culture opposes the politics of the experimental gardens that sprang up in the seventeenth century.[20] For instance, from the Civil Wars through the Restoration, the Oxford Botanic Garden, established in 1621 and the setting for book 2 of the *Plantarum*, was "a contested space of both natural and political order during a crisis of monarchy and the creation of new political structures."[21] Anna Svensson notes that during the same years when Cowley's original Latin text was published, an influx of monarchical funding beginning in 1660 ensured that "the garden became a Royalist monument retrospectively, after the Civil War and the recurring challenges to the throne in the late seventeenth century" (163). Control over this garden and others like it attests to the primacy of human governance. Charles II's work to retain power over the nation through its experimental gardens was mirrored by the labors of seventeenth-century naturalists who made sustained efforts not only to understand the material world but also to control it: for instance, the architecture of the Oxford Botanic Garden "not only regulated plants, but limited and regulated access for the public. The imposing walls and gate, along with yew hedges around the quadrants, formed several levels of defenses to protect the plants from being stolen or damaged by a careless boot, all under the careful eye of the Keeper" (Svensson, 166–67). Improvement and cultivation joined experimentation as dominant principles of the early Royal Society, whose acolytes used sites of botanical experimentation to carve out their territory of expertise.[22]

In response, Cowley defined his craft as the ability to delight in a vegetable world that lies beyond human control, and to digest its sweetness for the printed page. In fact, his epistle to the reader ends with his explanation that, although he had sworn off poetry, he wrote this text because "Fate drags me on against my Will, in vain, . . . / What can naked I, 'gainst armed Nature do?" (sig. b3r). The vegetable world exerts its force against the poet stripped bare of the power to resist. In Cowley's original, technical, tightly controlled, and far from spontaneous Latin, this claim seems ironic. But the irony is muted in the 1689 English version. When linked with Cowley's initial description of his poetic composition as the result of a process of plants coming indifferently into his purview, these claims about the futility of resistance resonate with Andrew Marvell's 1681 "The Garden," a slightly later poem, depicting a narrator immersed in and eventually overcome by a vegetable world that is vibrantly, energetically agential. Of course, this sense of nature's power is not new to the Restoration: Peggy McCracken finds in the twelfth-century *Roman d'Alexander* a challenge to the assumed powers of kingly virtues. As the titular monarch spends time in a forest filled with "flower maidens" who are half human and half vegetal, "Alexander encounters a place that he cannot win through force, since it does not resist him; he cannot rule through generosity, since he can give the women nothing that they do not already have; and he cannot demand tribute, since the maidens deny him nothing."[23] In this romance, vegetable life resists human domination not in its actions but in its fullness. Cowley's post-metamorphosed Ovidian flowers display the same sense of fulfillment in their consistent claims that they are happy in a way they never could be when they were human. Cowley's political deployment of the humanist commonplace (culled from Horace and promoted by texts such as Sidney's *Defence of Poesy*) that poetry should instruct and delight reverses the typical emphasis of edification over enjoyment. The shift to delight is also the shift from knowing nature through science to knowing nature through art instead.

In separating itself from scientific discourse, Cowley's verse herbal also distanced itself from the natural philosophical tradition underpinning it, which took its structure from classical and medieval notions of a cosmos connected to its divine creator in a hierarchy known as the Great Chain of Being. By placing all living things on this scale, naturalists followed Scholastics in situating humanity within nature rather than outside it:

> Everything, from the classification of the plant world according to a system of more or less "noble" plants to ideas about the growth of plants and their ability to reach upwards, reveals the extent to which late medieval and early Renaissance botanists, agronomists, and dietitians did not conceive of a strict separation between the natural world and the social world of man.[24]

The work of John Wilkins and early Royal Society members on how to conceptualize species began to differentiate ancient from modern notions of this interconnectedness by challenging venerable perceptions of the organicity of a divinely engineered cosmology, thus causing a "tension between sharp classification and gradual variation from one form to another in the Great Chain" that marked the movement to "the early stages of natural species realism, based on typological definitions, [from] species nominalism, based on the unreality of any divisions between them."[25] Nonetheless, in practice, the emerging life sciences retained hierarchical taxonomizing that separated lowly from elite forms of both human and nonhuman life. For instance, early adherents to the improver movement advocated for enclosures to counteract "despotic monarchs," since "through enclosure, a landowning class could arise with the means to defend the nation's liberty," while "the brightest lights of the society, including Boyle and Newton, turned attention to the problem of vegetative growth."[26] Despite the earthy commonwealth ideals driving midcentury naturalism, the realities of territorialization played out from the top down.

The difference between this scientific episteme and Cowley's poetic practice lies in the *Plantarum*'s rejection of the degraded nature of lowly plants. Jettisoning the implicit or covert assumptions of anthropocentrism, whereby low-growing weeds and vines were suspect and even dangerous, the poem embraces the lowly plants populating vegetable landscapes. Cowley also claims to reject elevated modes of versification: he warns his readers "not therefore to expect . . . the Majesty of an Heroick Style (which I never found any Plant to speak in) for, I propose not here to fly, but only to make some Walks in my Garden, partly for Health's sake, and partly for Recreation" (sig. b3r). Henri Lefebvre's theory of the scientific process helps explain the importance of Cowley's poetic recalibration of the botanical lexicon of seventeenth-century naturalism, as the poet shifts the register of not just the language itself but also the patterns of thought underlying it. Lefebvre argues that reconceptualizing the practice of science can also transform the spatial politics of the status quo:

> Conceptual thought explores ways, ventures on paths. It can precede practice, but cannot separate itself from it. Practice alone, freed from political obsession and released from state pressure, . . . can effectively realize what promises to be the simultaneous

use of concept and imagination (utopia). Theory opens the road, clears a new way; practice takes it, it produces the route and the space.[27]

Cowley appropriates the language of botany to put into praxis his form of an imagined community of nonhuman agents freed from inequitable social structures. In this way, his plant-based cosmology embodies the utopian promise of a vegetable world separate from the history of human injustices. Jeffrey Nealon notes that when vegetable existence becomes visible, it confronts its animal or human "other" with "the 'law' of plant-nature, . . . a kind of undifferentiated and uncontrolled growth that is finally anathema to the progress of spirit or law—and not because nature or the plant . . . is merely inert, but because they're dangerous."[28] This danger, Nealon continues, occurs because

> plant desire merely grows without telos. . . . In Aristotle, the vege-table *psukhe* or soul deploys a single power, the ability to grow. But that power is without entelechy, as plants have no ideal form toward which they grow—they just grow uncontrollably until they grow no more. (125)

This growth challenges human efforts to control nature and reveals the purposelessness at the heart of generation and destruction. Relinquishing control to nature births a new mode of worlding divorced from power struggles and violent conflicts.

Anna Tsing captures the broad social import, in Cowley's *poesis*, of a deeply networked, more-than-human, political ecology:

> The question of how the varied species in a species assemblage influence each other—if at all—is never settled. . . . Assemblages don't just gather lifeways; they make them. Thinking through assemblage urges us to ask: How do gatherings sometimes become "happenings," that is, greater than the sum of their parts? If history without progress is indeterminate and multidirectional, might assemblages show us its possibilities?[29]

As Cowley's apian narrator wanders through the possibilities of producing poetry that escapes the will of its author to touch the matter of collective life, he rejoices in the contingencies driving his natural history of plants. Delight for both the poet and his readership is the consequence of this immersion into the assemblage of flora, whose Ovidianism includes human society as well as ordinary weeds: in the first four books on herbs and flowers, other metamorphosed plants, such as Narcissus, join a panoply of humble simples recognizable to virtually every English eye. The botanical species supersedes the human in Cowley's poetic rendering of the messy mechanics of belonging and difference, which exposes a futurity incessantly shaped by the contingent collisions of discrete life forms, which, due to chance, fate, or shared experience, tangle together in a divergently generative landscape.

Even as Cowley promoted a mode of authority voiced by post-metamorphosed Ovidian flora happy to have escaped a narrative of human civilization driven by rape—anticipating a poetic authority of Marvell's speaker in "The Garden"—naturalists of the late seventeenth century made plant sexuality central to the new science of botany.[30] Within a handful of years of the initial Latin publication of the *Plantarum Libri Sex* in 1668, an Italian physician and the son of an English preacher issued their own books of plants under the auspices of the Royal Society.[31] The work of Marcello Malpighi and Nehemiah Grew introduced a new way of classifying flora, which moved away from traditional categories structuring the texts of practical herbalism to center plant identification instead on sexual function.[32] Lincoln Taiz and Lee Taiz identify their studies as seminal to the scientific sexualizing of plants:

> Malpighi's early work was first published in Bologna in 1671 under the title *Anatome Plantarum Idea*. Coincidentally, the Royal Society published Nehemiah Grew's preliminary anatomical studies, *The Anatomy of Plants Begun*, in the same year. Several years later, the Royal Society published Malpighi's comprehensive treatise, *Anatome Plantarum*, in two volumes: the first in 1675 and the second in 1679. In parallel, Grew presented a series of four shorter papers to the society between 1672 and 1676. The last of Grew's papers has since been cited in virtually every book

on the history of botany because it broke with the classical tradition by presenting a new sexual theory of plants.[33]

Malpighi's *Plantarum* mirrored the title of Cowley's text, but their treatment of plants was antithetical. The poet offered a vegetable world in which the speaking subjects express the joy of living as active, virtuous members of a post-metamorphic state emerging from sexual violence to exist as an organic whole. The naturalist developed a science in which sex was an inescapable feature of flora. Spearing argues that Cowley's text engages with the deeper political issues of his time; during England's transition from the Interregnum into the Restoration, the poet's plants embody a spirit of governance characterized by its constituents' diversity and oriented toward healing. In the following years, the naturalist's flora became passive specimens whose innate virtues disappear before a taxonomy in which sex dictated identity, a belief that joined with Grew's to shape the course of the twinned fields of botany and zoology that hardened into disciplines over the subsequent century. This system of classification organizes specimens into fixed hierarchies, whereas Cowley's approach to nature generates epistemic possibilities that exceed deeply ingrained patterns of human understanding.

In an interesting twist, Cowley's posthumous editors straddle this divide between Cowley's herbal poetry and the plant work of the Royal Society by imbuing the dead poet with the full force of the vegetable life he described on the pages of the *Plantarum*. In the 1689 transformation of Cowley's Latin folio into the smaller, cheaper quarto publication of the Englished *Six Books of Plants*, Nahum Tate translates Cowley's vegetable realm—accessible to anyone willing to relinquish control over it—to one that may only be accessed by reading Cowley. In Tate's introductory letter to Charles, Duke of Somerset, and to the general reader, the translator's patriotism shines forth, when he declares, "I proposed in setting forward this Work, that every English -Man, as far as was possible, should be master of their beloved Cowley entire" (sig. a1r). The expanded audience imagined for the Latin *Plantorum* is now deployed in the service of an English identity rooted in its soil as well as in its common language. The ordinary people, the "weeds," who, during the Interregnum, William Davenant had condemned for strangling out

England's Royalist character, were now the desired audience for his book of plants.[34]

Tate's paratext draws from the georgic ideals of the Royal Society to reterritorialize plants as passive specimens for Cowley's poetic experiments. He claims that although

> the nature of the Subject has sometimes furnish'd our Author with great and beautiful occasions of Wit and Poetry, so it must be confess'd, that in the main he has but a barren Province to cultivate, where the Soil was to be enrich'd by the Improvements of Art and Fancy. (sig. a2v)

The idea of improvement has crept into the discourse, with the poet now taking on the drive of the naturalist as he sets out to accomplish in verse what his society colleagues were striving for in agriculture and husbandry. No longer the industrious bee who takes pleasure in the vibrant confusion of plants around his Surrey house, Cowley now generates the innate vegetable life force he once only gathered:

> Our Author was oblig'd to animate his silent Tribe of Plants, to inspire them with Motion and Discourse. . . . He had the Judgment to perceive, that where the Subjects he was to treat of in their own naked Nature, and, simply consider'd, could afford but slender Matter; yet that many things were greater in their Circumstances than they are in themselves. (sig. a3r)

In Cowley's epistle to the reader cited above, he expresses Nature's supremacy over human will and refers to himself as "naked"; here, the plants lose their agency, "standing mute in their Beds, divested of that imaginary Life which might beautifie the Work" (sig. a3r). The poet is informed by the creative principle formerly attributed to nature; the vegetable world is the basic matter feeding his genius. In Tate's assessment, Cowley brings the liveliness into his inert botanical subject matter virtually *ex nihilo*: he is the agent manipulating the growth of flora into an artistic rendering, rather than the haphazard gatherer celebrating the innate and varied qualities in plants. In fact, Tate claims that the virtues of Cowley's work on plants "must be wholly ascribed to the Faculty of the Artist, with a *Materiem superavit Opus*," a phrase that is a variation of the classical adage *materiem superabat opus*, lauding the artist's aptitude while dismissing the inherent value of the material (sig. a2v). In Tate's revision, the past perfect is more definitive than the imperfect, revealing Cowley's mastery of his subject matter as not partial and in process rather than fully realized. Plants are worth nothing without their human improver.

Tate also revises the feeling of delight at the heart of Cowley's poetic botanical labor by emphasizing separation rather than entanglement. The translator assures his audience that despite the "Liberty" Cowley has taken in enlivening his subject matter, he is "no where diverted from his Point, Judgment, that is to say, a just regard to his Subject is every where conspicuous, being never carried too remote by the heat of his Imagination and quickness of his Apprehension" (sig. a3r). The poet has maintained his critical distance by reassessing "diverting Fables relating to several Plants" passed down by "Antiquity," in ways that transform that information from "stale Tradition" into "the pleasure of a Story first told" (sig. a3v). Judgment divides the author from his materials (both the plants themselves, and the stories told about them), allowing Cowley to offer his readers a novel form of enjoyment based on a critical distancing, which ultimately anticipates Kant's conceptions of aesthetic pleasure.

The close of Tate's epistle to the reader links this sense of dispassionate pleasure to his mastery of nationalism in his dedication to the Duke of Somerset. After surveying the substance of the six books, he concludes, "The impartial Reader may judge if *Virgil* himself has better design'd for the Glory of *Rome* and *August*[*us*], than *Cowley* for his Country and the Monarch of his time" (sig. a4r). Here again, the pleasure lies in the judgment—the assessment of the text's ability to promote royal nationhood—rather than in the beauty of the poetry itself. The poet should be judged by his ability to bring "the utmost force of Judgment and Invention" to an "artificial close," rather than to transmit information about the plants themselves (sig. a4r). Statist art rules over common matter, and Cowley's English translators accordingly truncate his copia of Latin notes on the natural history of plants to showcase the poet rather than his topic.

This translation enjoyed a long afterlife, with printings and new editions in 1700 (folio), 1708 (octavo), 1711 (octavo), 1721 (one octavo and two duodecimo), 1795 (duodecimo), with the final edition issued in 1815. As it was reissued and reedited, it shrank radically in size and cost, while the paratextual elements ballooned with additional dedicatory letters, editors' notes, and commendatory verses. For instance, the 1708 edition printed in London, called *The Third Part of the Works of Mr. Abraham Cowley: Being his Six Books of Plants*, is a pocket-sized octavo, the popularity of which is attested to by the sixty extant copies listed in the English Short-Title Catalogue alone. Its longer title boasts that it is "*Adorn'd with Proper and Elegant Cuts*" and "*Made English by several celebrated Hands. With necessary TABLES, and divers Poems of eminent Persons, in praise of the Author.*" This extended title reveals the mixed audience for whom this edition is intended, readers who appreciate the aesthetics of a definitive or commemorative edition of a poet, but who are not necessarily elite or Latinate. This is a book for the middle classes.

Following the title-page is a letter entitled "The Booksellers to the Reader" (sig. A2r). It begins by claiming the necessity of a new edition published two decades after the original translation: "The following Poems of Mr. *Cowley* being much enquir'd after, and very scearce, (the Town hardly affording one Book, tho it hath been Seven times printed), we thought this Eighth Edition could not fail of being well receiv'd by the World" (sig. A2r). The quick slippage from London to the world reflects the globalizing of Cowley, as the spatial politics of imagining London as a "World" coincides with the spread of the author's ideas. The booksellers assert, "There is no ingenuous Reader to whom the smallest Remains of Mr. Cowley will be unwelcome. His Poems are every where the Copy of his Mind" (sig. A2v). The material book is the physical vehicle of Cowley's spirit, conveying it to a broad public for whom the national is the global. Meanwhile, the current volume ensures that readers now "have the Picture of that so deservedly eminent Man from . . . the Bud and Bloom of his Spring, [to] the Warmth of his Summer, [to] the Richness and Perfection of his Autumn" (sig. A2v). Cowley's poetry continues to garner new readers, nourished by his poetic greatness. The booksellers' posthumous memorialization of Cowley marks a narrative of existence that grafts the creeping stem with the singular specimen, in which the widespread growth of literary history and English canonicity springs from a single poetic taproot.[35]

The 1708 edition includes several dedicatory verses eulogizing Cowley that also participate in memorializing the poet by creating a landscape of versification grounded in a singular source. One anonymous poet offers an encomium resonant with botanical images to celebrate Cowley's transcendence of temporal constraints through his vegetable poetics, which allows him to achieve a paradisical existence:

> In whom the double Miracle was seen;
> Ripe in his Spring, and in his Autumn green:
> With us he left his gen'rous Fruit behind,
> The Feast of Wit and Banquet of the Mind;
> While the fair Tree transplanted to the Skies,
> In Verdure with th'Elysian Garden vies;
> The Pride of Earth before, and now of Paradise. (sig. A5v)

Cowley's apotheosis takes a very earthy form: he is literally nourishing the "Mind," and leaving behind "gen'rous Fruit." He has replaced the Tree of Knowledge with his own worldly form of vegetable wisdom, while those who take sustenance from it are themselves fallen shadows of his paradisical production: the anonymous poet complains, "Thus faint our strongest Metaphors must be, / Thus unproportion'd to thy Muse and Thee" (sig. A5v). Despite replacing divine inspiration with Cowley as muse, his followers nonetheless are still precluded from participating fully in his poetic greatness. The system outlined thus does not place all on egalitarian footing, but rather maintains a hierarchy between the high and the low, albeit in secularized form.

Then follows a poem by Samuel Wesley (versifier, churchman, Royalist, and writer of satires, who was ridiculed in the *Dunciad*), titled "On Mr. Cowley's Juvenile Poems, and the Translation of his Plantarum" (sig. A6v). It too draws an image of Cowley as the arboreal source of poetic sustenance:

> These fair first Fruits of Wit young *Cowley* bore,
>> Which promis'd if the happy Tree
>> Should ever reach Maturity,
> To bless the World with better, and with more.

> Thus in the Kernel of the largest Fruit,
>> Is all the Tree in little drawn,
>> The Trunk, the Branches, and the Root. (sig. A7r)

Wesley's description of Cowley's seminal influence repeats Nehemiah Grew's influential articulation of how the seed contains the entirety of the next generation of plant. In this way, the poetic commemorator mixes the natural philosophic (after the fashion of the "experimenter") with the literary to place Cowley at the crux of both. Wesley declares,

> Hence Seeds of Numbers in thy Soul were fixt
> [. . .]
> And there they lurk'd, till *Spencer's* sacred Flame
>> Leapt up and kindled thine. (sig. A7v)

He establishes a transmission that is firmly botanical, and may be read within the same genealogy as that outlined by Grew in his contemporary work on plants for the Royal Society.

Wesley suggests that this national poetic lineage is encouraged to flourish and spread by the English translation of the *Plantarum*, which increases the accessibility of Cowley's poetry to a much broader public that includes the Englishwomen, assumed to lack Latin training, as well as the personified nation herself:

> But why should the soft Sex be robb'd of thee?
>> Why Should not *England* know,
>> How much she does to Cowley owe?
> How much fair *Boscobel's* for ever sacred Tree?
>> The Hills, the Groves, the Plains, the Woods,
>> The Fields, the Meadows and the Floods,
>> The Flowry World, where Gods and Poets use,
>> To Court a Mortal or a Muse? (sig. A8r)

The botanical knowledge voiced by Cowley, Wesley explains, was at least partly brought into print, in English, by a woman whose "Weakness" struggled against the dead poet's "Strength":

Soft *Afra* [Behn]
> . . . her own Sexes Pride,
> When all her Force on this great Theme sh'ad try'd,
> She strain'd awhile to reach th'inimitable Song,
> She strain'd awhile, and wisely dy'd. (sig. A8r)

In this passage, Wesley declares that Cowley is invaluable to both women's flourishing, and to the well-being of England. Boscobel House, the location of the Royal Oak where Charles II hid en route to his exile in France, is folded into the narrative in ways that evoke again the Tree of Life in the Garden of Eden; while under the poet's control, the natural English landscape becomes the site where the divine and the human blend together. All this, Wesley explains, has been hidden from women due to *Plantarum*'s use of Latin; the one woman capable of translating it proved too weak for the task that, ultimately, the poet asserts, killed her. It is a masculine vision of botanico-poetic knowledge, which proves at once necessary and fatal to the feminine voices defined by it: Behn's wisdom is to sacrifice herself to a task that is beyond her or her sex. Wesley implies that this botanical knowledge was the province of males, when he fails to mention that, in fact, Behn was only one of four "celebrated Hands" who translated the *Plantarum*, as the title-page and prefatory materials clearly state, while two at least of the other three were men (John Oldham and Nahum Tate; "C. Cleve" remains unidentified). In this way, Wesley retains the overarching masculinity of this literary expertise in the vegetable world, to which women have only a secondary and imperfect access.

The translation continued to enjoy numerous editions and reprints throughout the eighteenth century in a range of formats, from octavo to folio, that appealed to multiple audiences even as virtually all other herbals disappeared from the English print market. By making the ontology of plant life common knowledge, Cowley's poem presented an alternate version of expertise with the power to shape the order of things (to borrow a phrase from both Lucretius and Foucault), a model of poetic authority that grew rhizomatically in the untilled topographies of readers-cum-writers who at times hailed from groups generally excluded from official modes of literary, political, and scientific knowledge production. The irony of the translation is that, in making the *Plantarum* more available to this national public, its editors and bookmakers included paratextual materials that increasingly sort that public into social hierarchies that undermine the disorderly inclusiveness of Cowley's original.

CHAPTER NINE

Cowley's Singularity
Pindaric Odes and Johnsonian Values

Philip Smallwood

> You promised to get me a little Pindar.
>
> —Johnson to Boswell, August 31, 1772

Imitation and Poetry: Johnson on
Cowley's Second Olympique Ode

"If a man should undertake to translate *Pindar* word for word, it would be thought that one *Mad man* had translated another."[1] There could be no more disarming start to Cowley's preface to his precarious and original *Odes of Pindar* of 1656. Nor could there be a more accurate justification for his chosen creative technique. Not everyone, however, is disarmed. Several pages are devoted to Cowley's *Pindarique Odes* in Samuel Johnson's 1779 "Life of Cowley" (*Lives*, 1:56–64). These offer a close critique of a collection of verses by a poet once the widely celebrated favorite of Milton, Dryden, and of Pope, but who had fallen from grace after Johnson's day and has never really enjoyed a revival.

On Cowley's evasive account of his reworkings of Pindar, Johnson is amusingly wry. Quoting the preface to *Pindarique Odes* with his eye on Cowley's paraphrastical methods, Johnson wrote that "his endeavour was, not to shew *precisely what Pindar spoke, but his manner of speaking*" (1:125). "He was therefore not at all restrained to his expressions, nor much to his sentiments; nothing was required of him, but not to write as Pindar would not have written" (1:125).[2] Johnson—an imitator of Juvenal who had sealed his own creative tryst with classical poetry—had taken note of the free hand that Cowley had awarded himself as translator. And, given Johnson's use of Popean heroic couplets for his "Juvenal," there may be a double edge to these remarks. Johnson's blend of rigor and affection reveals Cowley's flawed and curious brilliance, but also Johnson's feeling for the singularity of the poems and the sense that only Cowley could have made them. Johnson's is a principled assessment; by extension, Cowley's Pindar is a litmus test for the merits and defects of all poetical practice. The several pages of the "Life of Cowley" devoted to the *Odes* mark a critical occasion that requires closer inspection.

Johnson finds reasons to admire the *Pindarique Odes* though reservations abound. Cowley's metrical organization is significant poetically, but bears its meaning unevenly. His lineation and patterns of indentation on the page are unpredictable; his rhymes are unsettled and scattergun. Shouldn't Johnson's verdict, therefore, be much harsher than it is? One thinks of Johnson's moral and aesthetic reaction to the Pindaric odes of Thomas Gray and his thumbs down for the regularizing eighteenth-century Pindaricists from Congreve on. Of Gray's "The Bard," Johnson complains, "The ode is finished before the ear has learned its measures" ("Life of Gray," 4:42). Johnson gives no clue that he thought Cowley unwise to attempt Pindar, and he is more accepting than we might expect of Cowley's lyrical irregularity, his demonstrable awkwardness, and his Pindaric willingness to go over the top in what Penelope Wilson calls "the hysterical sublime."[3]

Or, at least, for part of the time. Cowley published fifteen odes "Written in Imitation of the Stile and Manner of the Odes of Pindar." The two that Johnson reads most closely are the second Olympique and the first Nemæean odes; these poems do not imitate Pindar, as Johnson had Juvenal, nor do they translate him in the creative senses that the influential theories of Dryden or Roscommon promote. The poems offer rather forms of free adaptation: Colin Burrow has recently observed that Cowley "occupied a lexical gap between translation and imitation."[4] The two poems that have their source in Pindar are followed in *Works* of 1656 (and seventeenth-century editions thereafter) by Cowley's version of Horace's "Second Ode of the Fourth Book," which Cowley entitles "The Praise of Pindar." The remainder are original poems in a "Pindaric" style where Cowley simulates, or parallels, or analogizes Pindar's *unnavigable Song* (*Pindariques*, 18). In explaining, in his "Life of Dryden," how Dryden gave us "just rules and examples of translation," Johnson wrote that Cowley "spread his wings so boldly that he left his authors" (2:223). The headnote to his version of the second Olympique ode recognizes why Pindar might strike Cowley's modern readers as odd: "The *Ode* (according to the constant custom of the *Poet*) consists more in *Digressions*, than in the main subject: And the *Reader* must not be chocqued to hear him speak so often of his own *Muse*; for that is a *Liberty* which this kind of *Poetry* can hardly live without" (*Pindariques*, 1). Cowley correspondingly confesses in the preface to the *Works* that "I am in great doubt whether they [the *Pindarique Odes*] will be understood by most *Readers*; nay, even by very many who are well acquainted with the common Roads, and ordinary Tracks of *Poesie*" (*Works*, sig. C2v). But such doubts were not enough to deter him.

Cowley brings the explanatory apparatus of a learned edition to his Pindarics. Notes appear at the conclusion of all but two odes—"Brutus" and "The Extasie"—and, to show his workings, he supplies for the second Olympique and the first Nemean odes the Greek text of Pindar in prose (from the edition of Johannes Benedictus).[5] For both poems, Cowley provides a further Latin version of the Greek, and his elucidatory comments are keyed numerically to the verses. These additions are perhaps explained by Cowley's fearing his shockable readers might not deduce what he was trying to do from the poems alone or why he was trying to do it. Johnson writes with one eye on Cowley and one on Pindar, sometimes to Cowley's credit, and sometimes not. Thus, the beginning of the second Olympique ode "is, I think," writes Johnson, "above the original in elegance, and the conclusion below it in strength" (1:126). For what Johnson means by Cowley's "elegance" and "strength," we must turn to the verses themselves.

Cowley's Pindarics fill out the large empty ancient spaces of their spare Greek originals. Stripped of the music and dance of festal splendor, they incite invention and addition in any number of ways. The first "Turn," strophe, or verse paragraph of the second Olympique ode has thirty-six Greek words. Taking the lines imitated by Horace (*Odes*, 1.12) in order to expand his own imitation of Pindar, Cowley begins with the celebration of Thereon (or Theron) of Agracas, the noble victor in the chariot race of the seventy-seventh Olympic games in 476 BC. Johnson comes to his critical task with an aesthetic appreciation of Greek poetry, indeed a practitioner's eye in the art of Greek composition, and he registers general approval of Cowley's Pindaric invocation of the Muse. In their rousing harmony, words dance, and strings speak. If not quite justified by their source, the lines show Cowley at his rhapsodic and fanciful best:

> *Queen* of all Harmonious things,
>> *Dancing Words*, and *Speaking Strings*,
>> What *God*, what *Hero* wilt thou sing?
>> What happy *Man* to *equal* glories bring?
>>> Begin, begin thy noble choice,
> And let the Hills around reflect the *Image* of thy *Voice*.
>> *Pisa* does to *Jove* belong,
>> *Jove* and *Pisa* claim thy Song. (*Pindariques*, 1)

The king of the gods, and the city that hosts the games, make the Muses' song their own. Here the irregular line lengths (from eight to fourteen syllables) are balanced by a syllabic exactness scheduled predictably on cue through the beat of an incantatory music: Emerson's "grand Pindaric strokes, as firm as the tread of a horse."[6] In the second half of the first strophe, however, Cowley's Pindaric Pegasus takes flight only to fall lame; the relation between the sense and the syllables goes awry, and the verse is hobbled:

> The fair *First-fruits* of *War*, th'*Olympique Games*,
>> *Alcides* offered up to *Jove*;
>> *Alcides* too thy strings may move;
> But, oh, what *Man* to joyn with these can worthy prove!
> Join *Theron* boldly to their sacred *Names*;
>> *Theron* the next honour claims;
>> *Theron* to no *man* gives place,
> Is first in *Pisa*'s and in *Virtue*'s *Race*;
>> *Theron* there, and he alone,
> Ev'n his own swift *Forefathers* has outgone. (*Pindariques*, 2)

Cowley's breathless encomiastic energy, shared with Pindar's exultant choral lyric, invites us to intuit what he is trying to accomplish. The dissolution of painful present realities into the distance of myth may be a motive: Joshua Scodel suggests that Cowley is using the story of Theron's victory to divert contemporaries from triumphs of the recent past—seven years after the death of Charles I and three years into Cromwell's Protectorate.[7] David Fairer, meanwhile, sees Cowley's irregular Pindarics in general terms as a precedent for lazily achieved forms of poetic daring and blames him for the tedious tradition of "laureate odes and celebratory effusions" straining in their praise of princes and lords.[8] But for Cowley, a parallel poetical reality may override such real-world obligations: part of the appeal of Pindar to Cowley may have been that the very purity and intensity of his odes excluded politics. You will have noticed that Pope has visited this passage for another variety of victory song in the *Rape of the Lock*: "Behold the first in Virtue, as in Face!" (and, before that, in the context of a different kind of heroic life from that of Pope's combative modern young ladies, for his early version of the Homeric *Episode of Sarpedon*).[9]

The Loeb prose translation has simply that Theron was "the bulwark of Agracas" and "foremost upholder of his city from a line of famous ancestors."[10] In Cowley, the different parts of speech are syntactically intertwined and join hands in rhyme. We have the verb-noun rhyme of "belong"/"Song" in company with the noun "Names" and verb "claims." But we also have "alone"/"outgone," where Cowley pairs the adverb with a past participle and additionally achieves the likeness of rhyme in a pronunciation estranged from the modern ear. To share Cowley's sense of his task is to accept rhymes that slip between parts of speech, or relate words orthographically rather than acoustically—expressions of the poem's reckless drive. This is the "gaiety of fancy" and "dance of words" that Johnson also found in Cowley's "The *Chronicle*" (*Lives*, 1:51) and represents a Cowley unchained, not confined, by the classics, or rather, I should say, the preclassical, the archaic. As against the Beethovenian sublime, D. S. Carne-Ross writes of the "delicate, light-footed, deft, Mozartian Pindar."[11] Rhyme play pervades Cowley (but is far from the massive, if controversial, metrical default it became in the following century) and explains how he could bring not only couplet or triplet, but sextuplet repetitions to infuse the spirit of his performance. Such exuberance Pope could not quite countenance.

In appraising *Alexander's Feast; or, the Power of Musick* (1697), Johnson calls the absence of "correspondent rhyme" in Dryden's ode a "defect." But he adds that the "enthusiasm" of the verse means this will not ultimately matter ("Life of Dryden," 2:319). If we thrill for the same reason to the audacious anti-decorum of Cowley's strokes, we may not think that the tongue-twisting close of the first strophe of his second Olympique ode is simply a lapse. Such lines are not a half-hearted approach to later norms of fluency and pith that Cowley was too unskilled to master. They are rather an exuberant act of abandon—an escape from the ordinary. In precisely that carefree respect, they pay disciplined homage to Pindar's vers libre—the shock-inducing "Liberty" Cowley defends in his headnote to the second Olympique ode. The lines enact the Greek poet's other-worldly, awkward, enigmatic, remoteness, where meanings concatenate through rhyme. "Thou hast brought [Pindar] from the dust," writes Thomas Sprat, "And made him live again."[12] This is the sense in which William Cowper, writing in book 4, lines 723–30, of *The Task* (1785), could celebrate "Ingenious Cowley! . . . finding rich amends / For a lost world in solitude and verse."[13] Johnson's judgment of Cowley's superior "elegance" in the opening of the poem rests upon a distinction between the English and Greek construed as a difference in quality between translation and source. In his generally favorable verdict on Gilbert West's version of Pindar's first Olympique ode, Johnson compares the translation with the original, and assumes that they can be judged against a common standard ("Life of Gilbert West," 4:11–12). But Cowley's effort to push English rhyme and rhythm beyond its limits of stability may not be trying to compete with Pindar's lost world, but rather to comprehend its strangeness. A historical telos draws poetry to a more technically polished style that Johnson, writing in 1779, knows from the successive efforts of Denham, Waller, Dryden, and then Pope. For Cowley, writing within the limits of possibility in 1656, and before all this could be imagined, such style belongs to an unknow-able future of sweet, strong, elegant, and consistently fluid English verse, the normalization of which he had no reason to predict or desire.

Johnson goes on to show how Cowley "sometimes extends his author's thoughts without improving them." "We are told of Theron's bounty," he notes, "with a hint that he had enemies." The brevity of the original, Johnson remarks, "Cowley . . . enlarges in rhyming prose" (1:129). Johnson then quotes the lines from the final stanza he thinks the English poet has done too little to enhance:

> But in this thankless world the giver
> Is envied even by the receiver;
> 'Tis now the cheap and frugal fashion
> Rather to hide than own the obligation:
> Nay, 'tis much worse than so;
> It now an artifice does grow
> Wrongs and injuries to do,
> Lest men should think we owe. (as quoted in 1:129, with varia-
>   tions from *Pindariques*, 5–6)

Cowley "extends his author's thoughts" when he elucidates Pindar's sharply abbreviated praise for the victor. *Kópos* (literally "sufficient" or "enough") is the encompassing Pindaric term to curtail the wearisome unrestrained encomium that spoils a just assessment of a person through overstatement. Johnson is caustic: "It is hard to conceive that a man of the first rank in learning and wit, when he was dealing out such minute morality in such feeble diction, could imagine, either waking or dreaming, that he imitated Pindar" (1:130). Cowley is wrestling here with a tangle of ideas that recalls the terms Johnson uses to describe Shakespeare's "unwieldy" sentiments that "he cannot well express, and will not reject."[14] As Cowley upbraids his own unstoppable fertility at the poem's close, he cannot suppress a personal sense of the corrupt and miserable world from which he professed an ardent wish to retire. This ambition Johnson addresses satirically in the biographical section of the "Life."[15]

The ending of the poem may be underwhelming, but Johnson found much to enjoy in the body of Cowley's second Olympique ode:

> The connection is supplied with great perspicuity, and the
> thoughts, which to a reader of less skill seem thrown together

by chance, are concatenated without any abruption. Though the English ode cannot be called a translation, it may be very properly consulted as a commentary. (1:126)

It is a Johnsonian tribute to the art of Cowley that it is the "reader of less skill" for whom it is a matter of "chance." Johnson is here responding directly to comments in Cowley's preface to his *Pindarique Odes*: "It does not at all trouble me that the *Grammarians* perhaps will not suffer this libertine way of rendring foreign Authors, to be called *Translation*" (*Pindariques*, sig. T3v). In the collection as a whole, however, Johnson wrote that "the spirit of Pindar is indeed not every where equally preserved" (1:127). The calculated understatement is hard to miss.

"The Resurrection" and "The Muse"

Johnson thought the *Pindarique Odes* at their best where the material was shaped as far as possible from Cowley's own experience. In the second Olympique and the first Nemean odes, Cowley confined himself to originals, and in the details of his modern recreations, he still remains close to the subject matter of Pindar's Greek. With, however, the exception of his version of Horace, "In Praise of Pindar," Cowley turned to Pindar as a classical or preclassical authorization for a manner he had brought to a miscellany of topics personal to himself. "The Resurrection," "The Muse," "To Mr Hobs," "Destinie," "Brutus," "Life and Fame," "The Extasie," "To the New Year," "Life," "The 34 Chapter of the Prophet *Isaiah*," and "The Plagues of *Egypt*" are of this kind.[16] Johnson's attention to the first two of these poems follows their order in his edition of Cowley. He quotes from the second stanza of "The Resurrection," an ode that Cowley in the first of the notes to this poem calls "truly *Pindarical*, falling from one thing into another, after his *Enthusiastical manner*." Johnson again echoes Cowley's note:

> In the following odes, where Cowley chooses his own subjects, he sometimes rises to dignity truly Pindarick, and, if some deficiencies of language be forgiven, his strains are such as those of the Theban bard were to his contemporaries. (1:131)

Johnson sounds confident he could recognize the "truly *Pindarical*" when he heard it.

For Johnson, "dignity" could coexist with "enthusiasm." He, therefore, has no quarrel with Cowley on account of a taste for regular verse he cannot temperamentally betray, but complains where the poetic energy peters out. These reservations arise because of modern verses that come short of what in Pindar's time Johnson thinks Pindar was able to do. Describing the start of Matthew Prior's poetical career, Johnson wrote, in his "Life of Prior," that "we had not then recovered from our Pindarick infatuation" (3:77). Congreve corrected "a national error, . . . our Pindarick madness" ("Life of Congreve," 3:44). Watts's odes are "deformed by the Pindarick folly then prevailing" ("Life of Watts," 4:6). Whatever errors Johnson finds in the poems, Cowley is neither mad nor foolish.

Despite doubts about "Pindarick infatuation," Johnson approved, and enjoyed, Cowley's "The Resurrection." The poet explains how the enduring music of verse will accompany the dance of the years to come, until the annihilation of all things:

> Begin the song, and strike the living lyre:
> Lo how the years to come, a numerous and well-fitted quire,
>   All hand in hand do decently advance,
> And to my song with smooth and equal measure dance;
>   While the dance lasts, how long soe'er it be,
> My musick's voice shall bear it company;
>   Till all the gentle notes be drown'd
>   In the last trumpet's dreadful sound. (as quoted at 1:131,
>   with variations from *Pindariques*, 21)

"Who now shall charm the Shades where *Cowley* strung / His living Harp," writes Pope in *Windsor Forest* (ll. 277–78). But if Johnson can also rise with Cowley to such harmonious examples of the "tempestuous Pindar," he cannot conceal his contempt for the cobbled and crippled close of Cowley's poem: "After such enthusiasm who will not lament to find the poet conclude with lines like these!"

> But stop, my Muse——
> Hold thy Pindarick Pegasus closely in,
>   Which does to rage begin——
> ——'Tis an unruly and a hard-mouth'd horse——
>   'Twill no unskilful touch endure,
> But flings writer and reader too that sits not sure. (as quoted in
>   1:132, with variations from *Pindariques*, 22)

In a recent essay on "Hyper-Pindarics," Simon Jarvis has observed that Cowley is at this point himself metaphorically unhorsed, and the metrical horsemanship of any reader attempting to voice the line is similarly tested. This is notwithstanding the significant differences between the text that Johnson reproduces and the text as it appears with capitalizations and italics in the *Pindariques* of 1668.[17] Johnson does not spell out his despair with Cowley's "The Resurrection" with the minute particularity he notoriously accords to the logical absurdities of Gray's odes. But the lines spur Johnson to a crucial statement of theory, a credo that informs the judgments of the "Preface" to his edition of *Shakespeare* (1765), the celebrated definition of poetry in the tenth chapter of *Rasselas* (1759), and in this, the first of the *Lives*, an underpinning principle of the whole collection. Cowley's *Pindarique Odes* reinforces Johnson's encounter with his most oft-quoted critical homage—to the "grandeur of generality":

The fault of Cowley, and perhaps of all the writers of the metaphysical race, is that of pursuing his thoughts to their last ramifications, by which he loses the grandeur of generality; for of the greatest things the parts are little; what is little can be but pretty, and by claiming dignity becomes ridiculous. Thus all the power of description is destroyed by a scrupulous enumeration; and the force of metaphors is lost, when the mind by the mention of particulars is turned more upon the original than the secondary sense, more upon that from which the illustration is drawn than that to which it is applied. (1:133)

The Pindaric imitations are the part of Cowley's oeuvre where these criticisms carry the greatest weight. Cowley pursues his thoughts "to their last ramifications" when, in the final stanza of "The Resurrection," he insists on the literal horsiness of Pegasus; he loses "the grandeur of generality" by his reminders of the physical attributes of a real horse: thus Pegasus is "hard-mouth'd" (1:132) and is "Impatient of the *Spur* or *Bit*" (*Pindariques*, 22). The force of the metaphor is lost when the mind is turned more on the original sense of Pegasus, as a stubborn, difficult, and highly strung stallion, than on the secondary sense, as a mythical *winged* horse, combining the idea of poetical flight with an evocation of rhythmic, coordinated movement, the activity true both of the prancing steed and harmonious verse.

The subsequent poem is "The Muse," a piece that exhibits once again the quintessential weakness of the poetic technique that Johnson thinks "the fault of Cowley." "The Muse," in common with "The Resurrection," has the poet address the "Pindaric" part of his own poetical nature and to attempt, according to David Trotter, "a more extended definition of the expressive function of Pindaric verse" (*Poetry*, 21). The opening stanza furnishes another example of thoughts pursued to their last ramifications, and Johnson summarizes with some amusement the initial figure, where Cowley, wearing the mask of Pindar, has his Muse, or poetic alter ego, go to "*take the air* in an intellectual chariot, to which he harnesses Fancy and Judgement, Wit and Eloquence, Memory and Invention" (1:134). Johnson comments especially on the lines where faculties of the creative mind make up the team of horses supposed to be harnessed to the chariot of the Muse:

> Go, the rich *Chariot* instantly prepare;
>   The *Queen*, my *Muse*, will take the air;
> Unruly *Phansie* with strong *Judgment* trace,
>   Put in nimble-footed *Wit*,
>   Smooth-pac'd *Eloquence* joyn with it,
> Sound *Memory* with young *Invention* place. (*Pindariques*, 23)

In his note to these lines, Cowley claims a precedent for his metaphor in the sixth Olympique ode of Pindar, which he translates: "O, my *Soul*, joyn me the strong and swift *Mules* together, that I may drive the *Chariot* in this fair way" (*Pindariques*, 24n1).

Where poetry is the subject of poetry, Cowley frames literary creation in terms consistent with Johnson's personal vocabulary, and there is perhaps a hint of oversensitivity in Johnson's complaint: "How he distinguished Wit from Fancy, or how Memory could properly contribute to Motion, he has not explained" (1:134). Johnson had had the benefit of over a century's intensive thought by the critical community on this terminology and the cumulative experience of its practice in poetry. His personal definition of "Wit" had appeared at the structural center of the "Life," when he was commenting on all the metaphysical poets. Cowley distinguishes "*Wit*" from "*Phansie*" in the poem; for Johnson, they are different aspects of the same expression. He defines "Wit" in his *Dictionary* as "quickness of fancy."

To the extent that Cowley keeps all the terms of his poetical metaphor in play, Johnson observes that "we are . . . content to suppose that he could have justified his own fiction, and wish to see the Muse begin her career" (1:134). But tension is lost. Cowley cannot resist a "scrupulous enumeration" of the attributes of the departing Muse. As Johnson rather wearily notes: "There is yet more to be done" (1:134). The subsequent lines, again quoted loosely by Johnson, illustrate how the "grandeur of generality" is abandoned when great things are divided into small parts. Cowley depends on our conceiving of the grand abstraction of poetic inspiration in concrete form—a chariot drawn by a team of first-class horse-flesh, expertly picked to combine speed, stamina, and control. When, however, Cowley enumerates the details, awkward questions arise. In what sense, for example, can Nature mount the chariot of the Muse as her "*postilion*"?

> Let the *postilion* Nature mount, and let
> The *coachman* Art be set;
> And let the airy *footmen*, running all beside,
> Make a long row of goodly pride;
> Figures, conceits, raptures, and sentences,
> In a well-worded dress,
> And innocent loves, and pleasant truths, and useful lies,
> In all their gaudy *liveries*. (as quoted in 1:134, with variations
>   from *Pindariques*, 23)

Johnson records his distaste at the fuss and clutter of this passage by appealing to the common reader, but then warms to the stanza's conclusion: "Every mind is now disgusted with this cumber of magnificence; yet I cannot refuse myself the four next lines":

> Mount, glorious queen, thy travelling throne,
>   And bid it to put on;
> For long though cheerful is the way,
> And life alas allows but one ill winter's day. (as quoted in 1:135,
>   with variations from *Pindariques*, 23)

Life allows only one ill day of low spirits, because it is short. Johnson valued the "practical axioms and domestick wisdom" in Shakespearean plays, and he drew out the implied moral in many of the explanatory and critical notes in his edition of Shakespeare. Reminiscent of the Johnsonian moralist of the Shakespearean commentary or the essays of the *Rambler*, the axiomatic habits of Cowley's *Pindarique Odes* join with the Cowley of the *Anacreontiques* (*Pindariques*, 31–41). In all these locations, the shortness of life determines the present pleasures that one must seize, and the moral of the poem Cowley echoes in the lessons of his "Several Discourses by way of Essays, in Verse and Prose" (*Pindariques*, 79–148).[18] This may explain why Johnson had been willing to deploy an epigraph to *Rambler* 151 from Pindar's seventh Olympique ode, translated by West:

> But wrapt in error is the human mind,
> And human bliss is ever insecure:
>   Know we what fortune yet remains behind?
> Know we how long the present shall endure? (ll. 44–48, *Rambler*,
>   *Yale Edition*, 5:37)

Johnson's susceptibility to Cowley's "life alas" (1:135) recalls his taste for the "great thoughts" that "are always general, and consist in positions not limited by exceptions, and in descriptions not descending to minuteness" (1:158). Johnson thought that the metaphysical poets had missed the "sublime"—the very quality that Pindar was thought to epitomize. Cowley precisely seeks out the exceptional in his reaching for the sublime, but, for

Johnson, the exceptional, when unhinged from the rational, is the crucial limitation of poetic sublimity: "[The metaphysicals] never attempted that comprehension and expanse of thought which at once fills the whole mind, and of which the first effect is sudden astonishment, and the second rational admiration. Sublimity is produced by aggregation, and little-ness by dispersion" (1:58). In choosing the word "dispersion," Johnson distinguishes between the lines in the first stanza of "The Muse," which he liked, and Cowley's "cumber of magnificence" (1:135), which disgusted him, a reminiscence of the difference between the true and the false sublime developed one hundred years earlier by Boileau in his preface to Longinus's *Traité du sublime* (1674).[19] But for Johnson, as for Boileau, true sublimity is expressed not by rapture but by simplicity; it is an effect powerful by virtue of the apparent, but not actual, absence of a governing artistry. Johnson was to frame the conjunction apropos devotional poetry in the "Life of Waller," where "it will be found that the most simple expres-sion is the most sublime" (2:141). "Cowley seems to have possessed the power of writing easily beyond any other of our poets," Johnson had formerly concluded in *Idler* 77 (1759), "yet his pursuit of remote thoughts led him often into harshness of expression" (*Idler and Adventurer*, 2:242), and Johnson regarded Cowley's tendency to be carried beyond simplicity in the *Pindarique Odes* as a temperamental disability. Just as Shakespeare had sometimes suffered from a fatal attraction to the trivial comedy of quibbles or puns, Cowley, for his part, could not resist the temptation to put his knowledge on display. Johnson describes the vices of both writers in forgiving, even slightly affectionate, terms. The failure to hold back is a familiar and human one: "In the same ode, celebrating the power of the Muse, he gives her prescience or, in poetical language, the foresight of events hatching in futurity; but having once an egg in his mind he cannot forbear to shew us what an egg contains:

> Thou into the close nests of Time do'st peep,
>> And there with piercing eye
> Through the firm shell and thick white dost spy
>> Years to come a-forming lie,
> Close in their sacred secundine asleep." (as quoted in 1:136, with
>> variations from *Pindariques*, 24)[20]

Cowley actually prints "*Secondine*," from the Latin *Secundae*, defined in a note to his poem as "The thin *Film* with which an *Infant* is covered in the *Womb*, so called, because it *follows* the *Child*" (*Pindarique Odes*, 25). The equation of the "general" with the "poetical" is made explicit in Johnson's remark that "the same thought is more generally, and therefore more poetically, expressed by Casimir, a writer who had many of the beauties and faults of Cowley:

> Omnibus mundi Dominator horis
> Aptat urgendas per inane pennas,
> Pars adhuc nido latet, & futuros
> Crescit in annos."

[The Ruler of the world fits wings to all the hours to propel them through the void; some still lie hidden in the nest, and grow into future years] (1:136)

Johnson might have argued that the relative restraint of the Latin of Casimir leaves more for the reader's imagination. It is free from the oppressive sense of technical detail that Cowley's English version is fated to impose. The "general" is "more poetical" for Johnson because it liberates the mind to make for itself the connections between young chicks hatching and growing into winged creatures ready for flight, and the hours and years maturing in the nests of Time, ready to become the "flying hours" of temporary existence. Cowley's details tie the mind down to zoological, or, in the case of "*Secondine*," to obstetric facts.

Johnson's General Judgment of Cowley's *Pindarique Odes*

Johnson shifts the emphasis in the second half of his discussion of Cowley's *Pindarique Odes* from the problems of particular verses to issues that—as a collection in its own right—they are bound to raise: "Cowley, whatever was his subject, seems to have been carried, by a kind of destiny, to the light and the familiar, or to conceits which require still more ignoble epithets" (1:138). In expanding the scope of the commentary, Johnson moves from Cowley's delight in the poems' learned detail to the playfulness of the mind behind them. Johnson's comments return us to the security of his poetic judgment and the structure to which Johnsonian judgment belongs. He was perhaps enjoying a sly joke—that of judging Cowley by the laws of fate Cowley had applied both to mankind and to himself, as he does in "Destinie," the next, bar one, of the Pindaric versions. The center of this poem, as Cowley's note explains, is the thought that an angelic "unseen Hand" controls human action, though it appears independent (*Pindariques*, 30):

> This *Ode* is written upon an extravagant supposition of two *Angels* playing a *Game* at *Chess*; which if they did, the spectators would have reason as much to believe, that the pieces moved themselves, as we can have for thinking the same of *Mankind*, when we see them exercise so many, and so different actions. It was of old said by *Plautus*; *Dii nos quasi Pilas homines habent*. We are but *Tennis Balls* for the *Gods* to play withal, which they strike away at last, and still call for new ones: And S. *Paul* says, *We are but the Clay in the hands of the Potter*. (*Pindariques*, 32n1)

"Destinie" exemplifies Johnson's claim that "whatever was his subject," Cowley was carried "by a kind of destiny, to the light and the familiar" in order to explain the varied and motiveless natures of man. Like the pieces in an imaginary game of chess, which seem to move of their own accord, such natures, in fact, take their direction from some angelic power. From this extravagant parallel, the poem, like the note, turns irresistibly to Cowley's "familiar" expression.

Like Shakespeare, Cowley "approximates the remote" (*Johnson on Shakespeare*, 7:65). And even as a fellow metaphysical, Cowley's poetic self can rise above the ponderous and punning wordplay of John Donne's famously self-analytical "What thou hast done, thou hast not done" in his "A Hymn to God the Father." Cowley's lightheartedly philosophical delivery has an appealing directness. His Muse has dictated his Fate—

> With *Fate*, what boots it to contend?
> Such I *began*, such *am*, and so must *end*.
> The *Star* that did my *Being* frame,

> Was but a *Lambent Flame*,
> And some small *Light* it did dispence,
> But neither *Heat* nor *Influence*.
> No Matter, *Cowley*, let proud *Fortune* see,
> That *thou* canst *her* despise no less than *she* does *Thee*.
> Let all her gifts the portion be
> Of Folly, Lust, and Flatterie,
> Fraud, Extortion, Calumnie,
> Murder, Infidelitie,
> Rebellion and Hypocrisie.
> Do Thou not *grieve* nor *blush* to be,
> As all th'inspired *tuneful Men*,
> And all thy great *Forefathers* were from *Homer* down to *Ben*.
>   (*Pindariques*, 31)

—a celebration in this last line of a poetical ancestry paralleling the ancestral athletic talent that sustains Theron's sporting victory in the latest chariot race of the ancient Olympics. Cowley is familiarizing an abstruse subject at this point, but elsewhere makes light of large and serious considerations. "Life" is therefore "*Nothings younger Brother!*" he writes in "Life and Fame" (*Pindariques*, 39–40). Death, in "To the New Year," is the carelessly contemptuous breaking of the bottle that has been emptied of the wine of life:

> *Sowreness* and *Lees*, which to the bottom sink,
>   Remain for latter years to *Drink*,
> Until some one offended with the taste
> The *Vessel* breaks, and out the wretched *Reliques* run at last.
>   (*Pindariques*, 44)

To be set against the "fault of Cowley," Johnson writes that Cowley's "Destinie" discovers the characteristic "power," one also typical of the *Anacreontiques*, "to have been greatest in the familiar and the festive" (1:117). Unfortunately, Cowley is led by the same power to "conceits which require still more ignoble epithets" (1:138).[21] Johnson seems to have thought of colors, especially, as "ignoble": a slaughter in the Red Sea "new dies [paint(s)] the waters name" (from "The Plagues of *Egypt*") (1:138, *Pindariques*, 64); in Cowley's "To Dr. *Scarborough*," England during the bloody Civil War was "*Albion no more, nor to be named from white*" (1:138, *Pindariques*, 35). But it is as much the fit between the words and their contexts as the words themselves that disturbed Johnson: "Words become low by the occasions to which they are applied," he observes of Shakespeare's diction in *Rambler* 168 (*Rambler, Yale Edition*, 5:126). The adjectives of color in Cowley's poems are "ignoble" because of the trivial play of mere words within serious descriptions of two dreadful events, biblical and political.

Johnson illustrates just how feeble Cowley's thoughts can be by quoting the second part of the third stanza of "To the New Year," the fourth from the last poem of the *Pindarique Odes*. Governing the criticism is again a sense of Cowley's poetical temperament (reminiscent, I have suggested, of Johnson's notion of Shakespeare's creative "disposition"). In "The Muse," Cowley cannot "forbear to shew us that he knows what an egg contains." Here, "It is surely by some fascination not easily surmounted," that a writer professing to revive "*the noblest and highest* [kind of] *writing in verse*, makes this address to the new year" (1:138). Cowley is fixated by his own thought and forgets that he is imitating Pindar:

> Nay, if thou lov'st me, gentle year,
> Let not so much as love be there,
> Vain fruitless love I mean; for, gentle year,
>   Although I fear,
> There's of this caution little need,
>   Yet, gentle year, take heed
>   How thou dost make
>   Such a mistake;
> Such love I mean alone
> As by thy cruel predecessors has been shewn;
> For, tho' I have too much cause to doubt it,
> I fain would try, for once, if life can live without it. (as quoted in
>   1:138, with variations from *Pindariques*, 44)

Whatever Cowley's ambitions to revive his original, Johnson must sometimes conclude that he does Pindar no favors: "Even those who cannot perhaps find in the Isthmian or *Nemæan* songs what Antiquity has disposed them to expect, will at least see that they are ill represented by such puny poetry; and all will determine that if this be the old Theban strain, it is not worthy of revival" (1:139). From the poet's feeble thought, Johnson moves to Cowley's irregular verse: "To the disproportion and incongruity of Cowley's sentiments must be added the uncertainty and looseness of his measures" (1:140).

Cowley's "Measures"

As Horace wrote of Pindar's metrical liberties, Cowley's "measures" are "numeris lege solutis," "in metre freed from rule" (*Odes*, 4.2.11–12). No two poems from the *Pindarique Odes* follow quite the same pattern. Stanzas (or verse paragraphs) differ both in number and in length (even within the same poem). Rhymes within a given poem may be adjacent, or far apart. As I have noted above, a Pindaric poem by Cowley may contain up to six verses rhymed in succession. The distribution of long, short, and intermediate lines varies from poem to poem and from stanza to stanza. The arrangement of lines and stanzas is not *entirely* arbitrary. There is some consistency within the poems, if not between them, and Cowley's "The Extasie" follows a strict pattern through nine stanzas, or sections of verse, each of eight lines. But in the next poem, "To the New Year," the stanzas vary from two of ten, to one of twenty-four lines. Johnson notes a similar freedom (if not an anarchy), in the length of the line: "He takes the liberty of using in any place a verse of any length, from two syllables to twelve" (1:140).

Only one line has two syllables: "But *Fly*," in the third stanza of Cowley's "The Muse" (*Pindariques*, 24). There are many of twelve, and some, which Johnson does not mention (perhaps because they are exceptional), are fourteeners, as in "Whose gentler *Honours* do so well the *Brows* of *Peace* adorn" from the third stanza of the first Nemæan ode, or the last line of "To Mr Hobs": "And that which never is *to Dye*, for ever must be *Young*" (*Pindariques*, 28). But the nub of Johnson's criticism is not that Cowley has failed to anticipate the later conventions of stable versification; it is that there is little pattern of *any* kind in the stanzaic and polymetrical structure of the *Pindarique Odes*. No expectations of verse movement are disappointed because none are established.

At this point, Johnson turns to uncover the fallacy at the root of Cowley's imitative method. Focusing on his claim that "our Ears are strangers to the Musick of his [Pindar's] *Numbers*" (preface to his *Pindariques*, sig. T3r), Johnson insists that the old poetry be recreated in the known numbers of the ancient tongue as far as these can be discerned. In his rejoinder to Cowley, Johnson writes as a fellow imitator who takes the principled view that Cowley's loose and uncertain measures do not so much mangle Pindar as abandon him. Cowley's formal homage to the ancient poet is therefore undigested:

> The verses of Pindar have, as he observes, very little harmony to the modern ear; yet by examining the syllables we perceive them to be regular, and have reason enough for supposing that the ancient audiences were delighted with the sound. The imitator ought therefore to have adopted what he found, and to have added what was wanting; to have preserved a constant return of the same numbers, and to have supplied smoothness of transition and continuity of thought. (1:140)

The impersonal first-person plural of Johnson's "we perceive them" implies the consensus of a modern scholastic community. It is the presence of a pattern, Johnson asserts, contra Sprat, that identifies poetry, almost defines it: "The great pleasure of verse arises from the known measure of the lines, and uniform structure of the stanzas, by which the voice is regulated, and the memory relieved" (1:141). The style of Pindar is either like prose, or like poetry. It cannot resemble both.

One might think Cowley's experiments in rhyme and versification would endear him more than it has, if not to Johnson, then to present enthusiasts for late-modernist and postmodernist poetics. Jarvis has drawn a comparison between Cowley's "The Resurrection" and the British performance poet Keston Sutherland, where he suggests that Cowley's Pindarics are part of the "forgotten prehistory of free verse" (127–44). Johnson, for his part, deplores in his remaining remarks the fashion for "Pindarism" that Cowley's versions had inspired. Writing from the more distant perspective informed by the versification of Dryden and Pope,

Johnson places Cowley's Pindarics in their historical context as yet another literary fashion that rises, becomes dominant for a while, and then fades:

> This lax and lawless versification so much concealed the deficiencies of the barren, and flattered the laziness of the idle, that it immediately overspread our books of poetry; all the boys and girls caught the pleasing fashion, and they that could do nothing else could write like Pindar. . . . Pindarism prevailed above half a century; but at last died gradually away, and other imitations supply its place. (1:143)

Such comments display a philosophical mind at ease in articulating contradictory feelings and conscious of its own unstable position within the flux of taste. Other imitations may in time replace Pindarism, Johnson seems to say, but will themselves be replaced. Every present becomes a historical past.

In his concluding remarks, the uneven nature of Cowley's *Pindarique Odes* draws from Johnson both strong positive and strong negative reactions. The balance of the following is not that of an indifferent reader, but rather one pulled in opposite directions at once by Cowley's exuberance. "Johnson's singular qualification as a critic of Cowley," write Tom Mason and David Hopkins, "was his ability to rest easily within contradictory statements."[22] His closing judgments emerge in this light as a sequence of jostling sympathies and antipathies:

> The Pindarique odes have so long enjoyed the highest degree of poetical reputation, that I am not willing to dismiss them with unabated censure; and surely though the mode of their composition be erroneous, yet many parts deserve at least that admiration which is due to great comprehension of knowledge and great fertility of fancy. The thoughts are often new, and often striking; but the greatness of one part is disgraced by the littleness of another; and total negligence of language gives the noblest conceptions the appearance of a fabrick august in the plan, but mean in the materials. (1:144)

Had he seen the criticisms of Johnson, Cowley would probably feel no need to apologize for these vices. What he does, he does as he means to do; the free-minded poetry he writes stands as a proxy for the best outlook on living he is able to imagine. This Cowley makes crystal clear in the light and easy familiarity of his "Ode: Upon Liberty," from his "Several Discourses by way of Essays, in Verse and Prose", first published in 1668. Pindar legitimizes the freedom with which Cowley wishes to conduct his life:

> If Life should a well-order'd Poem be
>   (In which he only hits the white
> Who joyns true Profit with the best Delight)
> The more Heroique strain let others take,
>   Mine the Pindarique way I'le make
> The Matter shall be Grave, the Numbers loose and free.
> It shall not keep one setled pace of Time,
> In the same Tune it shall not always Chime,
> Nor shall each day just to his Neighbour Rhime,
> A thousand Liberties it shall dispense. (Cowley, *Verses
>   Written*, 90)

Johnson admired the *Essays, in Verse and Prose*, and the critical objectivity he sought when trying to write fairly about Cowley seems inadequate to the powerful yet contradictory sensations he felt. Nonetheless, it is on an eloquently positive note, with only a hint, perhaps, of the double edge, that he ends his summary, reminding us of Cowley's unique combination of powers: "Yet surely those verses are not without a just claim to praise; of which it may be said with truth, that no man but Cowley could have written them" (1:144).

Notes

Tribute to Mark Pedreira

1   This tribute is reprinted from the *Johnsonian News Letter* 73 (2022): 63–64, with the kind permission of the general editor, Robert DeMaria Jr.

Introduction

1   [Daniel Defoe], *The Pacificator. A Poem* (London: Printed, and are to be Sold by F. Nutt, 1700), 5.

2   John Evelyn, *Diary of John Evelyn*, ed. Guy de la Bédoyère (London: Boydell Press, 2004), 164.

3   Christopher D'Addario, "Abraham Cowley and the Ends of Poetry," in *Literatures of Exile in the English Revolution and Its Aftermath, 1640–1690*, ed. Philip Major (London: Routledge, 2010), 121–32; Niall Allsopp, *Poetry and Sovereignty in the English Revolution* (Oxford: Oxford University Press, 2020), chap. 4; Scott Black, *Of Essays and Reading in Early Modern Britain* (New York: Palgrave Macmillan, 2006), chap. 2; Jane Darcy, *Melancholy and Literary Biography, 1640–1816* (Basingstoke: Palgrave Macmillan, 2013), chap. 1; Paul Davis, *Translation and the Poet's Life: The Ethics of Translating in English Culture, 1646–1726* (Oxford: Oxford University Press, 2008), chap. 2; Alan De Gooyer, "Sensibility and Solitude in Cowley's Familiar Essay," *Restoration* 25, no. 1 (2001): 1–18; Richard Hillyer, *Four Augustan Science Poets* (London: Anthem, 2020), chap. 1; Richard Hillyer, *Hobbes and His Poetic Contemporaries: Cultural Transmission in Early Modern England* (New York: Palgrave Macmillan, 2007), chap. 3; David Hopkins, "Cowley's Horatian Mice," *Conversing with Antiquity: English Poets and the Classics, from*

Shakespeare To Pope (Oxford: Oxford University Press, 2010), 55–87; Theodore Kaouk, "'Perjur'd Rebel': Equivocal Allegiance and Cowley's *Cutter of Coleman Street*," *Restoration* 33, no. 2 (2009): 25–46; Kathryn R. King, "Cowley among the Women; Or, Poetry in the Contact Zone," in *Women and Literary History*, ed. Katherine Binhammer and Jeanne Wood (Newark: University of Delaware Press, 2003), 43–63; Margaret Koehler, "Odes of Absorption in the Restoration and Early Eighteenth Century," *SEL: Studies in English Literature 1500–1900* 47 (2007): 659–78; Simon Malpas, "'In No One Thing, They Saw, Agreeing': Communicating Experimental Philosophy in Cowley and Butler" *Restoration* 43, no. 2 (2019): 49–73; Tom Mason, "Abraham Cowley's Amiability," *1650–1850: Ideas, Aesthetics, and Inquiries in the Early Modern Era* 15 (2008): 189–218; Andrew Mattison, "Cowley's Dream of a Shadow: Imitation against Experience," *Modern Language Quarterly* 82 (2021): 55–80; Henry Power, "'Teares Break Off My Verse': The Virgilian Incompleteness of Abraham Cowley's *The Civil War*," *Translation and Literature* 16 (2007): 141–59; Adam Rounce, "The Digital Miscellanies Index and the Canon," *Eighteenth-Century Life* 41, no. 1 (2017): 158–78; Joshua Scodel, "The Cowleyan Pindaric Ode and Sublime Diversions," in *A Nation Transformed: England after the Restoration*, ed. Alan Houston and Steve Pincus (Cambridge: Cambridge University Press, 2001), 180–210; Elizabeth Scott-Baumann, *Forms of Engagement: Women, Poetry, and Culture, 1640–1680* (Oxford: Oxford University Press, 2013), chap. 3; Nathaniel Stogdill, "Abraham Cowley's 'Pindaric Way': Adapting Athleticism in Interregnum England," *English Literary Renaissance* 42 (2012): 482–51; Joseph Wallace, "True Poetry and False Religion in Abraham Cowley's *Davideis*," *Review of English Studies* 66 (2015): 895–914; and Thomas Ward, "Abraham Cowley's Odes 'Rightly Repeated,'" *Restoration* 42, no. 2 (2018): 39–64.

Chapter One: "Who Now Reads Cowley?": How a Major Poet Disappeared from the Canon

1   Alexander Pope, "The First Epistle of the Second Book of Horace Imitated" (1737), from Pope, *Poems*.

2   H.S.E. = "Hic Sepultus Est": "Here Lies Buried." These auxiliary names were cut into Cowley's gravestone in the nineteenth century at the direction of the Dean of Westminster Abbey, Arthur Stanley (1815–81).

3   Samuel Johnson, "Life of Cowley," *Lives*, 1:174. John Dryden, "Discourse," 1. The John Evelyn remark is cited by Philip Major in his introduction to *Royalists*, 2.

4   John Dryden, *Fables Ancient and Modern* (London: Jacob Tonson, 1700), sig. B2r.

5   James Boswell, *Boswell's Life of Johnson*, ed. George Birkbeck Hill, rev. L. F. Powell, 6 vols. in 2 (Oxford: Clarendon Press, 1934), 4:38.

6   Robert Hinman, in *Abraham Cowley's World of Order* (Cambridge: Harvard University Press, 1960), is the only person I have found who disputes identifying the poet Dryden laments as Cowley; Hinman too suggests Wycherley or Etherege (10–11).

7   See Adam Rounce, "The Digital Miscellanies Index and the Canon," *Eighteenth-Century Life* 41, no. 1 (2017): 158–78, for a discussion of what the DMI reveals about Cowley's popularity.

8   Quoted by Trevor Ross, *The Making of the English Literary Canon: From the Middle Ages to the Late Eighteenth Century* (Montreal: McGill-Queen's University Press, 1998), 252.

9   Quoted by Arthur H. Nethercot, *The Reputation of Abraham Cowley (1660–1800)* (Philadelphia: s.n., 1923), 48.

10   Rounce, in "Digital Miscellanies Index," also cites Arthur H. Nethercot, who slyly remarks that "though people, beginning with Dryden in 1700, were continually discovering that Cowley was 'sunk in his reputation,' when that discovery is made over and over again as a new and modern development, one begins to doubt" (164). From Nethercot, "The Reputation of Abraham Cowley (1660–1800)," *PMLA* 38 (1923): 588–641; the quotation is from 617.

11   These essays are reprinted in T. S. Eliot, *The Varieties of Metaphysical Poetry*, ed. Ronald Schuchard (London: Faber & Faber, 1993).

12   H. J. Grierson's *Metaphysical Lyrics and Poems of the Seventeenth Century* (Oxford: Oxford University Press, 1921).

13   The exception among post-Eliot anthologies would be Helen Gardner's *Metaphysical Poets*, 2nd ed. (1957; Oxford: Oxford University Press, 1967), which contains five poems by Cowley. Nonetheless, this is overbalanced by Donne (forty), Herbert (twenty-four), and Vaughan (seventeen). Unlike the other anthologies mentioned, Gardner is not featuring "major" metaphysical poets, but rather assembling an anthology that contains a wide variety of authors, most of them minor, including William Alabaster, Aurelian Townshend, Francis Kynaston, Owen Feltham, William Habington, Thomas Randolph, Sidney Godolphin, Thomas Stanley, John Hall, Thomas Heyrick, Richard Leigh, John Norris of Bemerton.

14   Noted by Joseph E. Duncan, in *The Revival of Metaphysical Poetry: The History of a Style, 1800 to the Present* (Minneapolis: University of Minnesota Press, 1959), 19ff.

15   *Ovid's Epistles, Translated by Several Hands* (London: Jacob Tonson, 1680), sig. a2r.

16   David M. Vieth, "Irony in Dryden's 'Ode to Anne Killigrew,'" *Studies in Philology* 62 (1965): 91–100.

17   F. R. Leavis, *Revaluation: Tradition & Development in English Poetry* (1936; reprint, London: Chatto & Windus, 1959), 39.

18   Geoffrey Walton, *Metaphysical to Augustan* (London: Bowes & Bowes, 1955), 14.

19   George Williamson, *Six Metaphysical Poets: A Reader's Guide* (New York: Farrar, Straus & Giroux, 1967), 174.

20   Donald Mackenzie, *The Metaphysical Poets* (New York: Macmillan, 1990), 15.

21   For an illustration of the chair itself, which is now sitting in the Divinity School, part of the Bodleian Library, Oxford, see Figure 1 in Kevin Cope's essay, in this volume.

22   Cowley, *Verses*, 15–17. Johnson does not discuss or quote the ode to Drake in his "Life of Cowley."

23   Kevin Cope, in his essay for this volume, regards metaphysical poets as "baroque"; I, however, regard them as manneristic, to borrow a term more familiar from art history—manneristic because of the cynicism, irony, paradox, strained metaphors, bizarre situations, and unresolved contradictions in their poetry, as opposed to baroque exuberance, optimism, overreaching, and transcendence. Nonetheless, we both agree that the problem besetting Cowley's reputation has been our inflexible concepts of literary genres—that we both see metaphysical poems belonging to different genres reinforces our argument that genres really are blurred, unstable, and overlapping.

24   The text used for all quotations of Donne is that of *The Poems of John Donne*, ed. Herbert J. C. Grierson, 2 vols. (Oxford: Clarendon Press, 1912).

25   Incidentally, the etymology is still operative in the word "university," since it derives from "universitas magistrorum et scolarium," i.e., "teachers and students rolled into one."

26   All allusions to Dryden's poetry rely on the text of *The Poems of John Dryden*, ed. Paul Hammond and David Hopkins, 4 vols. (London: Longman, 2000–2005). The Killigrew poem appears in vol. 3.

27   Of course, there are many scholars, too numerous to mention, who have expanded the canon of the English novel beyond this handful of authors. I focus here on Leah Orr's work because she is the first scholar, to my knowledge, to rely extensively on digital databases, specifically EEBO and ECCO, databases that are gradually becoming more accessible. The Renaissance Society of America (RSA) includes access to EEBO in its membership benefits, and, as I write this, the American Society for Eighteenth-Century Studies (ASECS) has just announced that its members will henceforth have access to ECCO. Where previous scholars working on the history of the novel were generally from major research universities, and had access to major research collections, now, a great many scholars, from schools large and small, urban and rural, have access to

an enormous amount of data, which should produce more scholarship that challenges established verities and our views of the canon. See also Ashley Marshall, *The Practice of Satire in England, 1658–1770* (Baltimore: Johns Hopkins University Press, 2013), based on her review of some 3,000 satires, accessed from EEBO and ECCO.

Chapter Two: Ease, Confidence, Difficulty, and Grasshoppers: Abraham Cowley's Segmented Baroque

1   See Cedric Reverand's essay, in this volume, for a rehearsal of the many modern anthologies of metaphysical poetry that exclude Cowley. As Michael Edson and Reverand note in their introduction, there are two relatively recent anthologies that, at long last, include Cowley, one edited by Julia Griffin for Penguin (1998), another edited by David Hopkins and Tom Mason for Carcanet (1994). However, the Griffin anthology, since it includes poetry by three poets—Edmund Waller, John Oldham, and Cowley—only has a selection of Cowley's poems. And the more extensive Hopkins-Mason anthology is currently out of print, although a paperback can be purchased, as we write this, for $115.99 on Amazon.com.

2   The multi-century history of the first two centuries of Cowley's reception is chronicled in exquisite detail by Arthur H. Nethercot in "The Reputation of Abraham Cowley, 1660–1800," *PMLA* 38 (1923): 588–641. It is worthy of note that, as recently as 1923, the prestigious *PMLA* allocated fifty-four pages to a study of Cowley.

3   The Open Textbook Library is online at https://open.umn.edu/open textbooks/textbooks/639.

4   Unless otherwise noted, all the references to Cowley's poetry in this chapter rely on Cowley, *Works* (1668).

5   The unrelenting lightness of Cowley's verse, which seems easygoing even when addressing challenging topics or soaring into Pindaric raptures, is one of the biggest impediments to his reputation during our era, when "serious" is treated as a synonym for "valuable" (as in "serious scholarship"). This inveterate frivolousness should not be regarded as an indication of triviality. As Tom Mason suggests, in "Abraham Cowley and the Wisdom of Anacreon," *Cambridge Quarterly* 19 (1990): 103–37, "Cowley's art in the *Anacreontiques* was the art of combining smallness and lightness with largeness and amplitude of thought: of expressing his deepest thoughts in the slightest of possible forms" (129).

6   During an attempt to align Cowley's definition of "wit" in "Ode. Of Wit," Scott Elledge, in "Cowley's Ode 'Of Wit' and Longinus on the Sublime: A Study of One Definition of the Word *Wit*," *Modern Language Quarterly* 9 (1948): 185–98, detects an analogous vacillation between the immense and the minute. Cowley, Elledge affirms, associates wit with both "the

sublime" and "decorum." Sublimity deals with the overwhelming, especially with anything very large; decorum, by contrast, deals with the fitting, including, perhaps paradoxically, that which befits the immense—for example, the decorum appropriate to an epic or tragedy (194).

7   Commenting on the "painted grapes" motif as well as on his attitude toward the new science, Simon Malpas, in "'In No One Thing, They Saw, Agreeing': Communicating Experimental Philosophy in Cowley and Butler," *Restoration* 43, no. 2 (2019): 49–73, observes that, for Cowley, "knowledge is something to be actively produced rather than passively received" (59). This point applies equally well to Cowley's frequent, highly creative use of formulaic language, familiar tropes, and stock literary gestures. Cowley's routine use of these old favorites calls attention to his manufacturing of new meanings, effects, and to producing information from them.

8   Cowley's approach to imitating either the ancients or their literary genres is more complicated than that of most long eighteenth-century writers. For an analysis of the complexities of Cowley's use of ancient models, see Andrew Mattison, "Cowley's Dream of a Shadow: Imitation against Experience," *Modern Language Quarterly* 82 (2021): 55–80.

9   The understanding of "insect" as a segmented, incised, sectioned creature began around the turn of the seventeenth century. See *OED*, s.v. "insect, n." (1).

10   Giovanna Garzoni, *Open Pomegranate in a Dish, with Grasshopper, Snail, and Two Chestnuts*, online at https://biblioklept.org/2018/09/10/open-pomegranate-in-a-dish-with-grasshopper-snail-and-two-chestnuts-giovanna-garzoni/.

Chapter Three: Sacred Calm: The Digressions of Cowley's *Davideis*

1   Unless otherwise noted, the text used for all quotations from Cowley is that of the 1656 *Poems*.

2   Maggie Kilgour, "Cowley's Epic Experiments," *Royalists*, ed. Major, 93–123, especially 102.

3   See Ross Chambers, *Loiterature* (Lincoln: University of Nebraska Press, 1999). Subsequent studies include Anne Cotterill, *Digressive Voices in Early Modern English Literature* (New York: Oxford University Press, 2004); *Digressions in European Literature: From Cervantes to Sebald*, ed. Alexis Grohmann and Caragh Wells (New York: Palgrave Macmillan, 2011); and *Textual Wanderings: The Theory and Practice of Narrative Digression*, ed. Rhian Atkin (London: Legenda, 2011).

4   For England and sublimity, see *Translations of the Sublime: The Early Modern Reception and Dissemination of Longinus's Peri Hupsous in Rhetoric, the Visual Arts, Architecture, and the Theatre*, ed. Caroline van Eck,

Stijn Bussels, Maarten Delbeke, and Jürgen Pieters (Boston: Brill, 2012) and Patrick Cheney, *English Authorship and the Early Modern Sublime: Fictions of Transport in Spenser, Marlowe, Jonson, and Shakespeare* (New York: Cambridge University Press, 2018). For the sublime during the Interregnum, see Philip Hardie, "Generic Dialogue and the Sublime in Cowley: Epic, Didactic, Pindaric," in *Royalists*, ed. Major, 71–92, especially 71.

5   Philip Shaw, *The Sublime*, 2nd ed. (2006; New York: Routledge, 2017), 22.

6   Longinus, *On the Sublime*, from *Aristotle: Poetics. Longinus: On the Sublime. Demetrius: On Style*, trans. Stephen Halliwell, W. Hamilton Fyfe, Doreen C. Innes, W. Rhys Roberts, rev. Donald A. Russell, Loeb Classical Library 199 (Cambridge: Harvard University Press, 1995), 269 (section 33).

7   Stella P. Revard, *Pindar and the Renaissance Hymn-Ode: 1450–1700* (Tempe: Arizona Center for Medieval and Renaissance Studies, 2001), 32.

8   *OED*, s.v. "inspiration" (3a).

9   Anthony Welch, *The Renaissance Epic and the Oral Past* (New Haven: Yale University Press, 2012), 120.

10   Royalist readings of the 1656 *Poems* include Thomas Corns, *Uncloistered Virtue: English Political Literature, 1640–1660* (Oxford: Clarendon Press, 1992), 256–68, and Stella P. Revard, "Cowley's *Pindarique Odes* and the Politics of the Interregnum," *Criticism* 35 (1993): 391–418. For antimonarchical/republican readings, see Nethercot, *Cowley*, 153 and Trotter, *Poetry*, 86–98.

11   John West, *Dryden and Enthusiasm* (Oxford: Oxford University Press, 2018), 46.

12   Joshua Scodel, "The Cowleyan Pindaric Ode and Sublime Diversions," in *A Nation Transformed: England after the Restoration*, ed. Alan Houston and Steve Pincus (Cambridge: Cambridge University Press, 2001), 180–210, especially 189.

13   Victoria Moul, "Abraham Cowley's 1656 *Poems*: Form and Context," in *Royalists*, ed. Major, 150–80, especially 159–62.

14   See Adam Rounce's essay in this volume.

15   See Plato, *The Symposium*, trans. Robin Waterfield (Oxford: Oxford University Press, 1994), 210a–212a and Marsilio Ficino, *Commentary on Plato's Symposium on Love*, trans. Sears Jayne (Dallas: Spring Publications, 1985).

16   James Howell, *Epistolæ Ho-Elianæ. Familiar Letters Domesic and Forren* (London: Humphrey Moseley, 1650), 202–203.

17   Stephen Guy-Bray, "Cowley's Latin Lovers: Nisus and Euryalus in the *Davideis*," *Classical and Modern Literature* 21 (2001): 21–42.

18   Cf. *Davideis*, 8–11 and *Aeneid*, book 7, ll. 406–74.

19 I have discussed this aspect of the *Davideis* more extensively in Ian Calvert, *Virgil's English Translators: Civil Wars to Restoration* (Edinburgh: Edinburgh University Press, 2021), 65–67.

20 See Chloe Wheatley, *Epic, Epitome, and the Early Modern Historical Imagination* (Burlington: Ashgate, 2011), 100.

21 *OED*, s.v. "patience" (1c, 1a).

22 Blair Worden, *God's Instruments: Political Conduct in the England of Oliver Cromwell* (Oxford: Oxford University Press, 2012), 35.

23 See Worden, *God's Instruments*, 43; John Spurr, "Virtue, Religion, and Government: The Anglican Uses of Providence," in *The Politics of Religion in Restoration England*, ed. Tim Harris, Paul Seaward, and Mark Goldie (Oxford: Blackwell, 1990), 29–47; and Alexandra Walsham, *Providence in Early Modern England* (Oxford: Oxford University Press, 1999).

24 See Frank Kermode, "The Date of Cowley's *Davideis*," *Review of English Studies* 98 (1949): 154–58.

25 Cf. *Davideis*, 19, *Aeneid*, book 6, ll. 645–78. The latter is quoted in Cowley, *Davideis*, 43.

Chapter Four: "Verse Loitring into Prose": Abraham Cowley's Prosimetric Ode

1 Frank Kermode, "The Date of Cowley's *Davideis*," *Review of English Studies* 25 (1949): 154–58, especially 156.

2 See Adam Rounce's essay in this volume.

3 Throughout this essay I distinguish Cowley's digressive notes from brief marginal glosses (e.g., "Queen Anne") and citations (e.g., "vide Virg. Aen. 6"), which were common features of the period's verse.

4 For Cowley's familiarity with Heywood's poem, see the "Preface" to Cowley's *Poems* (1656), sig. b3r; for his allusions to Prynne, see John Bruce, "Prynne, Cowley, and Pope," *Notes and Queries* 12 (1855): 67–69.

5 Cowley's biographer, Nethercot, in *Cowley*, suggests that Cowley's "Reason, The use of it in Divine Matters" was likely written in Jersey during the summer months of 1651 when he began the *Pindarique Odes*, refers to More and the Cambridge Platonists (132).

6 Daniel Defoe, for instance, cites Cowley as precedent to justify his annotation of *Jure Divino: A Satyr* (London, 1706), xxvi.

7 The limited internal evidence accords with Kermode's suspicion that the poems largely date from the 1650s. See *A Critical Edition of Abraham Cowley's* Davideis, ed. Gayle Shadduck (New York: Garland Publishing, 1987), 3–12 and Allsopp, *Poetry*, 117.

8 There is some evidence to support this conjecture. Nethercot, in *Cowley*, surmises that Cowley arranged his *Poems* in order of composition (133), and this view is supported by Hilton Kelliher's study of one of Cowley's

surviving manuscripts, "Cowley and 'Orinda': Autograph Fair Copies," *British Library Journal* 2 (1976): 102–108, especially 104. On Cowley's edition of Pindar, see Don Cameron Allen, "Cowley's Pindar," *Modern Language Notes* 63 (1948): 184–85.

9   See, for instance, the notes about Virgil and Homer included in the seventh stanza of Cowley's "The Second Olympique *Ode* of *Pindar*," which expand and add to those present in Benedictus's edition. See Cowley, *Pindariques*, 8–9 and Pindar, Πέριοδος, ed. Johannes Benedictus (Saumur, 1620), 56–57.

10   Regarding the latter work, Stella P. Revard, in *Pindar and the Renaissance Hymn-Ode: 1450–1700* (Tempe: Arizona Center for Medieval and Renaissance Studies, 2001), suggests that Cowley employs the philosophical ode "as an extension of the prose essay" (323).

11   Unless otherwise noted, the text used for all quotations from Cowley is that of the 1656 *Poems*.

12   Unless otherwise indicated, all translations are my own.

13   See Ian Calvert's essay in this volume.

14   "The Church-porch," *The English Poems of George Herbert*, ed. Helen Wilcox (Cambridge: Cambridge University Press, 2007), ll. 86–87.

15   Cowley, "The Garden," *Works* (1668), *Verses Written*, 114–15.

16   Pindar, *Olympian Odes, Pythian Odes*, ed. and trans. William H. Race, rev. ed., Loeb Classical Library 56 (Cambridge: Harvard University Press, 1997), 73.

17   John Dryden, "Discourse," l [Roman numeral]. In his "Preface" to *Ovid's Epistles, Translated by Several Hands* (London: Jacob Tonson, 1681), sig. A1r–a4r, Dryden misquotes a passage from Seneca (substituting "Nescivit" for "Nescit") in the same manner as Cowley's "To Mr. *Hobs*" (sig. A5v, and Cowley, *Pindariques*, 29). I have not located an instance of this misquotation other than Cowley's prior to 1681, which suggests the possibility that Dryden borrowed the passage from Cowley.

18   Revard, *Pindar*, 323 and John William Knapp, *Fiddled Out of Reason: Addison and the Rise of Hymnic Verse, 1687–1712* (Bethlehem: Lehigh University Press, 2019), 16.

19   Dryden's "Preface," *Ovid's Epistles*, sig. a1v.

20   David Lloyd, *Memoires of the Lives, Actions, Sufferings & Deaths . . . in our late Intestine Wars* (London: Samuel Speed, 1668), 620 and Gerard Langbaine, *An Account of the English Dramatick Poets* (Oxford: Printed by L. L. for George West, and Henry Clements, 1691), 84.

21   Cowley, *Pindariques*, 18–19 and William Congreve, "Discourse," sig. A1r.

22   "Tous les sublimes transports de l'ode doivent être réglés par la raison, tout ce désordre apparent ne doit être en effet qu'un ordre plus caché." Louis de Jaucourt, *Encyclopédie, ou Dictionnaire Raisonné des Sciences, des Arts et des Métiers*, 28 vols. (Paris: Briasson, 1751–72), s.v. "Ode."

23   Congreve, "Discourse," sig. A1r. See, for instance, Revard, *Pindar*, 48.

24   Congreve, *The Works of Mr. William Congreve*, 3 vols. (London: Jacob Tonson), 3:1102, 1100.

25   Lewis Theobald, *A Pindarick Ode on the Union* (London: Printed for T. C., 1707), sig. A1v.

26   On the rivalry between Hill and Pope, see Christine Gerrard, *Aaron Hill: The Muses' Projector, 1685–1750* (Oxford: Oxford University Press, 2003), 125–26.

27   Aaron Hill, *Gideon, or the Restoration of Israel* ([London, 1720]), 32; Richard Savage, "On Mr. Cowley's Introducing Pindaric Verse," *Miscellaneous Poems and Translations. By several Hands. Publish'd by Richard Savage* (London: Samuel Chapman, 1726), 93–97.

28   Samuel Wesley (who cites Cowley as precedent) had earlier integrated Pindaric verse into a biblical epic. See Wesley's *The Life of our Blessed Lord & Saviour Jesus Christ* (London: Charles Harper, 1693), 183–90, 220.

29   Aaron Hill, *Gideon; or, The Patriot* (London: A. Millar, 1749), 6–7.

30   Aaron Hill and William Bond, *The Plain Dealer: Being Select Essays on Several Curious Subjects*, 2 vols. (London: S. Richardson, 1730), 1:ii.

31   Samuel Johnson, *The Rambler*, vols. 3–5 of *The Yale Edition of the Works of Samuel Johnson*, ed. W. J. Bate and Albrecht B. Strauss (New Haven: Yale University Press, 1969), 5:77.

32   John Norris, *A Collection of Miscellanies: Consisting of Poems, Essays, Discourses, and Letters* (Oxford: Printed at the [Sheldonian] Theater, 1687), 1–15, 53–61.

33   Norris's imitator David Williams offers similar remarks—e.g., "This line hints at the Operations of the Eternal λόγος, the Word, or Wisdom of God in the Creation of the World"—in *A Pindaric on the Nativity of the Son of God* (London: Printed for St. John Baker, [1712]), 12.

34   J[ames] S[hute], *Virtue and Science: Pindarick Poems* (London, 1695), sig. a2v.

35   John Reynolds, *A View of Death: Or, The Soul's Departure from the World* (London: Printed for John Clark and Richard Hett, 1725), title-page, 35. The verse in Reynolds's poem is centered, unlike every other Pindaric I have encountered. For a discussion of Reynolds's place in the tradition of physicotheological poetry, see Megan Kitching, "'When Universal Nature I Survey': Philosophical Poetry before 1750," *Voice and Context in Eighteenth-Century Verse: Order in Variety*, ed. Joanna Fowley and Allan Ingram (London: Palgrave Macmillan, 2015), 83–100, especially 85–87.

36   Marjorie Hope Nicholson, *Newton Demands the Muse: Newton's Opticks and the Eighteenth-Century Poets* (Princeton: Princeton University Press, 1946), 56.

37   *The New Oxford Book of Eighteenth-Century Verse*, ed. Robert Lonsdale (Oxford: Oxford University Press, 1984), 80–81.

38   Joseph Addison, "An Account of the Greatest English Poets," *The Annual Miscellany, for the Year 1694* (London: Printed by R. E. for Jacob Tonson, 1694), 319–20.

39   Alexander Pope, *The Dunciad Variorum*, book 1, ll. 227–32.

40   William Mason, *Caractacus, A Dramatic Poem* (London: K. Napton, 1759), 89.

41   *Correspondence of Thomas Gray*, 3 vols., ed. Paget Toynbee and Leonard Whibley, rev. H. W. Starr (Oxford: Clarendon Press, 1971), letter 508.

42   Thomas Gray, *Poems by Mr Gray: A New Edition* (London: J. Dodsley, 1768).

43   On the relationship between these three works, see John Warner Taylor, "The Sources of Shelley's 'Queen Mab,'" *Sewanee Review* 14 (1906): 324–51, especially 325–26, and Dahlia Porter, "Formal Relocations: The Method of Southey's *Thalaba the Destroyer* (1801)," *European Romantic Review* 20 (2009): 671–79, especially 671.

44   See John Sitter, *The Cambridge Introduction to Eighteenth-Century Poetry* (Cambridge: Cambridge University Press, 2011), 9 and *The Cambridge Companion to Eighteenth-Century Poetry*, ed. Sitter (Cambridge: Cambridge University Press, 2001), 9.

45   On the ways in which colonial writers used this formal innovation to appropriate subaltern and indigenous forms of knowledge, for instance, see Kimberly Takahata, "A Caribbean Counter-Edition: *Digital Grainger* and the Breaking of James Grainger's *The Sugar-Cane*," *archipelagos: a journal of Caribbean digital praxis* 4 (2020), online at http://archipelagos-journal.org/issue04/takahata-counter.html.

Chapter Five: Black Comedy and Futility: Cowley's Notes to *Davideis*

1   For studies regarding Cowley's notes as excessive or aesthetically faulty, see Robert B. Hinman, *Abraham Cowley's World of Order* (Cambridge: Harvard University Press, 1960), 227–66; Trotter, *Poetry*, 83–108; Timothy Dykstal, "The Epic Reticence of Abraham Cowley," *SEL: Studies in English Literature 1500–1900* 31 (1991): 95–115; and *A Critical Edition of Abraham Cowley's* Davideis, ed. Gayle Shadduck (New York: Garland Publishing, 1987), 1.37–42, 42–62.

2   For recent studies of the allegory and notes in *Davideis*, see Joseph Wallace, "True Poetry and False Religion in Abraham Cowley's *Davideis*," *Review of English Studies* 66 (2015): 895–914; Lucinda Cole, *Imperfect Creatures: Vermin, Literature, and the Sciences of Life, 1600–1740* (Ann Arbor: University of Michigan Press, 2016), 49–80; and Andrew Mattison, "Cowley's Dream of a Shadow: Imitation against Experience," *Modern Language Quarterly* 82 (2021): 52–80.

3   For more discussion of Cowley's self-annotation in his *Pindarique Odes*, see Joshua Swidzinski's chapter in this volume.

4   Gerard Genette, *Paratexts*, trans. Jane E. Lewin (Cambridge: Cambridge University Press, 1997), 328, 327.

5   Anthony Grafton, *The Footnote: A Curious History* (Cambridge: Harvard University Press, 1999), 28.

6   See T. S. Eliot, "The Frontiers of Criticism" (1956), reprinted in *On Poetry and Poets* (London: Faber & Faber 1986), 103–18, especially 109–10.

7   D. T. Max, *Every Love Story Is a Ghost Story: A Life of David Foster Wallace* (New York: Penguin, 2013), 265.

8   Thomas Gray, *Poems by Mr. Gray: A New Edition* (London: Dodsley, 1768), 36.

9   *The Complete Poems of William Empson*, ed. John Haffenden (London: Allen Lane, 2001), 111.

10 All references to *Davideis* rely on Cowley, *Poems* (1656), cited by book and page number; note that each book includes a section of endnotes.

11 *The Complete Poetry and Prose of William Blake*, ed. David V. Erdman and Harold Bloom (New York: Doubleday, 1988), 146. Samuel Johnson, *The Idler* (1758–60), numbers 60 and 61.

Chapter Six: "More Famous by His Pen than by His Sword": Weaponizing the Classics in Abraham Cowley's *The Civil War*

1   The quotation in the title is from *The Weekly Intelligencer of the Common-Wealth Faithfully Communicating all Affairs both Martial and Civil* (April 17, 1655). See Allan Pritchard, *Abraham Cowley: The Civil War* (Toronto: University of Toronto Press, 1973), the text used throughout this chapter, indicated by book and line numbers. A shortened version (thirty-two pages) of the first book was published posthumously in 1679, but the text of the whole was thought to be lost (or burned), until two manuscripts surfaced in the 1960s. Pritchard's 1973 text, based on what he regarded as the more authentic manuscript, is, thus, the first edition of the three books Cowley completed.

2   Nethercot, *Cowley*, 21. Pending the discovery of the manuscript of all three books in the late 1960s, Nethercot, who published in 1931, had access only to the unauthorized, severely truncated, and posthumous Abraham Cowley, *A Poem on the Late Civil War* (London, 1679).

3   Thus David Norbrook, *Writing the English Republic: Poetry, Rhetoric, and Politics, 1627–1660* (Cambridge: Cambridge University Press, 1999), 83–85; Pritchard, *Cowley: The Civil War*, 34; and James Loxley, *Royalism and Poetry in the English Civil Wars: The Drawn Sword* (Basingstoke: Macmillan, 1997), 88.

4   Philip Hardie, "Generic Dialogue and the Sublime in Cowley: Epic, Didactic, Pindaric," in *Royalists*, ed. Major, 71–92; Henry Power, "'Teares Breake Off My Verse': The Virgilian Incompleteness of Abraham Cowley's

The Civil War," *Translation and Literature* 16 (2007), online at www. jstor.org/stable/40340065; and Edward Paleit, *War, Liberty, and Caesar: Responses to Lucan's Bellum Ciuile, ca. 1580–1650* (Oxford: Oxford University Press, 2013).

5   "Several Discourses by way of Essays, in Verse and Prose," Cowley, "Of My Self," *Works* (1668), *Verses Written*, 144–45.

6   This was of course to cause Cowley endless trouble when in the 1656 volume he appeared to come to an accommodation with the Cromwellian regime. For a recent discussion, see Allsopp, *Poetry*, 114–19.

7   On its importance as an early example of the genre, see Paul Davis, *Translation and the Poet's Life: The Ethics of Translating in English Culture, 1646–1726* (Oxford: Oxford University Press, 2008), 77–126 and Jane Darcy, *Melancholy and Literary Biography, 1640–1816* (Basingstoke: Palgrave Macmillan, 2013), 26–41.

8   Davis, *Translation*, 93–95, 110–15 and Darcy, *Melancholy and Literary Biography*, 31–37.

9   Caroline Spearing, "The Fruits of Retirement: Political Engagement in the *Plantarum Libri Sex*," in *Royalists*, ed. Major, 180–201. On Stoic withdrawal, see, particularly, Andrew Eric Shifflett, *Stoicism, Politics, and Literature in the Age of Milton: War and Peace Reconciled* (Cambridge: Cambridge University Press, 1998), 5–7.

10   [Abraham Cowley], *Poetical Blossomes* (London: Printed by B. A. and T. F. for Henry Seile, 1633).

11   See, for example, Sharon Achinstein, "Texts in Conflict: The Press and the Civil War," in *The Cambridge Companion to Writing of the English Revolution*, ed. N. H. Keeble (Cambridge: Cambridge University Press, 2001), 50–68.

12   Thomas Cogswell, "Underground Verse and the Transformation of Early Stuart Political Culture," *Huntington Library Quarterly* 60 (1997): 303–26; the quotation is from 314.

13   Pritchard, *Cowley: The Civil War*, 40–41; Power, "'Teares Breake Off My Verse,'" 154; and Paleit, *War, Liberty, and Caesar*, 296.

14   *Lucan's Pharsalia: or The Civil Warres of Rome, . . . The whole ten Bookes Englished by Thomas May*, trans. May (London: T. Jones and J. Marriott, 1627), 1.ll. 22–24.

15   See, particularly, Power, "'Teares Breake Off My Verse,'" 150.

16   An excellent discussion of the relationship between Apollo and the laurel can be found in Philip Hardie, *Ovid's Poetics of Illusion* (Cambridge: Cambridge University Press, 2002), 45–50.

17   For a contemporary example of the cypress denoting the elegiac genre, see Hugh Holland, *A Cypres Garland For the Sacred Forehead of our late Soueraigne King James* (London, Printed [by Nicholas Okes] for Simon Waterson, 1625). The personified laurel serves as the narrator of book 2

of Cowley's *Plantarum Libri Sex* (1663 and 1668), where he refers to her as "*mea Laurus*" (43).

18 Loxley, *Royalism and Poetry*, 18 and Maggie Kilgour, "Cowley's Epic Experiments," in *Royalists*, ed. Major, 93–123; the quotation is from 99–100.

19 David Quint, *Epic and Empire: Politics and Generic Form from Virgil to Milton* (Princeton: Princeton University Press, 1993), 5–10. See Pritchard, *Cowley: The Civil War*, 3–4; Paleit, *War, Liberty, and Caesar*, 296; Warren Chernaik, "Laurels for the Conquered: Cowley, Epic, and History," in *Royalists*, ed. Major, 46–70, especially 51; Gerald M. MacLean, *Time's Witness: Historical Representation in English Poetry, 1603–1660* (Madison: University of Wisconsin Press, 1990).

20 See, for example, MacLean, *Time's Witness*, 33–35 and Norbrook, *Writing the English Republic*, 23–62.

21 Victoria Moul, "Revising the Siege of York: From Royalist to Cromwellian in Payne Fisher's *Marston-Moor*," *Seventeenth Century* 31 (2016): 311–31 and Paleit, *War, Liberty, and Caesar*, 15–22.

22 See Paleit, *War, Liberty, and Caesar*, 297–98 and Power, "'Teares Breake Off My Verse,'" 150.

23 Pritchard, *Cowley: The Civil War*, 170. "Young" Vieuville, whose parents are anxiously watching for his return, was probably at least in his late twenties (as the eldest son of parents who married in 1611) and thus older than the poet.

24 *Mercurius Aulicus* (September 19, 1643): 38, cited by Pritchard, in *Cowley: The Civil War*.

25 For the trope in Homer, see Jasper Griffin, *Homer on Life and Death* (Oxford: Oxford University Press, 1983), 106–12.

26 Norbrook, *Writing the English Republic*, 86. See also Cowley's description of hell in 2:423–504, where rebels against the king are punished irrespective of the justice of their cause (445–48).

27 See, for example, Shadi Bartsch, *Ideology in Cold Blood: A Reading of Lucan's Civil War* (Cambridge: Harvard University Press, 2009), 15–17 and Martin T. Dinter, *Anatomizing Civil War: Studies in Lucan's Epic Technique* (Ann Arbor: University of Michigan Press, 2013), 37–39.

28 See Trotter, *Poetry*, 17–18. Trotter's discomfort with Cowley's generic hybridity is addressed by MacLean, in *Time's Witness*, who points to precisely this variation of genre as an important feature of contemporary epic (207).

29 See Raymond A. Anselment, *Loyalist Resolve: Patient Fortitude in the English Civil War* (Newark: University of Delaware Press, 1988), 162–64.

30 This use of the word "vandal" to mean "a wilful or ignorant destroyer of anything beautiful, venerable, or worthy of preservation" predates the earliest example (1660) given in the *OED*.

31 Accurate estimates of numbers benefiting from a grammar school education are notoriously difficult, but it seems that the vast majority of the sons of merchants and "superior shopkeepers" attended these establishments, along with some tradesmen and craftsmen. See Robert Black, "School," in *The Oxford Handbook of Neo-Latin*, ed. Sarah Knight and Stefan Tilg (Oxford: Oxford University Press, 2015), 217–32; Jenny C Mann, *The Trials of Orpheus: Poetry, Science, and the Early Modern Sublime* (Princeton: Princeton University Press, 2021); and David Cressy, "Educational Opportunity in Tudor and Stuart England," *History of Education Quarterly* 16 (1976), online at www.jstor.org/stable/368112.

32 Diane Purkiss, *Literature, Gender, and Politics during the English Civil War* (Cambridge: Cambridge University Press, 2005), 36–41.

33 The passage also evokes the severed hand at Virgil, *Aeneid*, 10:395–96 (see above).

34 "The contemporary accounts indicate that Cowley does not exaggerate its effect" (Pritchard, *Cowley: The Civil War*, 151).

35 This passage has received more discussion than any other in the work. See Trotter, *Poetry*, 19–20; Anselment, *Loyalist Resolve*, 163–65; MacLean, *Time's Witness*, 208–11; Loxley, *Royalism and Poetry*, 87–88; Power, "'Teares Breake Off My Verse,'" 154–57; Paleit, *War, Liberty, and Caesar*, 302–305; Hardie, "Generic Dialogue," 76–78; and Rebecca M. Rush, *The Fetters of Rhyme* (Princeton: Princeton University Press, 2021), 120–26.

36 For a recent treatment of the myth of Orpheus in this period, see Mann, *Trials of Orpheus*. His various associations are summarized at 6–17.

37 Paul G. Stanwood, "Community and Social Order in the Great Tew Circle," in *Literary Circles and Cultural Communities in Renaissance England*, ed. Claude J. Summers and Ted-Larry Pebworth (Columbia: University of Missouri Press, 2000), 173–86.

38 Ben Jonson, *The Underwood* (1641), from *The Cambridge Edition of the Works of Ben Jonson Online*, at https://universitypublishingonline.org/cambridge/benjonson/k/works/underwood/facing/#. See Hardie, "Generic Dialogue," 76–78; Victoria Moul, *Jonson, Horace, and the Classical Tradition* (Cambridge: Cambridge University Press, 2010), 48–53; and Rush, *Fetters of Rhyme*.

39 *Royalists*, ed. Major, 3 and Victoria Moul, "Cowley's 1656 Poems in Context," *Royalists*, ed. Major, 150–79, especially 162–63.

Chapter Seven: Cowley's *Essays*: Martial and the Ironies of Retirement

1   Unless otherwise noted, the edition I will be using for references to Cowley is that of *The Essays and Other Prose Writings*, ed. Alfred B. Gough (Oxford: Clarendon Press, 1915), hereafter *Essays*.

2   For the standard study of the seventeenth-century literature of retirement, see Maren-Sofie Røstvig, *The Happy Man: Studies in the Metamorphoses of a Classical Ideal*, 2 vols. (Oslo: Oslo University Press, 1954–58). For these and other retirement poets, see Michael Edson, "'A Closet or a Secret Field': Horace, Protestant Devotion, and British Retirement Poetry," *Journal for Eighteenth-Century Studies* 35 (2012): 17–41.

3   Philip Major, "Sacred and Secular in Cowley's *Essays*," in *Royalists*, ed. Major, 202–28; the quotation is from 220.

4   David Hopkins, "Cowley's Horatian Mice," *Conversing with Antiquity: English Poets and the Classics, from Shakespeare to Pope* (Oxford: Oxford University Press, 2010), 55–87; the quotation is from 60.

5   Dustin Griffin, *Satire: A Critical Reintroduction* (Lexington: University of Kentucky Press, 1994), 65–66.

6   Paul Davis, *Translation and the Poet's Life: The Ethics of Translating in English Culture, 1646–1726* (Oxford: Oxford University Press, 2008). Davis discusses Cowley on 75–126.

7   Davis, *Translation*, chap. 2; Jane Darcy, *Melancholy and Literary Biography, 1640–1816* (Basingstoke: Palgrave Macmillan, 2013), chap. 1; and Raymond A. Anselment, *Loyalist Resolve: Patient Fortitude in the English Civil War* (Newark: University of Delaware Press, 1988), 155.

8   For discussion of Cowley's finances, see Caroline Spearing, "The Fruits of Retirement: Political Engagement in the *Plantarum Libri Sex*," in *Royalists*, ed. Major, 181.

9   Alexander Pope, "Imitations of Horace: The First Epistle of the Second Book," Pope, *Poems*, l. 78.

10   Abraham Cowley, *Select Works of Mr. A. Cowley; in Two Volumes: With a Preface and Notes*, ed. Richard Hurd, 2nd ed., 2 vols. (London: Printed by W. Bowyer and J. Nichols, 1772), 2:261–62n.

11   Darcy, *Melancholy and Literary Biography*, 27. Among modern critics, Alfred B. Gough, editor of Cowley's *Essays*, found "unfeigned enthusiasm" (xxiii); Arthur H. Nethercot, in "Abraham Cowley's *Essays*," *Journal of English and Germanic Philology* 29 (1930): 114–30 thought it "betray[ed]" Cowley as he was (125); and Alan De Gooyer, in "Sensibility and Solitude in Cowley's Familiar Essay," *Restoration* 25, no. 1 (2001): 1–18, praised its "confessional immediacy" (10).

12   Cowley's letter to Sprat is reprinted in Johnson's "Life of Cowley," in Johnson, *Lives*, 199.

13   A. W. Ward, headnote to "Abraham Cowley," in *English Prose: Selections*, ed. Henry Craik, 4 vols. (New York: Macmillan, 1893–96), 2:575.

14   Tom Mason, "Abraham Cowley's Amiability," *1650–1850: Ideas, Aesthetics, and Inquiries in the Early Modern Era* 15 (2008): 189–218; the quotation is from 216.

15 Joseph Spence, *Observations, Anecdotes, and Characters of Books and Men*, ed. James M. Osborn, 2 vols. (Oxford: Clarendon Press, 1966), 1:192–93.

16 Onslow's comment, quoted from Johnson, *Lives*, 198n.

17 "The Preface to the Poems," *Essays*, 7.

18 Shane Herron, *Irony and Earnestness in Eighteenth-Century Literature: Dimensions of Satire and Solemnity* (Cambridge: Cambridge University Press, 2022), 5.

19 Scott Black, *Of Essays and Reading in Early Modern Britain* (London: Palgrave Macmillan, 2006), 49.

20 George Mackenzie had published *A Moral Essay, Preferring Solitude to Publick Employment* in 1665. In 1667, John Evelyn replied to Mackenzie in *Publick Employment and an Active Life Prefer'd to Solitude*.

21 See also Virginia Krause, "Montaigne's Art of Idleness," *Viator* 31 (2000): 361–80.

22 I take the translation from Horace, *Satires. Epistles. The Art of Poetry*, trans. H. Rushton Fairclough, Loeb Classical Library 194 (Cambridge: Harvard University Press, 1926), 360–61 (ll. 9–10).

23 Two such errors include: when quoting Virgil in "Of Solitude," for example, Cowley misquotes the original, "O qui me gelidis convallibus Haemi." Cowley has it: "O *quis* me gelidis *sub montibus* Æmi" (*Essays*, 133, italics mine). In "Of Avarice," Cowley wrongly attributes a quotation from Seneca the Elder to Ovid ("Desunt Luxuriae multa, Avaritiae Omnia") (*Essays*, 190).

24 For the backstory of Cowley's gaining a living at Chertsey, see Nethercot, *Cowley*, 244–50.

25 I take the translation from Ovid, *Tristia, Ex Ponto*, trans. A. L. Wheeler, rev. G. P. Goold, Loeb Classical Library 151 (Cambridge: Harvard University Press, 1924), 282–83 (ll. 35–36). Cowley replaces "cunctos" with "musas," either misremembering the original or wishing to stress that poets are especially drawn to rural subjects.

26 "The Motto" appeared in the *Miscellanies* section of Cowley's *Poems*, 1–2.

27 That "The Session of the Poets," a satire published the same year as Cowley's *Essays*, mocks the poet with the epithet "Savoy-missing Cowley" (l. 44), indicates that his ambitions were common knowledge at least in court circles of the time. The poem appears in *Poems on Affairs of State: Augustan Satiric Verse, 1660–1714*, ed. George deF. Lord et al., 6 vols. (New Haven: Yale University Press, 1963–75), 328–32.

28 In this passage, Cowley writes, "I do not remember the Name of any one Husbandman who had so considerable a share in the twenty years ruine," i.e., the English Civil Wars, "as to deserve the Curses of his Countrymen" (144). Gough, who ignores the possible irony and humor in this comment, nevertheless observes, "Numerous members of the landed

gentry, including Cromwell, may be said to have represented agriculture" (*Essays*, 328n20).

29   The passage reads, "The three first Men in the World were a Gardner, a Ploughman, and a Grazier; and if any man object, That the second of these was a Murtherer, I desire he would consider, that as soon as he was so, he quitted our Profession, and turn'd Builder. It is for this reason, I suppose, that *Ecclesiasticus* forbids us to hate Husbandry" (145–46).

30   For a discussion of Cowley's reputation and the long-standing bias against "metaphysical wit," see Cedric Reverand's essay in this volume.

31   Barry Slepian, "The Ironic Intention of Swift's Verses on his Death," *Review of English Studies* 14 (1963): 249–56.

32   David M. Vieth, "Irony in Dryden's 'Ode to Anne Killigrew,'" *Studies in Philology* 62 (1965): 91–100.

33   Evelyn to Cowley, March 12, 1667, from *The Letterbooks of John Evelyn*, ed. Douglas D. C. Chambers and David Galbraith, 2 vols. (paginated as a single volume) (Toronto: University of Toronto Press, 2014), 434–35.

34   See Brian Vickers, *Public and Private Life in the Seventeenth Century: The MacKenzie-Evelyn Debate* (Delmar: Scholars' Facsimiles and Reprints, 1986), which includes facsimiles of Evelyn's *Publick Employment and an Active Life Prefer'd to Solitude* as well as the work to which Evelyn replies, George Mackenzie's *A Moral Essay, Preferring Solitude to Publick Employment*. Vickers quotes Evelyn's letter (xii–xiii), but never mentions Evelyn's disowning of the perspective in his pamphlet or factors it into his interpretations of Evelyn's arguments.

35   For arguing *in utraquem partem* in the schoolroom, see Russ McDonald, *Shakespeare and the Arts of Language* (Oxford: Oxford University Press, 2001), 49 and Quentin Skinner, *Reason and Rhetoric in the Philosophy of Hobbes* (Cambridge: Cambridge University Press, 1996), 26–30.

36   Cowley's identifications of the epigrams are sometimes incomplete or differ from the modern numbering; for instance, he identifies 1.55 as Martial "Lib 2." I use the modern numbering for these epigrams throughout.

37   In *Abraham Cowley* (New York: Twayne, 1972), James G. Taaffe refers repeatedly to Cowley's "Horatian sentiments" (21), "Horatian viewpoint" (22), and "Horatian influence" (25). Hopkins, in "Cowley's Horatian Mice," also implies Cowley's debt to Horace above other classical writers in focusing on his *Satires* 2.6, although see Davis, *Translation*, 97–98, for the counterargument that Cowley's "self-righteous tone . . . is altogether foreign to Horace's poetic and moral sensibility" (98). By "first and last word," I mean that Martial is the first Latin poet Cowley translates (*Epigrams* 1.55 in "Of Liberty") and the last (*Epigrams* 10.96 in "Of My self") in *Essays*.

38 This is not to claim that Cowley had no interest in Martial before 1665. Cowley draws on Martial for his epigraph to "On the Death of Mr. William Hervey," in the *Miscellanies*, 16–20, epigraph on 16. Cowley also quotes or cites Martial in his notes to *Pindarique Odes* and *Davideis* (all from the *Poems* of 1656). See *Pindariques*, 45n, and *Davideis*, 41n, 70n, 111n, and 112n. Cowley also refers to Martial in his "Preface" to *Plantarum*, sig. a7r. Notably, Cowley also quotes from Martial, *Epigrams* 8.69 ("Tanti non est, ut placeam tibi, perire") in his "Preface" to his 1656 *Poems* when discussing his desire to make "a real *literal quitting* of this *World*" (sig. a3v).

39 Allan Pritchard, "Six Letters by Cowley," *Review of English Studies* 18 (1967): 253–63.

40 Cowley to Matthew Clifford, October 18, 1661, from Pritchard, "Six Letters," 260.

41 *Spectator* 62 (May 11, 1711), in *The Spectator*, ed. Donald F. Bond, 5 vols. (Oxford: Oxford University Press, 1987), 1:268.

42 Martial, *Epigrams*, 3 vols., trans. D. R. Shackleton Bailey, Loeb Classical Library 94 (Cambridge: Harvard University Press, 1993), 3:88–89. This is the text used for all subsequent references to the English translation of Martial.

43 For familiarity with Martial's epigrams, see the introduction to *Martial in English*, ed. J. P. Sullivan and A. J. Boyle (New York: Penguin, 1996).

44 For the associations of the epigram form, see James Doelman, *The Epigram in England, 1590–1640* (Manchester: Manchester University Press, 2015) and Victoria Moul, *History*, especially chap. 7.

45 Niall Livingston and Gideon Nisbet, *Epigram* (Cambridge: Cambridge University Press, 2010), 1.

46 Sullivan and Boyle, *Martial in English*, xxiii. Sullivan and Boyle discuss other Martial epigrams that clash with the epigrams dreaming of retirement.

47 Thomas May, *Selected Epigrams of Martial* (London: Printed for Thomas Walkley, 1629), sig. C4v; Robert Fletcher, *Ex Otio Negotium. Or, Martiall his Epigrams Translated* (London: Printed for T. Mabb, for William Shears, 1656), 19–20; and Henry Killigrew, *Epigrams of Martial, Englished* (London: Printed for Henry Bonwicke, 1695), 53.

48 To save space, I have refrained from quoting the Latin.

49 Fletcher's and Fanshawe's imitations are reprinted in Sullivan and Boyle, *Martial in English*, 67 and 78 respectively. For Randolph's translation, see *Poems: With The Muses Looking-Glass, and Amyntas: Whereunto is Added The Jealous Lovers* (Oxford: Printed for F. Bowman and are to be sold by John Crosley, 1668), 61–62.

50 Cowley neglects the economy of other Martial epigrams as well. Cowley's version of *Epigrams* 2.90 is twenty-four lines, while the Latin is ten lines. Cowley's *Epigrams* 5.20, published in his 1656 *Miscellanies*, was twenty-six lines, where the original was fourteen lines.

51   Cowley to Matthew Clifford, June 10, 1666, from Pritchard, "Six Letters," 262 and Spearing, "The Fruits of Retirement," in *Royalists*, ed. Major, 183.

52   Cowley to Evelyn, May 13, 1667, from *Diary and Correspondence of John Evelyn*, ed. William Bray (London: G. Routledge and Sons, 1900), 630.

53   Cowley to Clifford, October 4, [1663?], from Pritchard, "Six Letters," 261.

54   Cowley to Clifford, December 17, 1666, from Pritchard, "Six Letters," 262.

Chapter Eight: Abraham Cowley's *Six Books of Plants* and the Diversification of Textual Authority

1   The translators of the *Six Books* are John Oldham (books 1 and 2), C. Cleve (book 3), Nahum Tate (books 4 and 5), and Aphra Behn (book 6).

2   Cowley, *Six Books*, sig. Aaa1r.

3   Despite his widespread fame among authorial contemporaries and heirs, Cowley has suffered from a relative lack of modern scholarship; indispensable is the recent collection of essays in Philip Major's anthology, *Royalists and Royalism in 17th-Century Literature: Exploring Abraham Cowley*. Besides the works cited throughout, other well-known studies on Cowley include Joshua Scodel, *The English Poetic Epitaph: Commemoration and Conflict from Jonson to Wordsworth* (Ithaca: Cornell University Press, 1991) and Richard Helgerson, *Self-Crowned Laureates: Spenser, Jonson, Milton, and the Literary System* (Berkeley: University of California Press, 1983).

4   In Ode 4.2, Horace declares,

> ego apis Matinae
> more modoque
> grata carpentis thyma per laborem
> plurimum circa nemus uvidique
> Tiburis ripas operosa parvos
> carmina fingo. (ll. 28–32)
> [I, in manner and method like a Matine bee
> that with incessant toil sips the lovely thyme
> around the woods and riverbanks
> of well-watered Tibur, fashion in a small way
> my painstaking songs.]

Horace: Odes and Epodes, ed. and trans. Niall Rudd, Loeb Classical Library 33 (Cambridge: Harvard University Press, 2004), 222–23, online at www.loebclassics.com/view/horace-odes/2004/pb_LCL033.223.xml. Christopher Trinacty, in "The Fox and the Bee: Horace's First Book of Epistles," *Arethusa* 45 (2012): 55–77, argues that the Horatian bee is an element of "animal fables, [which,] as a 'low' feature of Horace's *sermo* in the *Epistles*, are often seen as devices for offering up folk wisdom and as befitting the moralizing found in this book" (60). Ernest Highbarger, in "The Pindaric Style of Horace," *Transactions and Proceedings of the American Philological Association* 66 (1935): 222–55, emphasizes the digestive aspect of this poetic identification: "Thus by wide reading and unlimited toil in composition Horace transmuted his Greek sources into a finished product which was all his own. Such was the honey which this Matinian bee distilled" (225). And Jacqueline Klooster, in "Horace, 'Carmen' 4.2.53–60: Another Look at the 'Vitulus,'" *Classical Quarterly* 63 (2013): 346–52, stresses Horace's insistence in this ode on "the dangers of emulating Pindar" (346).

5   Victoria Moul, in "The Transformation of Ovid in Cowley's Herb Garden: Books 1 and 2 of the *Plantarum Libri Sex* (1668)," in *The Afterlife of Ovid*, ed. Peter Mack and John North (London: University of London Press, 2015), 221–34, offers an incisive analysis of Cowley's Ovidianism in the *Plantarum*.

6   Caroline Spearing, "Abraham Cowley's *Plantarum Libri Sex:* A Cavalier Poet and the Classical Canon" (unpublished DPhil dissertation, University College London, 2017), 22.

7   In Thomas Birch, *The History of the Royal Society of London*, 2 vols. (London: A. Millar, 1756), Cowley is listed as among the founding members (1:4), but subsequent records of the society's daily activities and weekly meetings do not mention his involvement. His *Proposition for the Advancement of Experimental Philosophy* (1661) is one of the informing proposals that led to the establishment of the Royal Society in the first place.

8   For the influence of Sprat's biographical essay over Cowley's reputation, see Gail Mobley, "Abraham Cowley and the English Literary Canon," in *Royalists*, ed. Major, 124–49; for a reading that places this biography in the broader context of the Royal Society, see Joanna Picciotto, *Labors of Innocence in Early Modern England* (Cambridge: Harvard University Press, 2010), 329–30. See also Paul Davis, *Translation and the Poet's Life: The Ethics of Translating in English Culture, 1646–1726* (Oxford: Oxford University Press, 200), 77–126 and Jane Darcy, "The Emergence of Literary Biography," from *A Companion to Literary Biography*, ed. Richard Bradford (London: Wiley & Sons, 2019), 1–24.

9   Robert Hinman, *Abraham Cowley's World of Order* (Cambridge: Harvard University Press, 1960), 97, 100.

10   Cited in Richard Yeo, *Notebooks, English Virtuosi, and Early Modern Science* (Chicago: University of Chicago Press, 2014), 245.

11   For details, see Chantel M. Lavoie, *Collecting Women: Poetry and Lives, 1700–1780* (Lewisburg: Bucknell University Press, 2009), 85–87. Elizabeth Scott-Baumann, in *Forms of Engagement: Women, Poetry, and*

Culture, 1640–1680 (Oxford: Oxford University Press, 2013), reads Katherine Philips alongside Abraham Cowley as "writer[s] of retreat" who resisted the dominant politics of the Interregnum through recourse to Stoic models of retirement"—a mode that Scott-Baumann claims culminated in "Marvell's garden poems" (81).

12 Elaine Miller, *The Vegetative Soul: From Philosophy of Nature to Subjectivity in the Feminine* (Albany: SUNY Press, 2002), 8.

13 Douglas Chambers, "'Wild Pastorall Encounter': John Evelyn, John Beale, and the Renegotiation of Pastoral in the Mid-Seventeenth Century," in *Culture and Cultivation in Early Modern England: Writing the Land*, ed. Michael Leslie and Timothy Raylor (Leicester: Leicester University Press, 1992), 173–94; the quotation is from 177.

14 For details of Horace's adoption of Virgil, see Bernard Fenik, "Horace's First and Sixth Roman Odes, and the Second Georgic," *Hermes* 90 (1962): 72–96. Despite his influence on the foundation of the Georgicall Committee, Samuel Hartlib was not made a member of the Royal Society: Royal Society MS DM 5/63, cited by Anna Marie Roos, "Chymical Teaching in Early Modern Oxford: From Wilkins to Whiteside," in *John Wilkins (1614–1672): New Essays*, ed. William Poole (Leiden: Brill, 2017), 219–40, especially 220n8. On the Georgicall Committee, see Michael Hunter, *Establishing the New Science: The Experience of the Early Royal Society* (Woodbridge: Boydell, 1989), chap. 3.

15 Spearing, in "Cowley's *Plantarum*," explains that in Cowley's Latin poem, the "footnotes are one of the most remarkable features of the work": "Including information from classical, medieval, and early modern sources, and from prose texts as well as the poetry of Ovid and Virgil, they give details of the botanical and pharmacological properties of the plants and record contemporary controversies, particularly over nomenclature and identification" (31).

16 My reading here is influenced by the nascent field of critical plants studies, for instance, Michael Marder, *Plant-Thinking: A Philosophy of Vegetal Life* (New York: Columbia University Press, 2013); Vin Nardizzi, *Wooden Os: Shakespeare's Theatres and England's Trees* (Toronto: University of Toronto Press, 2013); Jeffrey Nealon, *Plant Theory: Biopower and Vegetable Life* (Stanford: Stanford University Press, 2015); and Antonia Szabari and Natania Meeker, *Radical Botany: Plants and Speculative Fiction* (New York: Fordham University Press, 2019).

17 Claire Preston, *The Poetics of Scientific Investigation in Seventeenth-Century England* (Oxford: Oxford University Press, 2015), 12.

18 Mauro Ambrosoli, *The Wild and the Sown: Botany and Agriculture in Western Europe, 1350–1850* (Cambridge: Cambridge University Press, 1997), 2.

19 The first botanist to divide flora according to British/native and non-British/foreign was Hewitt Watson, in *Outlines of the Geographic Distribution of English Plants* (Edinburgh, 1832, 1835, 1843), who judges plants on the basis of whether they are "good citizens" of the British Empire. My thanks to Emanuele Coccia for this information.

20 For the importance of these gardens to Baconian naturalism, see Vera Keller, "A 'Wild Swing to Phantsy': The Philosophical Gardener and Emergent Experimental Philosophy in the Seventeenth-Century Atlantic World," *Isis* 112 (2021): 507–30.

21 Anna Svensson, "'And Eden from the Chaos Rose': Utopian Order and Rebellion in the Oxford Physick Garden," *Annals of Science* 76 (2019): 157–83; the quotation is from 158.

22 For recent studies of this bias toward cultivation, see Frances Dolan, *Digging the Past: How and Why to Imagine Seventeenth-Century Agriculture* (Philadelphia: University of Pennsylvania Press, 2020) and Paul Slack, *The Invention of Improvement: Information and Material Progress in Seventeenth-Century England* (Oxford: Oxford University Press, 2015).

23 Peggy McCracken, "The Floral and the Human," in *Animal, Vegetable, Mineral: Ethics and Objects*, ed. Jeffrey Jerome Cohen (Washington: Punctum Books, 2012), 65–90; the quotation is from 88–89.

24 Allen Grieco, "The Social Politics of Pre-Linnaean Botanical Classification," *I Tatti Studies in the Italian Renaissance* 4 (1991): 131–49; the quotation is from 149.

25 John S. Wilkins, *Species: A History of the Idea* (Berkeley: University of California Press, 2009), 62–63.

26 Richard Drayton, *Nature's Government: Science, Imperial Britain, and the "Improvement" of the World* (New Haven: Yale University Press, 2000), 52.

27 Henri Lefebvre, "The Worldwide Experience," in *State, Space, World: Selected Essays*, ed. Neil Brenner and Stuart Elden (Minneapolis: University of Minnesota Press, 2009), 274–89; the quotation is from 288.

28 Jeffrey Nealon, "The Plant and the Sovereign: Plant and Animal Life in Derrida," in *Posthumous Life: Theorizing Beyond the Posthuman*, ed. Jami Weinstein and Claire Colkebook (New York: Columbia University Press, 2017), 105–35; the quotation is from 125.

29 Anna Lowenhaupt Tsing, *The Mushroom at the End of the World: On the Possibility of Life in Capitalist Ruins* (Princeton: Princeton University Press, 2015), 22–23.

30 Readings focusing on the asexual nature of vegetable relations in Marvell's poem include Jason Kerr, "Vulnerable Life in Marvell's Mower Poems," *Marvell Studies* vol. 4, no. 1 (2019): 1–27 and Marjorie Swann, "Vegetable Love: Botany and Sexuality in Seventeenth-Century England,"

in *The Indistinct Human in Renaissance Literature*, ed. Jean E. Feerick and Vin Nardizzi (New York: Palgrave Macmillan, 2012), 146–53.

31   For an overview of the society's first publications, see Charles A. Rivington, "Early Printers to the Royal Society, 1663–1708," *Notes and Records of the Royal Society of London* 39 (1984): 1–27.

32   Brent Elliott, in "The World of the Renaissance Herbal," *Renaissance Studies* (2011): 24–41, explains, "From Lobel onwards, a variety of classification schemes was tried, but until the mid-seventeenth century most herbalists were content to group plants by a mixture of criteria; medical, morphological, utilitarian, and sometimes etymological" (27).

33   Lincoln Taiz and Lee Taiz, *Flora Unveiled: The Discovery and Denial of Sex in Plants* (Oxford: Oxford University Press, 2017), 324.

34   In 1650, Charles I's poet laureate, Davenant, published his duodecimo in Paris, in which he complained that during the Interregnum "Vice overgrows Virtue, as much as Weeds grow faster than medicinable Herbs." See William Davenant, *A Discourse upon Gondibert* (Paris: Matthieu Guillemot, 1650), 88.

35   The booksellers' epistle is followed by Cowley's own, culled from *The Second Part of the Works of Mr. Abraham Cowley*, published in his lifetime, in which he likens writing poetry to being afflicted by poison ivy: "The Itch of Poesie by being angred increases; by rubbing, spreads further" (sig. a3v).

Chapter Nine: Cowley's Singularity: Pindaric Odes and Johnsonian Values

1   See Cowley, *Pindariques*, sig. T3r. Quotations from Cowley in this essay follow the text of Johnson's quoted excerpts in the "Life of Cowley," from Johnson's *Lives*, or, where indicated, from the *Pindariques* section in the *Works* (1668).

2   In his "Preface" to *Pindarique Odes*, Cowley had written that he had not made it "so much my aim to let the Reader know precisely what he [Pindar] spoke, as what was his *way* and *manner* of speaking; which has not been yet (that I know of) introduced into *English*" (*Pindariques*, sig. T3v).

3   Penelope Wilson, "'High Pindaricks upon Stilts': A Case-Study in the Eighteenth-Century Classical Tradition," *Rediscovering Hellenism: The Hellenic Inheritance and the English Imagination*, ed. G. W. Clarke with J. C. Eade (Cambridge: Cambridge University Press, 1989), 23–41; the quotation is from 27.

4   Colin Burrow, *Imitating Authors: Plato to Futurity* (Oxford: Oxford University Press, 2019), 303.

5   For detailed discussion of Cowley's Greek text, see Penelope B. Wilson, "The Knowledge and Appreciation of Pindar in the Seventeenth and Eighteenth Centuries" (unpublished DPhil. dissertation, University of Oxford, 1974). Wilson accepts the view that Cowley read Pindar in the Saumur edition of Johannes Benedictus (66).

6   Ralph Waldo Emerson, June 27, 1839, in *Journals of Ralph Waldo Emerson*, 15 vols. (Boston: Houghton Mifflin, 1909–14), 5:226. Quoted in John Hollander, *Vision and Resonance: Two Senses of Poetic Form* (New York: Oxford University Press, 1975), 119.

7   Joshua Scodel, "The Cowleyan Pindaric Ode and Sublime Diversions," in *A Nation Transformed: England after the Restoration*, ed. Alan Houston and Steve Pincus (Cambridge: Cambridge University Press, 2001), 180–210.

8   David Fairer, "Lyric and Elegy," *The Oxford History of Classical Reception in English Literature*, vol. 3, *1660–1790*, ed. David Hopkins and Charles Martindale (Oxford: Oxford University Press, 2012), 519–46; the quotation is from 527.

9   Pope, "Rape of the Lock," *Poems*, canto 5, l. 18. See also "The first in Valour, as the first in Place," *The Episode of Sarpedon* (1709), l. 38.

10   "For Theron of Agracas," Olympian 2, from *Pindar: Olympian Odes; Pythian Odes*, ed. and trans. William H. Race, Loeb Classical Library 56 (Cambridge: Harvard University Press, 2012), 63, strophe 1, ll. 6–7.

11   D. S. Carne-Ross, *Pindar* (New Haven: Yale University Press, 1985), 7.

12   Thomas Sprat, "Upon the Poems of the English Ovid, Anacreon, Pindar, and Virgil, Abraham Cowley, in Imitation of his own Pindaric Odes" (1656), in *The Works of the English Poets from Chaucer to Cowper*, ed. Alexander Chalmers, 21 vols. (London: C. Whittingham, 1810), 9:326.

13   William Cowper, "*The Task* and Other Poems, 1785," in *The Poems of William Cowper*, ed. John D. Baird and Charles Ryskamp, 3 vols. (Oxford: Clarendon Press, 1980–95), 2:205.

14   Samuel Johnson, "Preface" to *The Plays of William Shakespeare*, ed. Johnson, 8 vols. (London: J. and R. Tonson, 1765), 1:xxii.

15   "His vehement desire of retirement now came again upon him. . . . So differently are things seen, and so differently are they shown; but actions are visible, though motives are secret. Cowley certainly retired; first to Barn-elms, and afterwards to Chertsey, in Surrey. He seems, however, to have lost part of his dread of the *hum of men* [Johnson's note: L'Allegro of Milton]. He thought himself now safe enough from intrusion, without the defence of mountains and oceans; and, instead of seeking shelter in America, wisely went only so far from the bustle of life as that he might easily find his way back, when solitude should grow tedious. His retreat was at first but slenderly accommodated; yet he soon obtained, by the interest of the Earl of St. Albans and the duke of Buckingham, such a

lease of the Queen's lands as afforded him an ample income. By the lover
of virtue and wit it will be solicitously asked, if he now was happy. Let
them peruse one of his letters accidently preserved by Peck, which I
recommend to the consideration of all that may hereafter pant for solitude" (*Lives*, 1:42–45).

16 For discussion of Cowley's "To Mr *Hobs*," "Brutus," and "Destinie," see
Mark Pedreira's entry on Abraham Cowley for *The Encyclopedia of British
Literature, 1660–1789*, ed. Gary Day and Jack Lynch, 3 vols. (Oxford:
Wiley Blackwell, 2015). Pedreira observes that "these three Pindaric odes,
in particular, display Cowley's eloquent skill at conceptually integrating
vast domains of experience, human and divine" (1:321).

17 Simon Jarvis, in "Hyper-Pindaric: The Greater Irregular Lyric from
Cowley to Keston Sutherland," *Active Romanticism: The Radical Impulse
in Nineteenth-Century and Contemporary Poetic Practice*, ed. Julie Carr
and Jeffrey C. Robinson (Tuscaloosa: University of Alabama Press, 2015),
127–44, writes that "Cowley's final line, which seems entirely deliberately
to come off the horse, appears to suggest that the poem is a test of the
reader's or performer's skill as well as the writer's" (136).

18 See especially No. 9, "The shortness of Life and uncertainty of Riches,"
Verses Written, 136–39.

19 See "A Treatise of the Sublime, or The Marvellous in Discourse. Trans-
lated from the Greek of Longinus," from *The Works of Boileau*, 3 vols.
(London: E. Sanger and E. Curll, 1711–13), "Treatise," 2:11–88, "Critical
Reflections," 2:88–162.

20 J. D. Fleeman, in "Some Proofs of Johnson's *Prefaces to the Poets*," *The
Library* 5th Series 17 (1962): 213–30, points out that "though Johnson
corrected the erroneous 'the' to 'their' [in the same line], he did not alter
the equally erroneous 'fecundine.'" According to Fleeman, "All editions of
Cowley have this word as 'fecundine' or 'fecondine.'" He suggests that the
"u" instead of the "o" led Johnson to suppose that the word was derived
from "fecund," "and so to leave it, though no such word or derivation is
recorded by the NED" (216n1). As suggested by the Yale editors of *Samuel
Johnson: The Lives of the Poets*, vol. 21 of *The Yale Edition of the Works
of Samuel Johnson*, ed. John Middendorf (New Haven: Yale University
Press, 2010), it seems likely that the initial "f" is due to the compositor
misreading Johnson's long "ſ" (216n1). In his *Dictionary*, Johnson does
not recognize "fecundine," but does define "secondine," and quotes
Cowley. The compositorial mistake is repeated elsewhere, for example
when the compositor set "left" for Johnson's "beſt" in the later remarks
on Cowley's *Davideis*. The suggestion that Johnson supposed the word
he saw in the printer's proofs was derived from "fecund" is perhaps less
plausible than proposed because had he known the word "fecundine" he
would have defined it in the *Dictionary*, and the most likely explanation

is that, quite simply, he did not notice it. Fleeman's article gives ample evidence that Johnson was an impatient reader of proof.

21   More epithets or more ignoble ones? Perhaps he means ones more ignoble than those appearing in passages he has just been quoting, where the "nests of Time" are "close," the shell and white of an egg are, respectively, "firm" and "thick."

22   See *Abraham Cowley: Selected Poems*, ed. David Hopkins and Tom Mason (Manchester: Carcanet Press, 1994), xiii.

Notes on Contributors

Ian Calvert is Lecturer in English at the University of Bristol. He is the author of *Virgil's English Translators: Civil Wars to Restoration* (2021), as well as a number of articles on the translation and reception of classical epic in the seventeenth and eighteenth centuries. He is currently working on a critical edition of Pope's Homer.

Kevin L. Cope is a professor of English and Comparative Literature at Louisiana State University. His books include *Criteria of Certainty: Truth and Judgment in the English Enlightenment* (1990), *John Locke Revisited* (1999), and *In and After the Beginning: Inaugural Moments and Literary Institutions in the Long Eighteenth Century* (2007). He is also the editor and founder of the annual *1650–1850: Ideas, Aesthetics, and Inquiries in the Early Modern Era*.

Michael Edson is Associate Professor of English at the University of Wyoming and associate editor for *Eighteenth-Century Life*. His articles have appeared in *Journal for Eighteenth-Century Studies*, *The Eighteenth Century*, *Textual Cultures*, *1650–1850*, and *Studies in Eighteenth-Century Culture*. His edited book, *Annotation in Eighteenth-Century Poetry*, appeared in 2017.

Katarzyna Lecky is the Surtz Professor in English at Loyola University Chicago, a 2021–22 Solmsen Fellow at the University of Wisconsin–Madison, and the series editor of *Aperçus*. Her first book, *Pocket Maps and Public Poetry in Renaissance England*, was published in 2019. She has also published essays on topics such as naturalization, political medicine, and vegetable virtue ethics. Her work has earned fellowships from the ACLS and the Mellon Foundation, the National Endowment for the Humanities, the Renaissance Society of America, and the Folger Shakespeare, Huntington, and Newberry Libraries.

Cedric D. Reverand II is George Duke Humphrey Distinguished Professor Emeritus of English at the University of Wyoming. He has published extensively on literature of the period, especially Dryden and Pope; he has also written on art, architecture, and music. His recent publications include several books of essays: *Paper, Ink, and Achievement: Gabriel Hornstein and the Revival of Eighteenth-Century Scholarship* (2021) and *An Expanding Universe: The Project of Eighteenth-Century Studies. Essays Commemorating the Career of Jim Springer Borck* (2017) (both coedited with Kevin L. Cope), and *Queen Anne and the Arts* (2015). He is also the general editor of *Eighteenth-Century Life*.

Adam Rounce is Associate Professor in English Literature at the University of Nottingham. He has written extensively on various seventeenth- and eighteenth-century writers, including Dryden, Pope, and Johnson. He is coeditor of *Irish Political Writings after 1725* (2018) in the ongoing Cambridge edition of Jonathan Swift, and the author of *Fame and Failure* (2013).

Philip Smallwood is Emeritus Professor of English at Birmingham City University and at different times Honorary Visiting Fellow and Honorary Senior Associate Teacher in the English Department at the University of Bristol. He is the author of books on Johnson, Pope, modern criticism, and critical history, and is coeditor of the literary and aesthetic manuscripts of the British philosopher R. G. Collingwood.

Caroline Spearing currently holds a British Academy Postdoctoral Research Fellowship in the English Department at Exeter University, where she is researching the anthologies of occasional verse produced by the universities of Oxford and Cambridge between 1625 and 1660. She is particularly interested in the poetry of Cowley, whose *Plantarum Libri Sex* was the subject of her PhD. Recent work includes translations of Hadrianus Junius's pamphlet on the stinkhorn mushroom *Phallus Hadriani* (1564) and of Johann Faber's description of the legendary Canis mexicana (1628).

Joshua Swidzinski is Associate Professor of English at the University of Portland, where he teaches writing, introductory literature courses, and courses about literatures of the seventeenth and eighteenth centuries. His publications have explored intersections between poetry and scholarship in the writings of Alexander Pope, Thomas Gray, Robert Burns, and others. He is currently writing a biography of Abraham Cowley.

Index